Illustrated A-Z of Unde

STAR SIGNS

The History and Interpretation of Astrology

This is a Flame Tree Book
First Published in 2002

04 05 03

3 5 7 9 10 8 6 4 2

Flame Tree is a part of
The Foundry Creative Media Company Limited
Crabtree Hall, Crabtree Lane, Fulham, London SW6 6TY

Visit the Foundry website: www.foundry.co.uk

ISBN 1 904041 73 6

A copy of the CIP data for this book is available from the British Library

Printed in China

Special thanks to:
Ray Barnett, Tony Cohen, Karen Fitzpatrick, Julia Rolf, Colin Rudderham, Tom Worsley

Illustrated A-Z of Understanding

STAR SIGNS

The History and Interpretation of Astrology

Kim Farnell, Cat Javor, Helene Schnitzer
GENERAL EDITOR: KIM FARNELL

FLAME TREE PUBLISHING

CONTENTS

Introduction 7

Abscission of Light to Aztec Astrology......................................**10-32**
Babylonian Astrology to Byzantium...**33-39**
Cadent to Cycle...**40-58**
Dark Moon to Dryness **59-66**
Earth to Exaltation **66-75**
Face to Full Moon **75-83**
Galactic Centre to Guardians of Heaven **84-89**
Hamburg School to Hypothetical Planets **90-97**
Illness to Interpretation **97-100**
Joy to Jupiter Return **101-103**
Karma to Koch House System **103-105**
Latitude to Lunation **105-113**
Magnitude to Mystic Rectangle **113-124**
Nadir to Novile **124-129**
Obeying Signs to Oriental **130-132**
Parallel to Claudius Ptolemy **132-145**
Quadrant to Quotidian **146-148**
Radical to Rulership **148-155**
Sabian Symbol to Syzygy **155-177**
T-Square to Twelfth House **177-187**
Under Sunbeams to Ursa Minor **187-189**
Vettius Valens to Voice Signs **189-194**
Waning Moon to West Point **194-195**
Year to Zodiac **196-197**

Appendices **198-217**
Recommended Reading **218**
Author Biographies **219**
Picture Credits **220**
Index **221-224**

Each A–Z entry is tagged by themes which can be followed as threads throughout the book

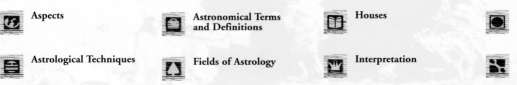

Aspects	Astronomical Terms and Definitions	Houses	Planets
Astrological Techniques	Fields of Astrology	Interpretation	Signs
Astrological Terms and Definitions	History and Background	Measurement and Time	

INTRODUCTION

Astrology. To most people that means reading a column in their daily newspaper that will tell them when they are going to meet a tall, dark, handsome stranger. Something to look at while drinking a morning coffee, a little light entertainment.

However, there is much more to astrology that that. It has a long and rich history, it is an integral part of our culture, and it is still used regularly by vast numbers of people. Serious astrology is very different to what we read in the popular press. It can be used as an adjunct to counselling, is associated strongly with psychotherapy, provides a guide to character and even predicts the weather. Its uses are innumerable.

The history of astrology goes back to ancient Babylon, where people first began to notice that cosmic phenomena were related to the seasons. The need to plan harvests and predict the weather led to more detailed observations being made. Over time more sophisticated observations enabled astrologers to offer predictions for states and rulers. By about 1700 BC the cast had been assembled. The seven planets, counting the Sun and Moon, the Sun's path around the earth and the twelve sections of that path, the Zodiac. What was essentially a farmer's calendar became an instrument for the foretelling of events.

By the third century BC astrology had reached classical Greece from Babylon. The mathematician Pythagoras placed his imprint on the concept of the movement of the heavens. The earth was maintained as the centre of the universe and was a sphere surrounded by other spheres fixed to a vast crystal sphere. As each moved at a different speed they were supposed to emit a note of a different pitch. This was the music of the spheres in which notes blended into one pure, harmonious sound. Greek mythology and culture permeated the whole of astrology and still retains an influence today.

The Egyptian writer Claudius Ptolemy, writing in the second century AD, produced the Tetrabiblos - widely regarded as the greatest astrology book ever written, and still in common use. By this time astrology was well established. It continued to flourish until the Dark Ages. In medieval times texts from Arabic scholars became available and these provided the next advances in astrology.

In the seventeenth century the first work in English was published, Christian Astrology, by William Lilly. However, with the move towards rationalism and the division of areas of study, astrology began a decline that was not to be reversed until the late nineteenth century.

In the early twentieth century astrology began to regain popularity, and in 1930 the first sun sign column appeared in the popular press. From this time onwards almost everyone would at least know the sign that their sun was in when they were born.

Astrology is still fundamentally the same, today, as it was several thousand years ago. A chart is cast for a specific moment in time, at a specific place, and by applying time honoured and tested rules the astrologer may describe the character of the subject and make predictions about what is likely to happen to them.

In casting a chart the astrologer calculates the position of the planets - including the Sun and Moon - and draws them on a circular chart at their zodiac degrees. The positions of the ascendant or rising sign and midheaven are then calculated. These vary by about one degree every four minutes of real time, and according to latitude. The ascendant is drawn on the left hand side of the chart and the midheaven at the top. From these points tables are used to calculate the other house cusps until the chart is divided into twelve sectors. Finally, the angular relationships between the planets - aspects - are calculated and the chart is ready to be interpreted.

The process of analysing a chart is very much like putting together a jigsaw. The planets represent defined energies. Their sign placements show how these energies are manifested and their house placements show in which areas of life they are apparent or most powerful. The aspects between the planets modify their meanings, allowing them to act in combination.

Depending on the astrologer's approach to their work, a number of refinements are often included at this stage to give more information. For example, note may be taken of the planet that rules, or has a strong affinity with a house. The position of this planet relates then to matters of that house.

When making predictions a variety of different techniques are available to the astrologer. These range from looking at the relationship between the positions of the planets at a specific date and comparing them to the birth chart (transit), to using a symbolic method (directions) to move the planets forward and comparing those positions to the ones in the birthchart.

To those who aren't used to astrological concepts, this may sound rather arcane. What use is it to know where the planets are and what their relationship is? The horoscope is basically a map of our lives. It describes the sort of person we are and who we can become. Few astrologers today would suggest that the planets cast down rays that affect our lives, as was believed in the past. But rather, most believe that the configurations and patterns made by celestial bodies are reflected down on earth. Centuries of observation enable us to interpret and judge a horoscope in amazing detail.

Once you have taken a look at what astrology can offer there is no going back.

KIM FARNELL

ABSCISSION OF LIGHT

Planetary combination preventing another combination. Derived from the Latin *abscissio* (from *abscindere* – to cut off), this is synonymous with frustration and describes a configuration that prevents something from happening. A common term in ancient astrology, it is only used in horary nowadays. When the planet that signifies the issue being considered makes an aspect to a planet that moves more slowly, or when two planets that signify the issue are about to reach an aspect but a faster moving planet makes an aspect with one of them before that can become exact, abscission occurs. In each case the light of the approaching significator is cut off by the rays of the third planet. It interferes with whatever is promised by the aspect between the two significators. For example, if the Moon is at 10 degrees of Taurus, and Saturn is at 15 degrees of Taurus, they are in conjunction. Jupiter at 12 degrees of Cancer makes a sextile to both. Jupiter 'cuts off' the rays of Saturn to the Moon. The difficult combination of the Moon and Saturn is eased by Jupiter.

➤ *Frustration, Horary Astrology, Sextile, Significator*

ABSOLUTE LONGITUDE

Term used to describe the position of a planet or chart point in the horoscope. Usually positions are given as degrees of a sign, for example, seven degrees of Gemini. Absolute longitude expresses this as part of the horoscope circle and, as Gemini begins at 60 degrees, in this case would be 67 degrees. It is necessary to convert to absolute longitude when performing some astrological calculations.

ABUMASSAR

Ancient Arab astrologer. Abu Ma'Shar (AD 787–886), known in the West as Abumassar, was born in Baghdad and died in Mesopotamia in March AD 886. He began his career as a student of the Hadith (a collection of traditions from the Prophet Muhammad) but he grew interested in astrology and eventually gave up the Hadith and turned his complete attention to astrology, in which he became a leading authority. His book *Introductorium in Astronomiam* was probably the first book on astrology to be printed after the invention of the printing press and

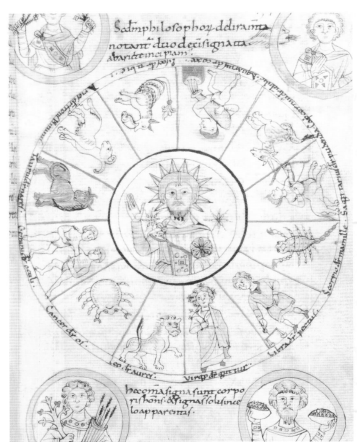

LEFT: *Montezuma, last king of the Aztecs, sights a comet. Comets were a subject of particular interest to Arab astrologer Abumassar.*
ABOVE: *Abumassar studied the significance of comets in the various signs of the zodiac.*

had an enormous influence on Renaissance astrologers. Abumassar displayed an astrological interest in comets, and his account of their significance in each of the signs of the zodiac was often repeated by Latin authors. He also dealt with the problem of Free Will and the degree of control exercised by the planetary bodies. He made a distinction between the influence of the planets and of fixed stars. His works contained a great amount of technical information, transmitted from antiquity, and formed the basis of much astrological theory.

)))➤ *Byzantium, Free Will*

ADAMS, EVANGELINE

Twentieth-century American astrologer. Various dates are given for her birth, but it is known that she died in 1933. Her astrological career began after she made a successful prediction in 1899, when she moved to New York. After this she became extremely well-known and successful, giving advice to some 100,000 people during her 40-year career. Her clients ranged from the poor and unknown to the famous and powerful. She taught astrology to John Pierpoint Morgan and was consulted by Enrico Caruso. In addition to her huge clientele, Adams wrote newspaper columns, published four books and presented a daily radio show. She was arrested in 1914 in New York City on a charge of fortune-telling. She came to court with a pile of reference books and illustrated the practice by reading a chart of the judge's son. The judge was so impressed by her that he ruled in her favour, concluding that astrology was a science. Adams met the renowned British occultist Aleister Crowley in 1916. In his autobiography, Crowley claims to have ghost-written at least two of Adams's books. He also claimed to have not received payment for this. Although the books continued to carry Adams's name they are commonly believed to be Crowley's work.

AFFLICTION

Weakening influence on a planet. Traditional astrology knows several forms of affliction, which weaken a planet or cause it to express its energies in a negative way. A planet can be afflicted by receiving a 'malefic' aspect from another planet. Instead of combining their forces, the planets involved are then at cross-purposes, especially when they are considered to be 'unfriendly' towards each other. Another affliction occurs when a planet is 'besieged', meaning that it is positioned between two other planets, thus obstructing its expression. A planet's position close to a fixed star of malefic description may also be regarded as an affliction.

)))➤ *Besiegement, Malefic*

social ideals and tries to realize them by connecting groups of people. Modern astrology associates the air signs with the thinking type of Jungian psychology, which focuses on the intellectual understanding of all phenomena, ignoring their emotional aspects and thereby often creating or experiencing emotional difficulties.

))))➤ *Earth Signs, Element, Fire Signs, Triplicity, Water Signs*

AL-BIRUNI, ABU RAYHAN

Ancient Islamic astrologer. Abu Rayhan Al-Biruni (973–1048) was born near Kath and the town where he was born is today called Biruni. He began his astrological studies at an early age under the famous astronomer and mathematician Abu Nasr Mansur. Al Biruni wrote over a hundred books and treatises on varied subjects such as mathematics and geography as well as astronomy and astrology. Classical learning was preserved by people such as Biruni during the Dark Ages and medieval and renaissance astrology is essentially Islamic astrology. His *Book of Instructions in the Elements of the Art of Astrology* follows a logical progression from first principles and discusses mathematics, astronomy, geography and chronology before going on to discuss astrology. Al Biruni occasionally criticizes certain techniques, although in the main he presents astrology as a natural part of Islamic philosophy and science. His texts have been reprinted in recent years and now form standard references for many astrologers. During his lifetime Biruni's fortunes changed drastically and he was often forced to spend time in abject poverty. He spent many years in India and is credited with translating a large number of works to and from Arabic and Sanskrit.

))))➤ *Byzantium*

ALCABITIUS HOUSE SYSTEM

Method of chart division. The Alcabitius house system is a time-based system. To derive the house cusps the portion of the circle made by the ascendant above the horizon (the diurnal arc of the ascendant) is divided

AIR SIGNS

Signs of the air triplicity. The signs expressing the element air are Gemini, Libra and Aquarius, ruled by Mercury, Venus and Saturn/Uranus, respectively. Traditionally, the active air element is connected with the thought process. Just as the air we breathe connects us all, the air signs are regarded as actively promoting connections between people in different ways. Mutable Gemini is constantly on the move in order to gather and distribute information and to organize useful practical relationships. Cardinal Libra directs its energies towards unification by smoothing out conflicts, intervening diplomatically and creating harmony using logical arguments. Fixed Aquarius creates the theoretical background for

ABOVE: One of the signs of the air triplicity is Aquarius, the water bearer, which can be seen in the top right-hand corner of this fifteenth-century manuscript.

into three. This circle runs parallel to the equator. This is done by dividing the time (in sidereal time) that it takes for the degree of the ascendant to reach the midheaven into three equal parts. The next three cusps are derived by adding these divisions to the sidereal time at birth and the houses below the horizon are calculated in reverse. This system was commonly used in medieval times and is the house system used by Nostradamus. It is attributed to Alcabitius, a Christian astrologer from Syria *c.* AD 950, who wrote a book on astrology. This was translated into Latin in the thirteenth century and became one of the most popular astrological works. However, Alcabitius did not actually invent this house system as is commonly believed, but merely promoted it. As it does not cause distortion at high latitudes, it is occasionally used where Placidus would be unsuitable.

))))▶ *House System, Placidus House System*

ALCOCODEN

Also Alchochoden. Planet that determines length of life. Meaning 'the giver of years', this term refers to the planet that reveals length of time a person is going to live. It was used extensively in medieval astrology. It is usually the almuten (the planet that holds most dignity) of the degree of the hyleg (the planet used to determine life length). It is rarely used in modern astrology, as present-day astrologers are less keen to predict the date of death.

))))▶ *Almuten, Alpheta, Anareta, Dignity, Hyleg*

ALDEBARAN

Fixed star used in astrology. Its name comes from the Arabic *Al Dabaran* meaning 'follower'. Aldebaran presently lies at almost 10 degrees of Gemini. It is a pale rose star marking the left eye of the Bull, Taurus. It is one of the four Guardians of Heaven – sentinels watching over other stars. It formed one of the four royal stars of Persia as Watcher of the East. Aldebaran is said to confer honour or power.

))))▶ *Fixed Stars*

LEFT: Nostradamus, a user of the Alcabitius House System
BELOW: Aldeberan, a fixed star and one of the four Guardians of Heaven, forms the left eye of the constellation of Taurus.

ALFRIDARIA

Also known as Fridaria; system of planetary periods. Derived from a Latin translation of the Arabic term *firdar*, this is a system of planetary periods that appears to be of Persian origin. The planets are assigned rulerships over periods of time in life, according to a specific scheme. There are two or more planets holding rulership over any particular time. The major ruler has a long period and is divided into sub-periods which are assigned minor rulers. The issues over which the planets have rulership are heightened and brought to the fore during this time.

ALMANAC

Popular astrological literature. Medieval almanacs had circulated in manuscript form but were intended primarily for students and physicians. It was during the Tudor period that the almanac rose to a position of enormous success. By 1600 there were over 600 different almanacs published in England and this number was increasing all the time. In the seventeenth century, over 2,000 were in circulation. William Lilly's almanac *Merlinus Angelicus* was selling 30,000 a year by 1649. Almanacs were issued to fit the varying meridians of different parts of the country. The information contained was carefully selected according to the readership. They were also extremely cheap. Astrological forecasts were only part of their contents. The frequency with which Elizabethan and Jacobean wits found it necessary to denounce almanacs illustrates the influence they exerted. Almanacs continued to be published into the nineteenth century, when their appeal began to wane. Today *Old Moore's* is still published, nearly 300 years after it first appeared.

))))➤ *William Lilly, Francis Moore, Renaissance Astrology*

ALMUTEN

Measure of a planet's strength. Meaning 'the strong holder', the almuten of any degree of the zodiac is the planet having most essential dignity at that degree. Some degrees may have more than one almuten (i.e. if two planets are equally dignified in that degree, they are both almuten). Because signs may have both day and night rulers, almutens may vary for the same degree of the zodiac, depending on whether it is a day or night

LEFT: Medieval almanacs, such as this one by Johann de Gamun Nider, were produced in manuscript form for a limited readership.

ABOVE: The altitude of an astronomical object must be measured from the observer's horizon.
RIGHT: The planet Anareta is concerned with physical death.

chart. The chart itself can have an almuten, which is often referred to as Lord of Chart. It is this meaning that is generally used today.

))))➤ *Dignity, Lord of Chart*

ALPHETA

Used to determine length of life. Also known as 'the giver of life', this was used in length-of-life calculations by Greek and medieval astrologers. Alphetical areas are defined in the birth chart and the Sun in a day chart, or the Moon in a night chart are taken to be alpheta if falling in the prescribed area. If neither of these fall in the correct place, the ascendant is used as alpheta. The term is rarely used in modern astrology.

))))➤ *Alcocoden, Anareta, Hyleg*

ALTITUDE

Astronomical measurement. Altitude is a measurement in mapping astronomical objects on the celestial sphere (the sky as visible from Earth). It is the angle of the object from the observer's horizon, measured against the plane of the horizon. If an object is on the horizon, its altitude is 0 degrees. If it is at the observer's zenith (directly above), its altitude is 90 degrees. Altitude is used to locate objects in the sky.

))))➤ *Celestial Sphere, Zenith*

ANARETA

Planet showing means of death. From the Greek for 'destroyer', this is the planet in the birth chart which shows how you are likely to die. It is concerned with physical death and there can be only one anareta in the chart. Although there are various methods of calculation, it is usually the planet that makes a difficult aspect to (i.e. has angular relationship with) the hyleg both in the birth chart and by direction. The twenty-ninth degree of a sign is said to be an anaretic degree.

))))➤ *Alcocoden, Alpheta, Hyleg*

ANGLES

The four cardinal points in the horoscope. From the Latin for 'corner', the angles are the ascendant, descendant, midheaven and immum coeli, or the cusps of the first, seventh, fourth and tenth houses. The most powerful of these is generally taken to be the ascendant, although some authorities believe the midheaven to be more powerful. Planets placed near these points are extremely potent positively or negatively, depending on the nature of the planet and the aspects (angular relationships) it makes in the chart. The signs found on these points reveal much about the individual's orientation to the basic experiences in life. As they are calculated according to the date, time and place of birth, these points are highly personal. In predictive work the angles are often moved forward, or directed, to describe what is likely to happen in the particular areas of life that they relate to. Planets in one person's chart falling on any of these four points in another's chart shows a strong bond between the two people concerned.

))))➤ *Angular, Ascendant, Descendant, Houses, Immum Coeli, Midheaven.*

ANGULAR

Type of house. The angular houses are those that have one of the angles – ascendant, midheaven, immum coeli or descendant on the cusp. That is the first, tenth, fourth and seventh houses. Planets placed in one of these houses are strengthened, though whether positively or negatively depends on the nature of the planet itself as well as any aspects it makes. A planet in the first house is stronger than one in the tenth, followed by the fourth and seventh houses in that order. Angular is also used to describe a planet being close – within five degrees – of one of the angles.

))))➤ *Cadent, Succedent*

ANTARES

Fixed star used in astrology. Antares presently lies at almost 10 degrees of Sagittarius and is a binary star, fiery red and emerald green. One translation of the name Antares is Anti-Ares, meaning 'rival of Mars', and ancient inscriptions make much of its connection with this planet. Antares was originally in Scorpio and it is strongly associated with this sign, often

LEFT: Birth charts, such as that of King George III, contain points called angles.
ABOVE RIGHT: Antares is strongly associated with Scorpio.

seen as a destructive influence. Antares is one of the four key stars in the heavens, also called archangel stars.

))))▶ *Fixed Stars, Mars*

BELOW: The rules of antipathy do not allow for the traditional friendliness between Mars and Venus, as depicted in Sandro Botticelli's painting.

ANTIPATHY

Planetary incompatibility. The term 'antipathy' is used in various ways, but it always indicates that the planets involved are incompatible or 'unfriendly', meaning that one planet weakens the other or obstructs its manifestation. Some planets have a natural antipathy according to their conflicting natures, such as the Moon to Mars and Saturn or Jupiter to Mars. The rulers of opposing signs are also said to be in antipathy towards one another, although this contradicts the traditional rule that Mars is friendly towards Venus. In synastry, planetary antipathy – even by aspect between the same planets in two charts – implies difficulties in the relationship.

))))▶ *Aspect, Synastry*

ANTISCION

Mathematical point on a chart; also known as 'solstice points'. To find the antiscia, a line is drawn from zero degrees of Cancer to zero degrees of Capricorn on the chart, and planets are reflected across that line to the corresponding degree on the other side. Therefore, if a planet is at 10 degrees Cancer, its antiscion is 20 degrees of Gemini. The opposite point is called the contra-antiscion. It is interpreted like a conjunction, although less strong, if occupied by another planet or if aspected by transit or direction. This technique is mainly used in horary astrology, but it can also be used in natal astrology and in synastry.

))))▶ *Aspect, Conjunction, Horary Astrology, Natal Astrology, Synastry*

describes the most obvious manifestations of the pattern and suggests possible solutions for the conflicts arising from this specific combination of planets and aspects. A transiting planet in conjunction or opposition with the apex planet usually triggers the whole pattern into action. Because it plays such an important role, the apex planet can flavour the whole chart and can almost act as chart ruler. The term belongs to modern astrology, which is increasingly interested in aspect patterns and their integration.

))))➤ *Aspect, T-square, Yod*

APHELION

Planetary orbit point. In a non-circular orbit around the Sun, the point at which a planet is furthest from the Sun; the opposite of perihelion. The distance of the planets from the Sun can vary widely. For example, Mercury can be between 46 and 70 million km away from the Sun at its perihelion and aphelion respectively.

The aphelion of the Earth occurs about 4 July each year. At this point it is moving at its slowest.

))))➤ *Perihelion*

APEX PLANET

Planet's position in aspect pattern. The term apex originates from geometry, where it refers to the angle opposite the basis of a triangle. In some triangular aspect patterns, like the T-square or the Yod, the apex planet is the one occupying that point. Two or more planets closely grouped together in this position will combine their forces and act as the apex planet. It is the most significant of all planets involved in the pattern and represents an outlet for the configuration, a focal point towards which its energies are directed. The apex planet

ABOVE: Mercury shown influencing a field of workers. The planet's aphelion is 70 million km from the Sun.

RIGHT: William Lilly translated a well-known work published in aphorisms.

APHORISM

Astrological statement. A short, pithy statement of truth, presumably based on experience. The term is applied in astrology to the summing up or synthesis of various configurations found in the chart. Many works on astrology were published in the form of aphorisms, especially during the sixteenth and seventeenth centuries. One of the most famous is *The Astrologers Guide,* written in 1675 by Guido Bonatus and translated by William Lilly.

))))➤ *Guido Bonatus, William Lilly*

methods can lead to very different results.

))))➤ *Perigee*

APPARENT MOTION

Movement of bodies. Motion viewed from the Earth and relative to the Earth as if it were stationary. It is traditional to speak of motions in terms of how they appear, rather than what they actually are. The rotation of the Earth makes the planets appear to travel in a westerly direction, although in reality they move in the opposite direction. The signs likewise appear to move west, although in reality they do not move at all.

))))➤ *Motion, Orbit*

APPLICATION

Movement of a planet. The movement of one planet towards another planet, house cusp or sensitive point approaching the formation of an aspect. The term 'mutual application' is used when a planet travelling direct is moving towards one that is retrograde and each of them is heading towards the other. Regardless of direction, the faster-moving planet 'casts its rays' to aspect the slower one. Although two planets need not be in aspect to apply to each other, the term is generally used when they are already in aspect and it is becoming exact. This is particularly important when considering timing in horary astrology.

))))➤ *Aspect, Horary Astrology, Retrograde, Separation*

APOGEE

Moon's cycle. Apogee refers to a point in the Moon's orbit when it is at its furthest point from the Earth; the opposite to perigee. In astrology the apogee marks the point of the black Moon, or Lilith – a hypothetical body used in chart interpretation. The variety of calculation

ABOVE: Apparent motion is the movement of celestial bodies as viewed from the Earth by stargazers such as the Alexandrian astronomer, mathematician and geographer Ptolemy.

AQUARIUS

Aquarius is the eleventh sign of the zodiac, a member of the fixed triplicity, masculine and of the air element. A human sign, the symbol for Aquarius is the water bearer. Its traditional ruling planet is Saturn, particularly by day, and its modern ruler Uranus. Often both planets are used as co-rulers. The Sun enters Aquarius around 20 January and exits around 18 February. People whose birthdays fall between these dates are said to be Sun-sign Aquarius. This is the second month of winter and the nature and qualities of Aquarius are closely associated with this time, when rain and snowfall level all and wash clean the past,

As an intellectual air sign, Aquarius is primarily concerned with thought, and the of mental images. Enormous amounts of energy are channelled into performing complex mental gymnastics, which can lead to such a preoccupation with the world created inside the mind that Aquarius often loses perspective of earthly limitations. As a fixed air sign, Aquarius will pursue intuitive thoughts until a principal or theory is arrived at, then keep it as building block for further ruminations; in this way Aquarius occasionally displays a stubbornness of mind. However, if conflicting information is brought to light which destroys this theory, Aquarius will happily adjust the concept to accommodate the new perspective.

the days grow longer and there is a certainty that the future will bring warmer weather.

In physical terms Aquarius rules the ankles and circulatory system. It is the ankles that lend grace and fluidity of movement to the way in which thoughts move around the Aquarian mind. The circulatory system distributes oxygen to the body, reflecting the manner in which Aquarius is impelled to distribute consciousness to the rest of humanity.

Aquarius represents a search for self through activity that communicates and affirms the place of every individual as an equal in the brotherhood of humanity.

Intellectual ability combined with intuitive inspiration makes Aquarius an original thinker, a natural scientist, inventor and innovator.

Aquarius is co-ruled by the planets Saturn and Uranus. In the case of Saturn this operates as a connection to the past and tradition, cold reasoning and logic. In the case of Uranus, it operates as aspirations towards the future and a new order, flashes of inspiration and innovation. Rarely does the sign concern itself with the here and now.

Aquarius has a reputation for being the bohemian of the zodiac, searching for the unusual in people, ideas and experience. They demonstrate an impetus towards experimentation and an eagerness to gather food for thought. Aquarius will try anything once. Motivated by community spirit, Aquarius enjoys the company of others that think in a similar way, seeking out clubs and societies

LEIMER 18 MAI 1924

LEFT: Venus in Aquarius may manifest itself as an interest in futuristic art forms, such as Variation VI by Wassily Kandinsky..
BELOW: The sign of Aquarius is ruled by Saturn.

ships Aquarius is first and foremost a friend – gregarious and social. They love being in the company of others, but due to the constant and exhaustive mental activity Aquarius also needs space to be alone and will at times appear aloof, cold and unfeeling. Despite a strong loyalty, partners will rarely be made to feel special, as Aquarius treats all equally.

Any planet in a horoscope found in this sign will operate through the energies connected with it. Venus in Aquarius, for example, may operate as an interest in modern and futuristic art forms, computer graphics, kinetic sculpture and electronic music, or as a romantic attraction to unusual, unconventional partners. Mars in Aquarius suggests a strongly opinionated person with an enthusiasm for intellectual debate or a desire to be a leader fighting for social reform.

Whatever part of the horoscope Aquarius is found in will be the arena of life in which there will be a concern for innovation and humanitarian ideals. Aquarius on the fourth house cusp, for example, suggests that the security of home and family is not found through connection to the traditional biological unit, but through being with those that one connects with on a spiritual and intellectual level.

that will work together for a collective objective. Aquarius is friendly, kind and compassionate; however, they are also quite impersonal in their dealings with others, treating everyone fairly and rarely playing favourites.

The social visionary qualities of Aquarius are considerable, and the desire to communicate these visions and concepts to others is very strong. Occasionally, however, what starts out as a sharing of inspiring thought can sometimes turn into a verbal diatribe. The need Aquarius feels for equality amongst humanity operates as an imperative to rebel against authority, dragging down hierarchical structures and a championing of the underdog. Aquarius has a revolutionary spirit, with high ideals for a human utopia and a true democracy. Sometimes the eagerness to cause revolution has Aquarius concocting eccentric ideas which work well intellectually but are inappropriate to the conditions of society in the real world.

In close personal relation-

In its most positive expression, Aquarius is friendly, gregarious and humanitarian, able to love all equally, an innovative and original thinker with an excellent ability to communicate ideas. In its negative expression, Aquarius can be cold, aloof, mentally chaotic and overly talkative, dictatorial in trying to impose their own ideas on others.

))))➤ *Air Signs, Fixed, Human Signs, Masculine, Saturn, Sun-Sign, Uranus*

AQUINAS, THOMAS

Astrologer. Born at Rocca Secca in the Kingdom of Naples, Thomas Aquinas (c. 1225–74) began his study of astronomy at the age of 11. He became a monk of the Dominican order in 1240 and was ordained a priest 10 years later. In 1257 he was made a doctor of theology. During the Middle Ages the teachings of Aristotle gained enormous popularity and Aquinas was one of the scholars of his time who subscribed to Aristotle's theory that the stars had an effect on human destiny; it was Aquinas's defence of Aristotle's works that ensured the former his place in astrological history. Aquinas wrote on natural science and alchemy and asserted that astrology played an important role in these disciplines. He believed that the divinatory arts were permissible as long as they had a natural base. Aquinas reflected in his works that if the Moon could influence the tides, there was no reason to deny that the planets could influence humanity. However, he did not believe that such knowledge should be used for predicting the future apart from in exceptional circumstances. Aquinas was canonized in 1323.

))))▶ *Aristotle*

ARABIAN PART

Mathematical point on chart. Arabian Parts (or Lots) are significant points that are arithmetical constructs of two or more components such as planets or house cusps. For example, the Part of Fortune is derived from adding the longitude of the Moon to the ascendant and subtracting the longitude of the Sun (Moon + Asc – Sun). So, if the Moon is at three degrees of Gemini (63 degrees of the circle), the ascendant at 22 Capricorn (292) and the Sun at six Libra (186), the Part of Fortune falls at 292 + 63 – 186 = 169 or 19 Virgo. The formula is often reversed for night births (Moon – Asc + Sun).

There are endless Parts including Parts of death, illness, marriage, treachery, journeys, etc. When aspected by natal

LEFT: Dominican monk Aquinas studied astronomy from an early age.
ABOVE: Aquinas defended the teachings and theories of Aristotle.
ABOVE RIGHT: The Moon's influence on the tides interested Aquinas.

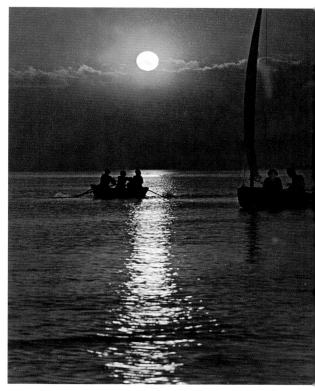

or transiting planets they are sensitive points in the chart. They are used when a specific issue is being examined in the chart. The history of Parts dates back to around 300 BC – certainly pre-Arabic times according to ancient texts – and so they are misnamed. Most of the Parts used are derived from a tenth-century text written by Al-Biruni. Although it is possible to use Parts in any form of astrology, only the Part of Fortune is generally used today.

))))▶ *Al-Biruni, Pars Fortuna*

ARC

Distance measurement. An arc is a portion of a curved line, such as a circle or ellipse, and is thus the orbital distance separating two bodies, or between two points. The diurnal arc is the arc that the Sun passes through from sunrise to sunset. The nocturnal arc is what remains after subtracting the diurnal from 360 degrees. The arc of direction is the distance between a significating planet and the point where it forms an aspect to a promittor.

))))▶ *Promittor, Significator*

ARIES

The first sign of the zodiac, a member of the cardinal triplicity, masculine and of the fire element. A bestial sign, the symbol for Aries is the ram; its ruling planet is Mars, traditionally by day. The Sun enters the sign of Aries around 21 March, the vernal or spring equinox, and exits around 19 April. People whose birthdays fall between these dates are said to be Sun-sign Aries. This is the first month of spring and the nature and qualities of Aries are closely associated with the awakening energy that follows the hibernation of winter, new growth and a burgeoning life force.

In physical terms, Aries rules the head and all the organs of the head including the brain. The mental facilities of the sign, however, are more intuitive and instinctual rather than intellectual, and manifest themselves as a rush of activity to fulfil the thought. The raw creative energy associated with this sign is a powerful impetus that propels it into action.

Like its symbol the ram, Aries rushes headlong at its goal with sometimes little more than the initial spark of an idea as motivation. This can occasionally result in regrettable situations, due to premature actions, and because of a lack of logical forethought. But Aries is a courageous and enthusiastic sign, and the brain a fast-working organ that quickly sparks another idea, so Aries is soon off again expressing a new energy.

Aries represents a search for self through activity that reaffirms existence as an individual, set apart from the rest of the crowd. Aries experiences and understands the world from a totally subjective position and judges all that is presented for consideration entirely from a personal perspective. This can be perceived as egotistical, arrogant and selfish, as Aries is oblivious to all outside thoughts and ideas. Learning to share and co-operate – traits associated with Libra, Aries' polar opposite sign in the zodiac – must be cultivated to fully realize the creative potential inherent in Aries. There is a constant need to

test the limits of selfhood by taking the initiative whenever the opportunity arises and by engaging in competition with other individuals. For this reason Aries is seen as the sign of the sportsperson and soldier and, due to its courageous and bold spirit, can have a strong inspirational influence on others.

The leadership qualities in Aries are considerable, as is the need to be the instigator of action, along with a pioneering spirit and an apparent self-confidence – all of which mean that others are attracted to this charismatic energy. For the same reasons Aries is not comfortable in a

ABOVE: The Sun is in Aries, the ram, during the first month of Spring. Consequently, those born under this sign are linked to awakening energy and new growth.

position of obeisance, resenting those in authority. There is a distinct inability to listen to and consider the advice of others. The enormous rush of energy that propels Aries in its quest for leadership is impulsive, leaving little room for diplomacy. Occasionally Aries may try using force to obtain authority and a position of superiority; overcoming an attitude of 'might makes right' is an important lesson Aries must learn.

Aries does not respond well to routine and repetition; once a task has been completed and mastered, there is an inbuilt need to move on to the next. There is a constant desire for spontaneity and the freedom to pursue new goals, so any chosen career path should offer up plenty of opportunities to follow new areas of activity that will not require going over the same old ground.

It is important that Aries carry through and bring to completion any creative project or pursuit once it has been instigated. It is only through achieving the individual goals set by the self that Aries feels secure and vital.

In personal relationships Aries likes to make a conquest and can be powerfully romantic, although it can also be selfish and demanding. Aries is fiercely protective towards its nearest and dearest and exhibits strong passionate feelings towards lovers and marriage partners.

Any planet in a horoscope found in this sign will operate through the energies connected with it. The Moon in Aries, for example, suggests that all emotional and instinctive responses are

ABOVE: *The two faces of Mars, which is the ruling planet of Aries.*
LEFT: *Aries' competitive nature makes it the sign of the soldier.*

subjective and focus on the need to be assertive and self-starting in the pursuit of emotional security. Saturn in Aries operates as tendency toward the setting up of rigorous ego structures and boundaries through which the enthusiastic creative energies must pass or else remain unexpressed and stagnant.

Whatever part of the horoscope in which Aries is found is the arena of life in which there will be an aggressive and opportunistic need for action. For example, Aries on the third house cusp suggests the manner of speech and communication will be approached with the fire of initiative and an enthusiastic, forceful energy.

In its most positive expression, Aries is direct, decisive and enthusiastic with an ability to use personal initiative, courageous, enthusiastic and inspirational to others. In its negative expression, Aries is egotistical, combative and lacking in subtlety; there is an inability to be objective and a foolhardy, zealous approach to goals.

)))➤ *Bestial, Cardinal, Fire, Mars, Masculine, Sun-Sign*

ARIES POINT

The first degree of the chart. Another word for zero degrees Aries, or vernal point. This is the point where the celestial equator intersects the ecliptic in the east. This marks the vernal equinox and the beginning of the tropical zodiac. It is considered significant when working with midpoints, especially if a birth time is not available. It represents a point of social contact. It indicates day-to-day activities, the type of people you meet and how you are viewed.

)))) *Ecliptic, Midpoint, Tropical Astrology*

ARISTOTLE

Philosopher. Aristotle was born in 384 BCE. at Stagirus in Thrace. He studied under Plato and later began to lecture on his own account. His divergence from Plato's teaching prevented him from being elected to leadership of the Academy. He was the tutor of Alexander (the Great) and set up his own school at the Lyceum. On the death of Alexander in 323 BC the Athens government was overthrown. A charge of impiety was trumped up against him and to escape prosecution he fled. Complaining of a stomach illness he died in 322 BC. Aristotle and Plato are responsible for reinforcing astrological thought through attempts to define time. Aristotle wrote a summary of astrology accounting for planetary motion. His views were based on philosophical speculation rather than observation, although he did acknowledge the

RIGHT: Aristotle studied under Plato and was the teacher of Alexander the Great. His work was popular in the Middle Ages.

importance of 'scientific astronomy'. He also believed that celestial bodies were composed of ether – in addition to the four other elements of earth, air, fire and water. Aristotle was responsible for developing a mechanistic view of the universe as opposed to the earlier models that focused on the divine. Through Thomas Aquinas and others' writings, Aristotle gained great popularity in the Middle Ages and was a common source for all astrologers. Numerous texts were falsely attributed to him. Aristotelian thought was re-introduced to Europe through Arabic writings.

)))) *Thomas Aquinas*

ARMILLARY SPHERE

Astrological tool. A representation of the celestial sphere used by the Greeks from the third century BC. Its name comes from the Latin *armilla*, meaning 'circle' or 'bracelet'. Armillary spheres were used well into the seventeenth century to teach the concepts and coordinate systems of spherical astronomy. The Earth is at the centre of the device and rings represent the horizon, equator, tropics and ecliptic. The cage as a whole revolves around the axis of the celestial poles.

Armillary spheres sometimes incorporate models showing the motion of the Sun, Moon and other planets.

ASCENDANT

Sign rising in the east, and the degree of the zodiac that appeared on the eastern horizon at the moment for which

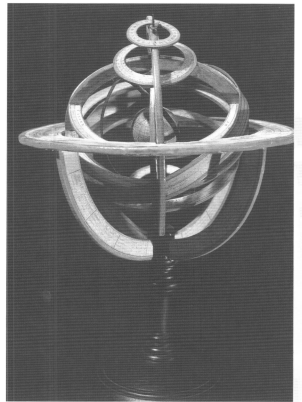

the chart is cast. It is often loosely applied to the whole of the rising sign and sometimes to the entire first house, as well as specifically to the exact degree on the horizon. Older texts refer to the ascendant as the horoscope. Planets close to the rising degree are said to be in the ascendant. It is the first point on the chart wheel and forms the cusp of the first house. It represents the face a person presents to the world and their physical body. It can act as a mask, hiding some aspect of your inner self that you do not choose to reveal. Along with the Sun and Moon, the ascendant forms one of the three most important chart points in natal astrology. The ascendant is highly individual, as its calculation is based on the time, date and place of birth. It moves about one degree every four minutes.

)))➤ *Angle, Angular, Descendant, First House*

ABOVE: A wooden Ptolemaic armillary sphere.

RIGHT: Ptolemy, shown here with various astronomical instruments, believed that there are five major aspects, based on the division of the circle..

ASCENDING

Description of planetary position. A planet is rising if it falls close to the ascendant, generally taken to be up to five degrees either side of the ascendant. A planet in this position is particularly strong and has a close relationship with the ascendant, and how the person presents themselves to the world. In older texts the term may refer to any planet on the left-hand side of the chart or a planet in the first house.

)))➤ *Ascendant, First House*

ASPECT

Angular relationship between planets. The term (from Latin for 'looking at') relates to planets facing each other at a specific angle within the horoscope. This angle is referred to as 'aspect'; the relevant planets are 'in aspect' with each other, meaning that they combine their forces and form a harmonious or conflicting relationship, depending on the angle in question. According to Ptolemy, there are five 'major' aspects, based on the division of the circle into one, two, three, four and six segments:

conjunction, opposition, trine, square and sextile. The so-called minor aspects are based on different divisions and were added later on. There are various forms of aspects: a planet can, for example, form an angular relationship with certain points in the horoscope, like the ascendant or the nodes. Transiting planets can activate any point in the horoscope by temporarily forming an aspect with it. Aspects between transiting planets are called 'mundane', while planets with the same declination form 'parallel aspects'. In order to work fully an aspect should be exact, but there is a sphere of influence on either side of the exact angle, within which its influence can still be felt. This margin of several degrees is called orb and varies according to the combination of planets and the aspect in question. Unfortunately, there is no consensus as to the width of orbs.

)))➤ *Major Aspects, Minor Aspects, Moiety, Orb, Parallel*

ASPECTARIAN

List of astrological occurrences. An aspectarian lists the occurrence of specific astrological phenomena in chronological order and is found in modern ephemerides, calendars or almanacs. It saves the astrologer the trouble of having to calculate the times of these occurrences by hand and is therefore a useful astrological tool. Aspectarians in calendars are largely limited to the phases of the Moon. Almanacs, astrological calendars and ephemerides often include eclipses, void-of-course Moon, ingresses of the Moon and other planets, retrograde periods, daily aspects of the Moon or the exact points of aspects formed by other planets.

))))➤ *Aspect, Ingress, Retrograde, Void of Course*

ASTEROID

Celestial body. Also called 'planetoid' or 'minor planet' if of a larger size. More than 10,000 asteroids have orbits sufficiently well known to have been catalogued and named, but thousands more exist. Most asteroids are irregularly shaped, unlike the spherically shaped major planets. The largest known asteroid, Ceres, has a diameter of 1,000 km (630 miles), the three next largest are Pallas, Vesta and Juno. Only Vesta can be seen with the naked eye. Many asteroids are so small that their sizes cannot be measured with any equipment currently available. The orbits of most asteroids lie partially between the orbits of Mars and Jupiter. Asteroids with orbits in the outer Solar System are known as Centaurs. The origin of asteroids is unclear; one theory states that they were formed from material that could not condense into a single planet because of perturbation effects involving Jupiter. Some asteroids are actually nuclei of comets that are no longer active. The four main asteroids are used for interpretation by some modern astrologers and the influences of the asteroids are strongly linked to the mythological legends for which they are named.

))))➤ *Planetoid*

ASTRO*CARTO*GRAPHY

Location-based astrology. Astro*carto*graphy is based on the traditional astrological tool of relocating a chart for where the person lives at that time, involving recalculating the chart. The resulting chart shows what the person's life would have been like if they had been born in the new place. The most important factor in a relocated chart is when planets become angular, or placed near the cusps of the first, fourth, seventh or tenth houses. In astro*carto*graphy a computer calculates the places on Earth where each planet would be on those points. The nature of the planet concerned describes the type of experience a person could be expected to have in that location. For example, if Jupiter is highlighted, it suggests a feeling of well-being and financial benefit. Astro*carto*graphy is primarily used as a technique when someone is considering moving and wants to know how they relate to a particular place, or if they want to know where to move to achieve something specific. It was devised by the American astrologer Jim Lewis.

))))➤ *Local Space, Relocation*

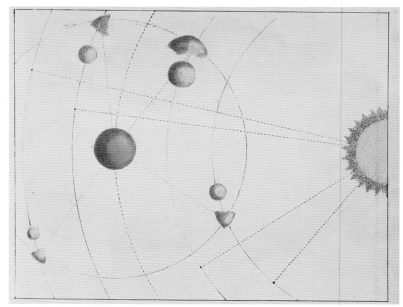

BELOW: Asteroids are celestial bodies of irregular shape and uncertain origin. This is one interpretation of how asteroids are formed.

LEFT: An Italian astrolabe from around 1630.
BELOW: Astrologers cast horoscopes during celebrations for the birth of Timur
or Tamerlaine, conquerer of the Islamic faith.

Astrology fell out of favour during the eighteenth century, and when it was revived towards the end of the nineteenth century it was no longer an academic subject, but was practised by those versed in occult arts. During the twentieth century it has become both an adjunct to psychotherapy and a form of popular entertainment.
➤ *Astrology*

ASTROLABE

Astrological tool. The principles of astrolabe projection were known before 150 BC and astrolabes were being made by around AD 400. The astrolabe was highly developed by AD 800 and was introduced to Europe from Spain in the early twelfth century. The astrolabe is an instrument for computing problems relating to time and the position of the Sun in the sky. In its heyday, the most popular version of the instrument was the planispheric astrolabe, on which the celestial sphere was projected on to the plane of the equator. A typical astrolabe was made of brass and about 15 cm (6 in) in diameter. An astrolabe shows how the sky looks at a specific place at a given time. This is done by drawing on the face of the astrolabe and marking it so that positions in the sky are easy to find. To use it you adjust the moveable components. Once set, the whole sky is represented on the face of the instrument.

ASTROLOGER

One who studies celestial patterns and makes analysis of character and predictions based on them. For many centuries the terms 'astrologer' and 'astronomer' were synonymous – meaning one who studied the movements of the skies. It is only in relatively recent times that the two have been separated into a science, and, as regarded by many, a belief system. In the earliest times astrologers were priests and scholars. Astrology was studied at universities and astrologers worked for the most important people in the land. By the sixteenth century astrology was closely allied with medicine and male practitioners were physicians.

ASTROLOGY

Astrology is classed as a type of divination that consists of interpreting the influence of the planets and stars on earthly affairs, to predict or affect the destinies of individuals, groups or nations. At times regarded as a science, astrology has exerted an extensive or a peripheral influence in many civilizations, both ancient and modern. Its origins lie within the astral religion of ancient Mesopotamia of the third and second millennia BC. From Mesopotamia, astrology spread to the adjacent regions, changing its form as it went. For many centuries the terms astronomy and astrology were synonymous. Astrology is often defined as a pseudo-science and considered to be diametrically opposed to the findings of real science. Although there have been periods when astrology has fallen out of favour, it has never completely disappeared. Although scientists continue to rail against the discipline, it has gained in popularity since the late 1980s. Astrology is now part of popular culture and everyone has a smattering of knowledge of it, even if it only extends as far as knowing their Sun-sign.

))))➤ *Astrologer, Sun-Sign Astrology, Synchronicity*

ASTROMETEOROLOGY

Long-range weather forecasting by astrology. Predicting the weather through astrology is one of its oldest uses. During the mid-nineteenth century the struggle between scientific weather prediction and more traditional forms was highlighted. A number of nineteenth-century astrologers, including Zadkiel, were members of the London Meteorological Society. It ceased to be fashionable at the end of the century and is rarely practised today. Astrometeorology, also known as long-range weather forecasting, is the science of forecasting weather, fierce storms, floods, droughts, freezes, hurricanes, earthquakes and volcanic eruptions, and is one of the oldest-known systems of organized knowledge. Astronomers in the past had observed that when the planets in geocentric longitude moved through the various constellations or zodiacal signs, seismic activity occurred and weather patterns differed according to the influence of that particular sign. Using the Sun, Moon and Planets, their angular positions in relation to each other and to the Earth, astrometeorology seeks to predict the time, location and severity of weather or seismic activity at any given time, for any geographical location on the planet.

))))➤ *Zadkiel*

LEFT: The signs of the zodiac are now widely recognised, as astrology has permeated popular culture.

LEFT: *Astronomy personified in a sixteenth century Italian publication.*
BELOW: *Saint Augustine, originally a believer in astrology but later disillusioned, is shown in his cell in this painting by Sandro Botticelli.*

Chinese, Indians, Egyptians and Babylonians, who succeeded in laying the foundations of the science. When astronomy became a Greek science it underwent a transformation. Attempts began to be made to render the appearances of the sky intelligible. Descriptive astronomy took its rise from the invention of the telescope. For many centuries the terms astrology and astronomy were interchangeable, the term natural astrology being used to describe what we would nowadays think of as astronomy.
))))➡ ***Astrology***

AUGUSTINE, SAINT

Philosopher. Augustine (AD 354–430) was born at Tagaste (now Souk-Ahras) in Numidia. In his youth he consulted astrologers and shared the common belief in the efficacy of their art. According to his *Confessions*, this belief was undermined on the day that he discovered a very wealthy landowner had been born at the same moment as one of the slaves on his estate. His final condemnation of astrology came in *The City of God*, written after the Sack of Rome in AD 410. He claimed that astrology was a fraud and an elusion which usurped God's power over the Universe. If a planet could predict a future event, this limited the Creator's power to alter that event. Primarily because of Augustine's writings, astrology was dismissed as a fool's

goal for more than four centuries. However, it was never formally proscribed by the Church and an underground movement kept the art alive in Europe.

ASTRONOMY

Science of the heavens. From Greek *astron* meaning 'star' and *nemein*, 'to distribute'. Today astronomy is divided into two main branches: astrometry and astrophysics; the former concerned with determining the places of the investigation of the heavenly bodies, the latter with the investigation of their chemical and physical nature. In antiquity, astronomy revolved around attempts to fix the apparent positions of the objects on the sphere. Systems of astronomical knowledge were early established by the

AYANAMSA

Calculation between tropical and sidereal zodiacs. The ayanamsa is the figure used in calculations to convert the tropical zodiacal positions, used in the West, to the sidereal positions used in Vedic astrology. Depending on the method used, and the date of the chart to be calculated, it can vary from 19 to 23 degrees. The figure is the difference between the actual zero degrees of Aries and the tropical zodiac's symbolic zero degrees of Aries. The variation is due to disagreement about the precise date when the two zodiacs coincided and the rate of precession – approximately 50 seconds a year. Tables are available in Vedic text books giving the ayanamsa for each year. The number given is subtracted from the positions given in tables of tropical positions and the new positions drawn on the chart. Or it is simply added to a sidereal position to convert it to a tropical one.

)))➤ *Precession, Sidereal Astrology, Tropical Astrology, Vedic Astrology, Zodiac*

AZIMENE

Measure of a planet's strength. A planet is said to be azimene when it is placed in certain weak or lame degrees which, if rising at birth, is said to make the subject blind, lame or otherwise physically afflicted. If the ruler of the chart or the Moon falls in one of these degrees it is said to have a similar effect. The degrees are 0 Aries, 6–10 Taurus, 0 Gemini, 9–15 Cancer, 18, 27, 28 Leo, 0 Virgo, 0 Libra, 19, 28 Scorpio, 1, 7, 8, 18, 19 Sagittarius, 2–29 Capricorn, 18, 19 Aquarius and 0 Pisces. This traditional judgement of planetary strength has now fallen out of popular use.

)))➤ *Critical Degree*

AZIMUTH

Measurement to help locate celestial objects. Azimuth is a measurement used to map the position of astronomical objects. It is the angle from the observer's north point projected onto the horizon. If an object is at due north its azimuth is 0 degrees. If it is due east its azimuth will be 90 degrees. By using altitude along with azimuth an object can be located in the sky.

)))➤ *Altitude*

AZTEC ASTROLOGY

Ancient astrology. The Aztecs and Mayans were obsessed by time and so became accurate calendar keepers. Their astrology appears to have developed in the Yucatán or Peru and spread from there; however, much of their knowledge was destroyed when the Spanish invaded their lands in the sixteenth century. Their calendar

BELOW: As well as displaying an interest in astrology, the Aztecs were obsessive time-keepers. Their calendars were accurate and comprised 365 days.

RIGHT: Saturn is considered 'barren', in that it can prevent the conception, birth and survival of children.
BELOW: The cosmos as perceived by the ancient Babylonians.

comprised 365 days – just short of the solar year. Their astrological system features circles within circles. The largest circle is the 52,000 years it takes for our Solar System to go around the Pleiades and the smallest the 'Tzol'kin', or Sacred Calendar. This is a combination of 13 numbers and 20 'day names'. In one sense there is no beginning day and no end day, because a circle is in continuous flow. Like other astrological systems, Aztec astrology is able to describe basic personality and behaviour. Each day has basic and predictable characteristics that can be calculated. Energies go through cycles described in terms of north (direction of winter and rest), west (direction of autumn and harvest), south (direction of summer and rapid growth) and East (direction of spring and beginnings).

BABYLONIAN ASTROLOGY

Ancient astrology. Babylonia is seen as the original home of astrology as we know it. Around 2000 BC it was deduced that the changing seasons were produced by the movement of astronomical bodies. From there proceeded the observation that there was a high and low point in summer and winter as well as in the seasons. After more sophisticated observations were made, by 1700 BC the planets, Sun, Moon and zodiac were incorporated into the developing system. Gradually the system was developed away from a simple chronology to that of mapping the future on a general scale. Later, the individual's fate dominated interest. Both were linked to the concept of measuring time. By 2000 BC human affairs were being predicted on a broad scale – mundane astrology – and by 600 BC the personal horoscope had come into being. Astrology has remained unchanged in its essentials since this date. It is unknown what changes occurred in these centuries to cause new skills to emerge – although the first appearance of Venus is one theory among many.

)))➤ *Astrology, Mundane astrology*

BARREN PLANETS

Traditionally, the planets Mars and Saturn are regarded as 'barren', that is they prevent the conception, birth or survival of children, especially when placed on the ascendant, in the fifth or eleventh houses, where they retrograde or negatively aspect the rulers of the same. In modern astrology, the Trans-Saturnians, especially Uranus, sometimes signify barrenness or artificially induced conception. Though not a planet, the Moon's south node (the dragon's tail) is also regarded as barren.

)))➤ *Barren Signs, Children, Fifth House, Retrograde*

BARREN SIGNS

 One of the manifold divisions of the zodiac, used in traditional and ancient astrology. These divisions are rarely – if ever – used in modern astrology. However, in the judging of a horary chart, when a barren sign appears of the ascendant or fifth house cusp, it suggests that any further action invested in the matter questioned will not produce any worthwhile results. There are three barren signs: Gemini, Leo and Virgo.

)))⯈ *Gemini, Horary Astrology, Leo, Virgo*

BEHOLD

Term to describe relationship between planet and sign. When two planets are within orb of an aspect, they are said to behold one another. Signs that have the same declination, or are at equal distances from the tropics, i.e. Aries/Virgo, Taurus/Leo, Gemini/Cancer, Libra/Pisces, Scorpio/Aquarius, Sagittarius/Capricorn, are also said to behold each other. Zodiac signs can behold one another in one of three ways: by major aspect (conjunction, sextile, square, trine, opposition), by antiscion, or by contra-antiscion.

)))⯈ *Antiscion, Aspect*

BENEFIC

Traditional planet classification. The planets Venus and Jupiter are classified as benefics, meaning their

BELOW: Perhaps the best-known reference to astrology in the bible is the Three Wise Men following the star to Bethlehem.

+SCS BALTHASSAR +SCS MELCHIOR +SCS GASPAR

influence is generally positive. Venus and Jupiter are also often referred to as the 'Lesser Benefic' and the 'Greater Benefic', respectively. The Sun, the Moon and the north node of the Moon (the dragon's head) are also regarded as benefics if they are dignified or well aspected. The term benefic is also applied to aspects. The trine is regarded as positive, because the planets in question operate within signs of the same element, whereas the sextile involves planets in signs of either feminine or masculine disposition.

)))► *Aspect, Debility, Dignity, Element, Malefic, Sextile, Trine*

BESIEGEMENT

A trapped planet, bound on either side by an unhelpful planet which limits its scope. A besieged planet is taken to be unfortunate in traditional astrology. Generally, besiegement involves a planet that falls between Saturn and Mars in the horoscope and is within orb of an aspect (angular relationship) with both planets. In the past, planets that lay between Venus and Jupiter were said to be fortunately besieged and were considered to be positive in meaning. Today, however, the term is used in its negative sense and restricted to horary astrology.

)))► *Horary Astrology*

BESTIAL SIGNS

Also known as quadrupedian signs; one of the divisions of the zodiac used in traditional and ancient astrology. It refers to those signs in the zodiac represented in their symbol by four-footed creatures. The bestial signs are Aries the Ram, Taurus the Bull, Leo the Lion, Sagittarius the Centaur and Capricorn the Goat.

Referring to them by this name such suggests that each represents characteristics and behavioural tendencies associated with its respective creature.

)))► *Aries, Capricorn, Leo, Sagittarius*

BIBLE AND ASTROLOGY

There are numerous references to astrology in the Bible. The most popularly known is that of the Three Wise Men following the star to discover the Christ child: 'Saying, Where is he that is born King of the Jews? For we have seen his star in the east, and are come to worship him' (Matthew 2:2). In some passages astrology is condemned: 'There shall not be found among you any one … that useth divination…' (Deuteronomy xviii, 10–11).

Christianity and astrology had an uneasy truce in the past, but coexisted, particularly in England where many priests were students and covert practitioners of astrology. Most of the objections cited in opposition to astrology today are from the King James version of the Bible and many have been proven to be based on mistranslations. Several Christian groups state that the Bible clearly opposes astrology and often make the case that astrology itself is unscientific, but there are arguments to the contrary. The largest astrological library in the world is that held at the Vatican.

)))► *Thomas Aquinas, Saint Augustine*

LEFT: Leo the lion, shown here on a Tarot card, is one of the bestial signs.
ABOVE: The Bible opposing astrology: An astrologer holds up a celestial sphere as proof of his claims, but the monk refutes him from the Holy Book.

BI-CORPOREAL SIGNS

Also known as double-bodied signs; one of the divisions of the zodiac used in traditional and ancient astrology. It has also found a use in modern psychological astrology. The term refers to those signs of the zodiac represented by symbols of two bodies. These are Gemini the Twins and Pisces the Fish. The name describes the nature of bi-corporeal signs as having two modes of behaviour, or being able to express two different perspectives on one matter.

))))→ *Gemini, Pisces*

BI-QUINTILE

Minor aspect. The bi-quintile is one of the aspects introduced by Johannes Kepler and it is based on the division of the circle into five segments. The bi-quintile (double-quintile) covers an angle of 144 degrees and is generally allowed an orb of two degrees or, if one of the lights is involved, three degrees. Like the other Keplerian aspects, it is seen as relating to the subtler functions of the human mind. The planets involved can be used in the development of creative or occult abilities far above the ordinary. The bi-quintile is associated with clairvoyance, magic and a general interest in hidden or occult forces. When separating, it denotes almost genial powers of creative self-expression. In both cases, the 'tools' used by the individual are described by the planets involved, their placement in signs and houses and by the houses they rule.

))))→ *Aspect, Johannes Kepler, Minor Aspects, Quintile*

BIRTH MOMENT

Time used to cast a horoscope. A horoscope is calculated for the time, date and place that a person

is born, or that an event takes place. In horary astrology the chart is cast for the birth time of a question. For an individual's horoscope the moment of birth is classed as when the child takes its first breath or makes its first cry after being completely out of the mother. Recorded times of birth are often later than this. It has always been a source of controversy, as many believe that conception marks the beginning of life.

))))→ *Data, Horary Astrology*

BIRTHSTONE

Astrological talisman. Astrology associates a variety of gems and precious stones with certain signs or planets. To wear a stone associated with one's Sun-sign or the ruler thereof is believed to offer protection and to promote the wearer's health and success in life by filtering and focusing cosmic energies. Such a stone is referred to as the birthstone. This ancient tradition is still much used in Vedic astrology, whereas in the West birthstones are often only commercially exploited. Unfortunately, there is no conclusive answer as to which stone belongs to which sign or planet, the following list can therefore only give an indication:

Sun	diamond, ruby
Mercury	yellow topaz, citrine
Venus	jade, emerald
Mars	carnelian, jasper
Jupiter	lapis lazuli, amethyst
Saturn	falcon's eye, black star
Uranus	turquoise
Neptune	labradorite
Pluto	granite

The colour of the stone may be seen as a general indicator of its planetary connection. It is advisable to consider that a birthstone may enhance not only one's strength and fortune, but also the negative qualities of the planet by which it is ruled.

))))→ *Colours, Metals, Rulership, Sun-Sign, Vedic Astrology*

ABOVE: The birthstone turquoise, shown here in a Tibetan pendant, is associated with the planet Uranus.

BLUE MOON

Second of two full Moons in one month. The expression 'blue Moon' usually refers to the second full Moon that occurs in a calendar month. Because the Moon and our calendar are not in sync and all the months except February are longer than the Moon's cycle, a blue Moon occurs about seven times in 19 years. Blue Moons were actually printed in blue in older planetary tables, although it is not known where the term comes from. No blue moon will occur at all in the years 2003, 2006, 2011, 2014 and 2017.

》》 *Moon*

BODY, PARTS OF

The tradition of assigning signs and planets to the parts of the body has often been illustrated by pictures of the 'Melothesic Man', a figure with the zodiac symbols arranged along the body. The traditional correspondences are:

Aries	head
Taurus	neck, throat
Gemini	shoulders, arms, lungs
Cancer	breasts, ribcage
Leo	heart
Virgo	stomach, bowels, womb
Libra	kidneys, lower back
Scorpio	sexual organs
Sagittarius	hips, thighs, liver
Capricorn	bones, joints, skin
Aquarius	shins, ankles, circulatory system
Pisces	feet

There are diverse views on planetary correspondences. Some are based on the traditional system listed above, others include the modern planets as well as the findings of modern medicine, such as the functions of the glandular

ABOVE: The signs of the zodiac and how they influence a man's body.
ABOVE LEFT: How the body is influenced by the sun and six planets, according to Jean Belot, French chiromancer and diviner.

systems. According to Ptolemy the traditional rulerships are:

Sun	brain, sight, heart, right-hand side
Moon	sense of taste, stomach, belly, womb, left-hand side
Mercury	tongue, bile, buttocks
Venus	sense of smell, liver, flesh
Mars	left ear, veins, kidneys, genitals
Jupiter	sense of touch, arteries, lungs, semen
Saturn	right ear, spleen, bladder, bones

》》 *Medical Astrology, Illness*

EFFIGIES TYCHONIS BRAHE O. F.
ÆDIFICII ET INSTRUMENTORVM
ASTRONOMICORVM STRVCTORIS
A° DOMINI 1587 ÆTATIS SVÆ 40

Tycho Brahe in seiner Sternwarte „Uranienburg" auf der Insel Hven
Nach einem Kupferstich zu Tycho Brahes „Astronomiae instauratae Mechanica" vom Jahre 1602

of his work was based on his own experience. He made his living by advising princes, and was for some time employed by Count Guido de Montefeltro. When that prince was involved in a dispute that led to military action, Bonatus would climb to the top of his castle, and at the auspicious moment strike the bell once for the Count and his men to don their armour, again for them to mount their horses, and a third time for them to ride forth to battle. Filippo Villani, a contemporary historian, claims that Montefeltro won many battles by following his astrologer's advice. Bonatus died around 1300 after being assaulted by robbers. He was the astrologer Dante described as one of the sufferers who had spent too much time trying to predict the future, and were now condemned to pace about with their heads on backwards.

BRAHE, TYCHO

Astrologer. Tycho Brahe (1546–1601) was born in Skane, then in Denmark, now Sweden. Brahe lost part of his nose in a duel with another student at Wittenberg in 1566 and for the rest of his life wore a

BONATUS, GUIDO

Medieval astrologer. Guido Bonatus (c. 1230–c. 1300) was born in Friaul. Professor of astrology at Bolgna University, he wrote a book on astronomy and a theory of the planets, as well as books on astrology. Much

ABOVE: Sixteenth century Danish astrologer Tycho Brahe, at work in his observatory in Uranienborg, Sweden

metal insert over the missing part. He returned to Denmark in 1570; in 1572 he observed the new star in the constellation Cassiopeia and published a brief tract about it the following year. In 1574 he gave lectures on astronomy at the University of Copenhagen. He was convinced that the improvement of astronomy hinged on accurate observations. Brahe accepted an offer from Frederick II to fund an observatory, which he built near Copenhagen. He designed and constructed new instruments, calibrated them, and instituted nightly observations. He also ran his own printing press. Brahe trained a generation of young astronomers in the art of observing. After falling out with Christian IV in 1597, he left Denmark; he settled in Prague in 1599 as the Imperial Mathematician at the court of Emperor Rudolph II and died there in 1601.

BUCKET

Chart shape, horoscope pattern. The 'bucket' – also known as 'wedge' or 'funnel' – is an easily recognizable chart shape. It consists of a tight group of planets within 180 degrees of one hemisphere ('bucket') and a singleton planet ('handle') in the opposing hemisphere. Two planets in close conjunction may also be counted as a singleton. The closer the planets of the 'bucket' are grouped together, the more energies are being generated in the areas defined by their house position. These energies are then focused

LEFT: The planetary system devised by Tycho Brahe, who lectured on astronomy at Copenhagen University.
BELOW: Constantinople, previously Byzantium, in the sixteenth century.

towards the singleton and released through it, in a manner according to its position in sign and house.

))))➤ *Chart Shape, Stellium*

BYZANTIUM

Ancient astrology. Byzantium is the name given to the state and culture of the Eastern Roman Empire in the Middle Ages. After the fall of the Roman Empire in AD 410, there was a decline of learning in western Europe. With the loss of the Greek language, in which most astrological texts had been written, knowledge of astrology survived only as a passing reference. In the Byzantine East a high culture and civilization continued to flourish for another 1,000 years. Despite successive injunctions against divination, the ongoing usage of the Greek language insured the production and survival of new astrological works. Many scholars emigrated to Persia and India where astrological writings were translated and preserved. By the seventh century, the practice of astrology had declined, but texts were still available. It was the Islamic world that was responsible for transmitting the legacy of the Babylonian astral religion to medieval Europe. The revival began around 1000, when some European scholars began to study at Islamic universities. There they rediscovered Aristotle, Ptolemy and astrology.

))))➤ *Aristotle, Ptolemy*

CADENT

Type of house. The cadent houses are those that precede the angular houses, that is, the third, sixth, ninth and twelfth houses. A cadent planet is one that occupies a cadent house. These houses are considered weaker than angular houses. The word cadent means 'fallen'; a planet in a cadent house has been carried away from the cardinal position of the angular house and symbolizes a falling from grace and weakening of power. Originally the cadent houses represented foreign places and situations. They referred to a lack of familiarity and the fear and danger that can arise from it. The most afflicted are the sixth and twelfth houses as they have least relationship with the ascendant. When timing an event from a chart, a cadent planet indicates that it is likely to take months, rather than weeks or days. Although the distinction is particularly important in horary astrology, and is used in other traditional forms, modern astrology does not distinguish between the houses in this manner.

))))➡ *Angular, Succedent*

CALENDAR

The roots of our modern civil calendar lie in ancient Rome. The original Roman calendar started on 1 March and consisted of 10 months totalling 304 days, numbering the years from the foundation of Rome. Later, the months of January and February were

BELOW: A thirteenth century calendar showing the months July to December, including signs of the zodiac.

introduced and the year increased to 354 or 355 days.
After some years, however, it was noted that the calendar
year was out of sync with the solar year and an extra
month was introduced in some years. In 45 BC Julius
Caesar reformed the calendar, approximating the year at
365.25 days, achieved by having a leap year every four
years. The Roman year now began at 1 January. There
were still problems, however, and to resolve such errors
the calendar was reformed again by Pope Gregory XIII in
1582. Catholic states adopted the new Gregorian
calendar immediately but Protestant states took longer. In
1752 the English civil calendar was reformed; the start of
the English legal year was moved from 25 March to 1
January, adopting the civil year observed in other
countries.

CAMPANUS HOUSE SYSTEM

Method of chart division. The Campanus system is
a space-based system. The thirteenth-century mathematician Johannes Campanus designed this system using
the prime vertical, a great circle which passes through the
east and west points of the horizon as well as the zenith
and the nadir. He divided it into equal 30-degree
segments and the great circles, which passed through these
points, and the north and south points of the horizon,
became the house cusps. The main drawback of the
Campanus system manifests in higher latitudes, where the
angle of the ecliptic to the prime vertical becomes more
acute, causing the longitudinal position of house cusps in
relation to the ecliptic to become unequal and the houses
markedly distorted. Campanus also believed that the cusp
should mark the centre of a house, rather than its start.
Houses in this system can be extremely wide or narrow in
comparison to other systems. It was popularized in the
twentieth century by the astrologer Dane Rudhyar.

➤ House System

CANCER

Cancer is the fourth sign of the zodiac, a member of the cardinal triplicity, feminine and of the water element. A fertile sign, the symbol for Cancer is the Crab, its ruling planet is the Moon. The Sun enters the sign of Cancer around the time of the summer solstice on 22 June and exits around 23 July. People whose birthdays fall between these dates are said to be Sun-sign Cancer. This is the first month of summer and the nature and qualities of Cancer are closely associated with the maturing life energies that were in its early creative growth stages through the spring. This is the time when life needs tending and nurturing to maximize the potential of its eventual yield.

In physical terms, Cancer rules the chest and breasts, which symbolize in both sexes the protective and nurturing qualities connected with this sign. Cancer operates on emotional instinct and, just as its ruler the Moon is constantly going through phases of full, half, crescent, new and back again, so do the emotional moods of Cancer pass through an ever-changing cycle. There is enormous sensitivity to atmosphere and environment in Cancer, being receptive to vibrational energy that is then interpreted through the personal and subjective feeling senses. Cancer has a strong instinctive nature and is extremely intuitive, picking up on the slightest emotional nuance. There is an inability to regulate and control the thoughts and emotions; Cancer is subject to the mood of the moment and behaves accordingly. Like the sign's symbol, the crab, it is necessary for Cancer to develop a tough outer shell in order to protect the soft and vulnerable inner self from damage.

Cancer represents a search for self through what is felt on an emotional level. In order for any information to be absorbed it must first be intuited and processed through the senses. Initially Cancer has a problem with being pinned down, scuttling sideways in order to avoid being trapped. The strong need for self-protection ensures that a lot of effort must be made to pierce the outer shell and touch the gentle centre. However, once the powerful emotions have been engaged, Cancer embraces with full attachment and then finds it very difficult to disengage. It is for this reason that the sign has a reputation for being smothering. Home and family, both blood and chosen, are very important to Cancer, which is often seen as the sign of Mother the nurturer. In all ways, that which is familiar and offers comfort assists in the feeling of security – a much sought-after commodity by Cancer. Cancer is a hoarder and collector of mementoes and treasures; many items they possess have sentimental value and represent memories of time spent feeling safe and warm.

The theme of nurturing runs strongly through Cancer, whether it be as the one giving or receiving, and it operates on many levels. Cancer is happiest when feeling loved, protected and well-fed, and they would like to offer the same to their nearest and dearest. Cancer can provide enormous amounts of tea and sympathy, and they come into their element when playing host over a table groaning with food. Cancer is not above playing emotional games in order to test those that profess to love and want them, but the rewards for passing the test are great and partners and friends are offered the gentle, cosy and loving private world of home sweet home.

Cancer can be found in any career pursuit where the financial rewards are potentially great. Due to the cardinal qualities of the sign, Cancer is also extremely active and very resourceful; the ambitious nature can be seen in the tenacity that

ABOVE: Like their symbol, the crab, those born with the Sun in Cancer need tough outer shells to protect their inner frailties.

RIGHT: Cancer's ruler, the Moon, perceived as a boat by ancient Egyptians.

Cancer displays when searching for and holding on to a secure income. Financial and material wealth are important as they provide the stable outer security necessary to assist in the fostering of inner emotional security.

BELOW: Cancer enjoys hosting banquets, like the one shown in this Limbourg Brothers painting from Les Tres Riches Heures du Duc de Berry.

BELOW: Cancer enjoys hosting banquets, like the one shown in this Limbourg Brothers painting from Les Tres Riches Heures du Duc de Berry.

Any planet in a horoscope found in this sign will operate through the energies connected with it. Venus in Cancer for example suggests a love and artistic ability related to the domestic environment, an indulgence in beautiful surroundings and luxury, the mark of a good interior designer. Saturn in Cancer might operate as a harsh disciplinarian attitude around the home, demanding exacting standards in the search for a safe and secure environment.

Whatever part of the horoscope in which Cancer is found is the arena of life in which there will be a concern for emotional comfort and security. For example, should Cancer be found on the eleventh house cusp, there is a strong need for making emotional connections with friends and associates of like mind, and a desire to nurture humanity as a whole rather than just those in the immediate environment.

In its most positive expression, Cancer is imaginative, sensitive, caring and gentle, understanding of the human condition, nurturing the best qualities in those of close connection. In its negative expression, Cancer is moody, selfish, irritable, over-sensitive to imagined insults, excluding others that are not members of their personal clan.

)))➤ *Cardinal, Feminine, Moon, Solstice, Sun-Sign, Water signs*

CAPRICORN

Capricorn is the tenth sign of the zodiac, a member of the cardinal triplicity, feminine, and of the earth element. A bestial sign, the symbol for Capricorn is the mountain goat, its ruling planet is Saturn. The Sun enters the sign of Capricorn at the time of the winter solstice on 22 December and exits around 19 January. People whose birthdays fall between these dates are said to be Sun-sign Capricorn. This is the first month of winter and the nature and qualities of Capricorn are closely associated with this time of year when the attention of nature is turned inwards and energy goes into the plans which must be laid down for the coming spring. There is hope in this apparently barren season, as the hours of daylight are getting gradually longer.

In physical terms, Capricorn rules the knees, that part of the body which must be strong so as not to buckle under the weight of a heavy load, and the bending of which allows the body to climb upwards towards the goals of the mind. As a

ABOVE: The sign of Capricorn and killing a goat, from a mid-fifteenth century French calendar and book of hours.
BELOW: The phases of Saturn, Capricorn's ruler.

cardinal sign Capricorn is goal-oriented and puts enormous energy into achieving personal objectives, but the earthy nature of the sign requires that each step along the way be perfectly planned and grounded in the reality of the physical world. Like its symbol, the mountain goat, Capricorn makes sure of each foothold before looking for the next, as it steadily advances higher up the mountain.

Capricorn represents a search for self through activity that puts in place the structures and supports necessary to manifest its aspirations and affirm its place in the hierarchy of society. Capricorn works within the structures it creates and is keen to utilize these as frameworks to achieve solid and measurable advancement upwards. There is respect for tried-and-tested methods and society's widely accepted modes of behaviour, traditional values and inherited resources are the building blocks for growth in Capricorn's world.

Very little of practical consequence will escape the notice of the ambitious Capricorn; they are adept at handling material resources and very effective at coordinating their energy to a pre-planned strategy.

Capricorn is pragmatic and patient in achieving ambitions, disciplined enough to wait and plan for the right opportunity before making a move and seizing advantage. Once set on a course of action Capricorn will not be deterred, being precise and methodical in the execution of a task, working hard to achieve recognition and status for a job well done. There is a persistent desire in Capricorn for the attainment of worldly power; if wealth and fame are important, respect and position are paramount. The link to time through the sign's ruling planet Saturn means that many Capricorns must wait until later life before acquiring the position and success to which they aspire. At whatever age, Capricorn enjoys the trappings of success and finds security in the prestige of high financial independence. Seemingly contrary to this there is also a nagging intuition that spirituality and the advancement of the soul are equally important – if not more so – as worldly status. Capricorn has a sense for the divine source that governs all physical matter.

There is an intense physical energy connected to Capricorn; calm and self-assured on the outside, it seems that just beneath the surface is a well-contained explosion just waiting to happen. But it never does – Capricorn conserves this energy until it can be channelled in the right direction for maximum impact and the achievement of ambitions, whatever form they take.

In personal relationships Capricorn appears cool and dispassionate. There is a touch of the social climber about Capricorn. Although there is an intense physical desire in the sign, Capricorn is not given to emotional display and has been known to choose a mate based as much on the prestige the match will bring as on love. Capricorn has a wonderful appreciation for the absurd and ironic, however, and makes an engaging companion and a steadfast and trustworthy friend.

ABOVE RIGHT: One of the negative qualities of Capricorn is a tendency to be miserly and cold, like Scrooge in Charles Dickens' A Christmas Carol.

Any planet in a horoscope found in this sign will operate through the energies connected with it. Mercury in Capricorn, for example, suggests a logical, orderly mind, slow to take things in but with an excellent retentive memory and a reluctance to speak unless sure of a good impact. Jupiter in Capricorn might operate as a need to push the boundaries of career, obtaining enormous pleasure and great knowledge through pursuing ambitions.

Whatever part of the horoscope that Capricorn is found is the arena of life in which there will be a concern for patient discipline in the attainment of ambitions. Capricorn on the eleventh house cusp, for example, might suggest a need to join with others of like mind and create a framework for the advancement of the group as a whole, or desiring membership of a club or society that has prestigious advantage.

In its most positive expression, Capricorn is industrious, trustworthy and loyal with good organizing skills and a deep spiritual understanding. In its negative expression, Capricorn is demanding, dictatorial, miserly and cold, opportunistic for position and prestige, pessimistic and brooding.

)))➤ *Bestial signs, Cardinal, Earth, Feminine, Saturn, Solstice, Sun-Sign*

CAPUT ALGOL

Fixed star used by astrologers. Also called simply Algol, this is a malefic fixed star representing the Gorgon, whose hair consisted of hissing snakes and who was decapitated by Perseus, which is analogous to losing one's head in a matter. It has been classed as an evil star in many cultures. Algol is now at about 26 degrees Taurus.

))))➤ *Fixed Stars, Malefic*

CARDAN, JEROME

Astrologer; also known as Cardanus Hieronymous or Cardano Girolamo (1501–76). He taught mathematics and wrote commentaries on Ptolemy. Cardan was born Pavia, Italy and entered the university there in 1519. He completed his studies at Padua in 1526, earning a doctorate in medicine and setting up a practice locally. Marrying in 1531 he had two sons and a daughter. Beset by

financial problems, Cardan turned to gambling in an attempt to make his fortune. In 1534 the family moved to Milan where he took up teaching. His reputation in medicine grew and he was appointed Chair of Medicine at Pavia. In 1560 his son was beheaded after being charged with poisoning his wife while in childbirth. Cardan fled from Milan in disgrace and became professor of medicine at Bologna. In 1570 he was imprisoned by the Inquisition for casting the horoscope of Christ. In 1571 he went to Rome where he received a pension from the pope and resumed his profession. Cardan was the astrologer for Henry VII and Edward VI. After Henry's death, he came to England expressly to calculate

ABOVE: Jerome Cardano, Italian mathematician and scholar.
LEFT: The star Caput Algol represents the Gorgon (or Medusa), who had snakes for hair and is depicted here by Caravaggio.

the chart of Edward VI. Having cast his own horoscope predicting he would live to the age of 75, he committed suicide on 21 September 1576.

CARDINAL

Quality of sign or house. The signs of the zodiac and the houses of the horoscope are not only divided by elements and modes, but also by qualities, which describe the direction and distribution of energies within the signs. The cardinal signs, also known as 'initiating' or 'leading' signs, are Aries, Cancer, Libra and Capricorn. Traditional astrology also calls them 'moveable signs', because they mark the change of the seasons. The term 'cardinal' is derived from the zodiacal position of these signs on the cardinal angles (Aries – east, Cancer – south, Libra – west, Capricorn – north) and is also applied to the corresponding houses. The nature of the cardinals is activating, initiating and creating primary experience. Planets in these signs and houses are generating motivational forces. Individuals with a strong cardinal emphasis in their horoscope are often initiators of ideas and actions who seek to actively influence or direct their environment. Since their energies are so much focused on contact and exchange with the outside world, the cardinal signs are sometimes in danger of losing contact with the inner self.

))))⟩ *Fixed, Mutable, Quadruplicity, Quality*

CARDINAL POINTS

Specific zodiac degrees. The four cardinal points are at 0 degrees of the cardinal signs Aries, Cancer, Libra and Capricorn. The annual passage of the Sun over these

points marks the astro-logical beginnings of the seasons and in ancient astrology they were used to mark the four quarters of the heavens, i.e. to compute time. They also refer to the four main directions and some astrologers regard planets in these degrees as especially powerful. The cardinal

points are often used to mark the angles of a horoscope, when the time or even the place of an event are unknown.

))))⟩ *Cardinal, Degree, Equinox, Solstice, Tropical Year*

CAZIMI

Planetary position related to the Sun. An Arabic term meaning 'in the heart of the Sun', cazimi describes a position up to 17 minutes either side of the Sun. Traditionally, a planet in this position is strengthened. The specific qualities it imparts vary depending on the planet involved. It may indicate a particularly close relation-ship in a horary chart. Because of the closeness of the path of Mercury's orbit to that of the Sun, Mercury is the planet most commonly cazimi. It is rare but nowadays generally used simply to describe a position rather than for interpre-tation, except in horary astrology.

))))⟩ *Combust, Horary Astrology*

CELESTIAL EQUATOR

Coordinate. The celestial equator is the earth's equator projected into space. Just as the earth's equator divides the sphere of the earth into two hemispheres – northern and southern – the celestial equator divides the apparent sphere of the sky into a northern and southern celestial hemisphere. Like the equator of the earth the celestial equator lies halfway between two poles, the north celestial pole and the south celestial pole.

))))⟩ *Equator*

CELESTIAL LATITUDE AND LONGITUDE

Astronomical measurement. Celestial longitude is measured east or west along the ecliptic and celestial latitude north or south of the ecliptic. They are the equivalent of geographical latitude and longitude projected out into space. The celestial latitude lines represent the celestial coordinates known as declination. The correspon-ding coordinate to longitude in the sky is called right ascension. Unlike longitude, which is measured in degrees and minutes, right ascension is usually measured in hours and minutes.

))))⟩ *Declination, Latitude, Longitude*

LEFT: The cardinal points, from a fifteenth century treatise. These zodiac degrees were used to mark the four corners of the heavens.

danio sup ipsū postea, xii. uircutib; que eū uoluerō de oriente inoe
cidente delup er subter er de piprir eas nemrod quoin flant omis
in una partem ad firmandū quod locutus est.

de vii. foertitudi
 nentium in oriente

nb; que flaint
ur terrantium.

o dum audiffet ioanton a magistro suo g septem errancia nso firma
ta in celo dicit ioanton magist meus uideo celum uoluens in mensura
directa er cognoui gō ista. vii. currencia nso firmata incelo ut oecere
stelle er p gs uircutes alias currunt festinabilic er alia p spacin. er alia de

LEFT: A fifteenth century representation of the Celestial Sphere.
RIGHT: Astronomer-priests of
Chaldea observe stars from the Tower
of Babylon (Babel).

CHALDEAN

Ancient astrology. Chaldean astrology is attributed to priests and is based on the finding of tablets dated about 670 BC, which reported astrological information. The location of Chaldea is subject to speculation. Chaldeans are seen as the magi of Babylonia, astrologers and diviners and 'the wise men from the East'. The chief object of their worship was the Sun, Belus. They did not worship the stars as God but worshipped those they believed He had appointed as mediators between Himself and man. In the time of Alexander the Great (around 356 BC) the Chaldeans alleged that their astrology had existed for 473,000 years.

))》 *Chaldean Order*

CELESTIAL SPHERE

Astronomical measurement aid. When viewed from the Earth, the sky resembles an inverted bowl and the stars and other bodies appear to be on the inside of a large sphere with the Earth at its centre. This large imaginary globe forms the celestial sphere. Within this, the Earth rotates on its axis from west to east, and to an observer on Earth the celestial sphere appears to move westwards. This apparent movement causes the Sun and other bodies to appear to rise east of the observer's meridian. The coordinate system used in astronomy is based on this sphere.

CHALDEAN ORDER

Order of planets. The Chaldean order of planets is Saturn, Jupiter, Mars, Sun, Venus, Mercury, Moon. The first (furthest from the Earth) Chaldean planet, Saturn, is the 'heaviest' or 'slowest', and the seventh or last (closest to the Earth) Chaldean 'planet', the Moon, is the 'lightest' or 'swiftest.' The order is used when calculating planetary hours, for example. In modern astrology the planets tend to be listed in the reverse of this order and the Sun placed first.

))》 *Planetary Hour*

CHART SHAPE

Horoscope pattern. Some visually distinctive planet configurations or aspect patterns are referred to as chart shapes. The distribution of planets in the horoscope gives the astrologer an impression of what kind of chart he is dealing with. Certain chart shapes have always been looked upon as special, for example, the five- or six-pointed star, the kite or the mystic rectangle. In addition to the traditional chart shapes, Marc Edmund Jones introduced and named several planetary patterns and described the personal characteristics they signify. These chart shapes, also known as 'Jones patterns', are quite popular among modern astrologers.

))))▶ *Bucket, Configuration, Locomotive, See-Saw, Tripod*

CHILDREN

To answer questions concerning children, the astrologer will look at the fifth house, an area of the natal horoscope connected to recreation, procreation and, in psychological astrology, to the child within. Planets in the fifth house – as well as the general condition and aspects of its ruler – will provide information about children and the relationship with them. Traditional astrology uses more elaborate methods and looks at the ascendant and its ruler as well as the condition of the Sun and Moon. If the ascendant or fifth house has a barren sign on the cusp or contains a barren planet, the chances of having children are considered to be slim. The same judgement applies if the Sun, as representative of the individual's creative powers, is considered to be in bad shape or if the Moon, significator of female fertility, is weak or afflicted. On the other hand, fruitful signs on the relevant cusps, benefics involved with the significators and Sun and Moon dignified promise numerous happy and healthy offspring.

))))▶ *Barren Planets, Barren Signs, Benefic, Cusp, Fifth House, Fruitful Signs, Significator*

CHIRON

Controversial new planet. Chiron, discovered in 1977, was named after the centaur in Greek mythology. Too large to be classed as an asteroid and too small for a planet, the new body inspired the term 'planetoid' ('planet-like'). Chiron's rotational cycle varies from 49 to 51 years; its orbit is highly elliptic and connects the orbits of Uranus and Saturn. This astronomical profile has given Chiron the nickname 'maverick', meaning 'outsider' or 'drop-out'. Many astrologers still dismiss Chiron as irrelevant; others have extensively researched Chiron's astrological significance.

Mythological Chiron, an immortal healer and teacher of homeopathy, suffered from a fatal wound and could neither live nor die. Accordingly, astrological Chiron is said to describe a physical or psychological 'wound' which may be incurable, but can lead to an understanding of similar suffering in others. In analogy with its orbit, Chiron is also said to describe the native's ability to combine traditional Saturnian limitations with the pioneering and rebellious spirit of Uranus.

))))▶ *Asteroid, Planet, Saturn, Uranus*

CIRCUMPOLAR

Type of star. Circumpolar literally means 'to circle around the pole' and circumpolar stars are those of the north circumpolar region, at the North Pole. They are those that circle overhead all night, without setting or dipping below the horizon. They move in an anticlockwise direction. They include Ursa Major and Minor, Cassiopeia, Cepheus and Draco constellations. Most stars are farther away from Polaris, and fall below the horizon. These appear to rise in the east and set in the west.

)))))➤ *Ursa Major, Ursa Minor*

DRACO AND URSA MINOR.

COLLECTION OF LIGHT

Planetary combination in chart. Collection occurs when a slower planet receives aspects from two faster planets that are not themselves in aspect, or forming an angular relationship to one another. In horary astrology the slower planet is said to collect the light of the faster planets and symbolizes that the matter in question may occur, or be brought about, through an intermediary described by the slow third planet. Traditionally, the slow planet should be in a degree of the zodiac where each of the faster planets is dignified, for example, in a sign it rules or is exalted in.

LEFT: Two examples of circumpolar constellations are Draco and Ursa Minor.
BELOW: Colours, represented here by Henri Matisse's L'Escargot, indicate *planetary correspondences.*

COLOURS

Planetary correspondences. To identify planetary influences in objects of daily life, which is of special importance in horary astrology, the astrologer looks for correspondences with the nature of the planet. This can be the material, the use, the shape or the colour of the object. Since there are about as many lists of colour correspondences as there are astrological works, the following can but provide general indications: Moon – white, silver, pale green; Mercury - yellow, azure, spotted or striped mixtures; Venus – pastels, light blues and greens, indigo; Sun – gold, orange, yellow; Mars – deep red, magenta,

COMET

Celestial body. The word comet comes from the Greek *komete*, meaning 'the hairy one'. Before 1600, comets were essentially considered to be heavenly omens and were not established as astronomical, rather than meteorological, phenomena. Then followed two centuries of mostly positional measurements with emphasis on the motions and the orbits, until the early nineteenth century, when the era of cometary physics was inaugurated. The next major step occurred in 1950 with the sudden emergence of the modern picture of comets as essentially very old Solar System objects made of primordial ice and dust, generally in unstable orbits. The earliest extant records of cometary observations date from around 1000 BC in China and probably from about the same time in Chaldea. Ideas about the true nature of comets are available from the time of the rise of Hellenistic natural philosophy at about 550 BC, when the Pythagoreans considered comets to be kinds of planets that were seen infrequently and mostly near the horizon in the morning or evening sky. For centuries they were believed to portend evil.

COMMANDING SIGNS

One of the divisions of the zodiac used in traditional and ancient astrology. It refers to the first six signs of the zodiac – Aries, Taurus, Gemini, Cancer, Leo and Virgo – and describes the nature as commanding, due to the placement of these signs on the horoscope and their connection to the developmental stages of growth centred around the projection of the self in the world and the fulfilment of the self's needs.

)))➤ *Aries, Cancer, Gemini, Leo, Taurus, Virgo*

deep orange; Jupiter – purple, violet, all sky blues; Saturn – black, brown, green, all dark colours; Uranus – all electric or metallic shades; Neptune – greyish pastels, sea colours, changeants; Pluto – black, blood red.

)))➤ *Birthstone*

COMBUST

Planetary position related to the Sun. A planet is combust if it lies in the same sign as the Sun and is within eight and a half degrees of its position. It is a form of debility and damages the planet concerned, as it is believed to be burned by the Sun and its power thereby reduced. Traditionally, the Moon is especially debilitated when combust. A combust Moon is a new Moon. It can indicate fear or being overpowered by another person in a horary chart. Combust is a traditional description, rarely used today except in horary astrology.

)))➤ *Cazimi, Horary Astrology*

ABOVE: Morehouse's Comet, photographed from Greenwich in 1908. The word 'comet' comes from the Greek for 'the hairy one'.

COMMON SIGNS

One of the divisions used in traditional astrology, 'common' refers to the signs Gemini, Leo, Sagittarius and Pisces. It describes them as retaining a property or nature that partakes of the signs preceding and following its position in the zodiac. Gemini therefore retains properties of Taurus and Cancer, Leo includes properties of Cancer and Virgo, Sagittarius has properties of Scorpio and Capricorn and Pisces contains properties of Aquarius and Aries.

COMPOSITE CHART

Horoscope describing a relationship. One of the methods of analysing a relationship is the composite chart. This is an artificial horoscope, based on the natal horoscopes of the persons involved and must be distinguished from the relationship chart. It is erected by calculating the midpoints between the charts for each planet. For example, if person A's Sun is at 10 degrees Aries, and person B's Sun is at 10 degrees Gemini, the composite Sun will be at 10 degrees Taurus. The composite houses are calculated either on the basis of the midheaven midpoint or the ascendant midpoint. The results of either method are only slightly different, but may affect the timing of events by solar-arc progression or transits to the angles. The location for the chart is the one where the relationship takes place. The idea behind this method is that two or more people combine their forces and blend their energies to create an artificial third entity, the relationship, which then starts to lead a life of its own.

)))⯈ *Midpoint, Relationship Chart, Synastry*

RIGHT: Sagittarius is one of the four common signs.
BELOW: The Hireling Shepherd in William Holman Hunt's painting could have his relationship analysed in a composite chart.

CONFIGURATION

Horoscope pattern. The term 'configuration' has various meanings. It is mainly applied to certain important aspect patterns, like the grand trine, the grand cross, the T-square or the mystic rectangle – all of which focus the horoscope's energies in special ways. Sometimes the term is used to describe certain planetary patterns or chart shapes, such as the 'locomotive', the 'see-saw' or the 'bucket'. Traditional astrology at some point referred to all aspects as configurations.

))))➡ *Chart Shape, Grand Cross, Grand Trine, Mystic Rectangle, T-Square*

CONJUNCTION

Major aspect. The conjunction is in fact rather a position than an aspect, but classified as such for simplicity's sake. It entails a close gathering of two or more planets, ideally with the same zodiac degree and symbolizes close cooperation of the planets, ehich combine their potentials and reinforce each other. Whether this has positive or stressful results largely depends on the nature of the relevant planets. The admissible orb for the conjunction is still a subject of discussion and ranges from three to as much as 10 degrees. Ancient astrology even worked with a 'conjunction by sign', which regarded planets in the same sign as conjunct, even if they were 29 degrees apart. This practice is still used in Vedic astrology. Conjunctions with the Sun have a special set of traditional rules. A planet within five degrees of the Sun is called 'combust' and is regarded as weak or even ineffective by most astrologers, while a planet within 17 minutes of arc from the Sun is called 'cazimi' and is supposedly much strengthened.

))))➡ *Aspect, Cazimi, Combust, Major Aspects, Parallel, Stellium, Vedic Astrology*

CONSIDERATIONS BEFORE JUDGEMENT

Technique to ascertain whether a chart is fit to be judged. The considerations are applied to horary charts before they are judged. If any of them are present then the chart is deemed unfit. They are also termed 'strictures' or 'cautions'. The chart is valid if the ruler of the hour and ascendant are of the same triplicity or nature, a factor which is frequently ignored. When less than three or more than 27 degrees rise, the chart is considered unfit. If the Moon is in the later degrees of a sign, the chart is unsafe – often ignored. If the Moon is in via combusta (between 15 degrees Libra and 15 degrees Scorpio) or void of course (cannot form an exact aspect before changing sign) the chart is unfit. If Saturn is in the first or seventh houses or the seventh cusp is afflicted, the chart is unfit. If the ruler of the seventh is badly placed or ruler of the ascendant combust, the chart is unfit. These definitions do not apply to birth-chart analysis.

))))➡ *Horary Astrology, Ruler, Triplicity, Via Combusta, Void of Course*

ABOVE: Considerations are applied to charts by astrologers, such as the noted Paris astrologer Barlet, shown here working with some his feline associates.

CONSTELLATION

Group of stars. Astronomers officially recognize 88 constellations covering the entire sky in the northern and southern hemispheres. Currently, 14 men and women, nine birds, two insects, 19 land animals, 10 water creatures, two centaurs, one head of hair, a serpent, a dragon, a flying horse, a river and 29 inanimate objects are represented in the night sky (the total comes to more than 88 because some constellations include more than one creature).

Our modern constellation system is derived from that of the ancient Greeks. The oldest description of the constellations as we know them comes from a poem called *Phaenomena*, written about 270 BC by the Greek poet Aratus. It seems likely the Greek constellations originated with the Sumerians and Babylonians of ancient Mesopotamia. In AD 150 Ptolemy published *The Almagest*, which contained a summary of Greek astronomical knowledge, including a catalogue of 1,022 stars, together with estimates of their brightness, arranged into 48 constellations. These formed the basis for our modern constellation system. Over the years astronomers have added constellations in the gaps between Ptolemy's figures and map the uncharted regions of the sky near the South Celestial Pole.

)))) *Galaxy, Ptolemy, Solar System, Universe*

CONTRA PARALLEL

Aspect by declination. Two planets with the same degree of declination are said to be 'in parallel'. While traditional astrology ignores the northern or southern position of the planets, modern astrology calls a parallel between a planet of northern and another of southern declination contra parallel. It is said to have the same connotations as an opposition. Many astrologers only consider parallel aspects if the planets are also connected by another aspect in the chart.

)))) *Opposition, Parallel*

CONVERSE DIRECTION

Method of prediction. The term 'direction' refers to various ways of moving the planets around the horoscope according to a certain key formula and then judging their new positions in relation to the natal chart. One of these methods of direction is the so-called secondary progressions, which use the daily motions of the planets to describe a whole year. Thus, the first day after birth describes the first year of life, the second day the second year and so on. Converse directions use the same formula, but instead of moving forward, the planets are progressed backwards through the zodiac.

)))) *Directions*

ABOVE: *The ceiling from the Sala del Mappamondo fresco by G de Vecchi and da Reggio, showing the constellations.*

COORDINATE

Astronomical measurement. Celestial coordinates specify which direction something is in respect to the Earth, but not distance from it. For objects inside the Solar System (comets, planets, moons, asteroids) distance is often specified in Astronomical Units (AU). An AU is the average distance from the Earth to the Sun or 149,597,870 km (92,955,730 miles). Any of two measurements that determine position – for example, longitude and latitude – can be referred to as a coordinate. Coordinates used in astronomical measurement include declination, right ascension, celestial latitude and longitude and altitude. They are usually measured in degrees, although right ascension is often measured in units of time.

)))➤ *Declination, Latitude, Longitude*

COPERNICUS, NICOLAS

Founder of modern astronomy. Born in Poland, Copernicus (1473–1543) studied mathematics at Cracow University and canon law at Bologna. He was appointed canon in the cathedral of Frauenburg, and it was from here that he carried out his astronomical observations from a turret situated on a wall around the cathedral. In 1530 Copernicus completed his great work *De Revolutionibus*, in which he asserted that the Earth rotated on its axis once a day and travelled around the Sun once a year. This heliocentric (Sun-centred) system overthrew the traditional geocentric (Earth-centred) view of the Universe. The work was clearly controversial and Copernicus was in no hurry to publish it, although it was circulated. His work was banned by the Church in 1616 and only removed from the Index in 1835. Copernicus died in 1543 and was never aware of what a stir his work caused. It forever changed the position of man in the cosmos.

ABOVE: Polish astronomer Nicolas Copernicus.

BELOW: The universe as understood by Copernicus, with the Sun as its centre, circled by the Earth and other planets, and by the signs of the zodiac.

COSIGNIFICATOR

Second significator. Like the significator, this planet represents a certain person, matter or area of life. Generally, the ruler of an intercepted sign is the cosignificator of the house that contains the interception. It provides additional information, but weighs less in interpretation than the main significator. In horary astrology, certain houses are assigned signs or planets as cosignificators. For example, the Moon is always looked at as cosignificator of the ascendant, i.e. the querent.

))))➤ *Interception, Significator*

COSMOBIOLOGY

Modern astrological method. The word 'cosmobiology' was first coined in 1914 by the medical scientist Feerhow and was adopted by Reinhold Ebertin and his associates in Germany during the 1920s. The discipline is concerned with the possible correlation between the cosmos and the individual, and the effects cosmic movement and stellar motions have on the individual as a whole in a given environment. As a scientific discipline, it is also concerned with researching the effects of stellar influences on individuals. Ebertin published *The Combination of Stellar Influences* in 1940, and this remains the standard guide to this method. Cosmobiology does not make use of the houses as traditional astrology does. House systems were discarded as unreliable; most people do not have the exact

ABOVE: Cosmobiology explores links between the cosmos and the individual, as shown in this illustration from Les Tres Riches Heures du Duc de Berry.

time of birth needed to plot them accurately. Cosmobiology relies on using the positions of the planets by signs and in relation to one another, and relies heavily on the use of midpoints. It also emphasizes the need to consider the person's background and environment. It is particularly popular as a system in Europe.

))))➤ *Reinhold Ebertin, Midpoint*

COSMOGRAM

Astrological tool. The cosmogram is a tool used in cosmobiology. It is a 90-degree dial on which one degree represents one degree of the zodiac. The numbering begins at the top of the dial and moves in an anticlockwise direction. The first 30 degrees represent the cardinal signs (Aries, Cancer, Libra, Capricorn), the next 30 the fixed signs (Taurus, Leo, Scorpio, Aquarius) and the last 30 the mutable signs (Gemini, Virgo, Sagittarius, Pisces). When all the planets are placed around the dial the conjunctions, squares and oppositions can be seen easily. The instrument was designed to reveal these aspects or angular relationships.

))))➤ *Cardinal, Cosmobiology, Fixed, Mutable*

CREATIVE ASTROLOGY

Modern astrological method. Creative astrology is an astrological interpretation technique closely allied to psychological astrology. It came into being during the 1970s, developing out of humanistic psychology, in which the client is empowered to enter into a dialogue with their unconscious. The horoscope is often seen as an aid to psychology. Creative astrology also has strong links with esoteric astrology. Techniques such as guided imagery and drama are used extensively. The person whose horoscope is under discussion is encouraged to participate in the chart reading. Unlike in other forms of astrology, the horoscope is treated as a means to self-discovery, and it is assumed that it is not possible to read the birth chart and predict specific events. With the recent rise in interest in traditional forms of astrology, creative astrology has largely fallen out of favour, although it is still used by astrologers who also work as therapists.

))))➤ *Psychological Astrology*

ABOVE: *In creative astrology, a modern astrological method, the querent is encouraged to participate.*
BELOW LEFT: *The crescent moon is shown over a landscape.*

CRESCENT MOON

Phase of the Moon. The Moon forms a crescent shape twice in its cycle. The waxing crescent Moon can be seen after the new Moon. It will grow larger until it looks like the first quarter Moon. The waning crescent

Moon can be seen after the last quarter Moon. It will grow smaller every day, until it looks like the new Moon.

))))➤ *Full Moon, New Moon, Waning Moon, Waxing Moon*

CRITICAL DEGREE

Zodiac degree classification. The critical degrees of the zodiac are the cusp degrees of the lunar mansions. They are primarily used in medical astrology, which predicts the progress of an illness using the transits of the Moon. Days on which the Moon passes over such a point are called 'critical degree days' and usually mark a change in the course of events. Some astrologers only regard the cusps of the first, eighth, fifteenth and twenty-second lunar mansion as critical. In natal astrology, a planet within two to three degrees of a critical degree is said to gain strength similar to exaltation. Some sources class 29 degrees of any sign as critical

))))➤ *Cusp, Exaltation, Illness, Lunar Mansions, Transit*

CULMINATION

Positional measurement. A celestial body culminates when it meets the upper meridian. In astrology the term describes when a planet arrives at the midheaven, or the cusp of the tenth house, by direction, progression or transit. It is sometimes used as a term to indicate the completion of an aspect – the arrival of a planet at an exact degree. 'Culminator' is a term used to describe a planet that reaches such a critical position.

))))➤ *Aspect, Midheaven, Tenth House*

CULPEPER, NICHOLAS

Astrologer and herbalist. Nicholas Culpeper (1616–54) is a legendary figure in the field of herbal medicine and is popularly regarded as the figurehead of alternative medicine. A member of an old noble family, he was born fatherless in Surrey, squandered a fortune in Cambridge and tried to elope with a rich heiress who was killed by lightning. His study of astrology began at the age of ten, and he was taught astrology by William Lilly in 1635. Although it was intended that he should study theology, he began attending anatomy lectures and was disinherited by his family as a result. He trained as an apothecary in London, and by producing an unauthorized critical translation of the *London Dispensatory* he became the enemy of the physicians. Working as an astrologer and herbalist he saw up to 40 patients a day. During the Civil War he joined the Parliamentarian forces and was wounded. He fought a duel and was accused of witchcraft. In 1652 he wrote his famous herbal, *The English Physician,* and before that the first English textbook on midwifery and childcare.

))))➤ *William Lilly*

CUSP

Boundary of sign or house in horoscope. The cusp of a sign or house is the point at which it begins. Therefore, zero degrees of Aries is the cusp of Aries. As the Sun changes signs on slightly different dates each year, people often refer to being born on the cusp when their birthdate is a day that the Sun changes sign. However, the Sun is in one sign or another, and an astrologer will calculate the precise time that it changes signs. The cusp of a house is generally regarded as the most powerful part of the house. Therefore, a planet that is up to five degrees before the cusp may be regarded as being in that house. The planet that rules the sign that the house cusp is in is said to rule that house.

CYCLE

Patterns of motion. The Universe has many cycles. The Milky Way turns like a wheel and all the stars within it revolve around its centre. The Solar System moves within this galaxy. The Sun spins on its axis once every 24 days and 16 hours. The planets turn on their axis and orbit the Sun. Moons orbit their planets. Astrologers

ABOVE: Nicholas Culpeper was a famous herbalist and wrote his own herbal work. These healing herbs are from an earlier, fourteenth century manuscript.

are most interested in the cycles of the planets as they orbit the Sun. They each take a differing amount of time to complete an orbit, and the length of this, as well as its halfway and quarter points, are astrologically significant. For example, the Sun returns to its place in the birth chart approximately one year later, an occasion we celebrate on our birthday. The time at which a planet returns to its original place in the birth chart is referred to as a 'return' and charts are cast for these times.

)))➤ *Orbit*

DARK MOON

Hypothetical planet or focal point of the lunar orbit; also called Lilith. The dark moon constitutes a rather confusing issue: the name was given to a hypothetical second moon orbiting the Earth, which is said to be visible only when passing between the Earth and the Sun. The American astrologer Ivy Goldstein-Jacobson published an ephemeris which gives the dark moon a rotational cycle of 126 years. The term, dark moon, can also refer to the focal point farthest from Earth of the Moon's elliptic path. This point has a rotational cycle of 3,232 days. French astrologer Joëlle de Gravelaine describes it as the dark, destructive side of the feminine principle, analogous to Adam's first wife Lilith in Rabbinic mythology. Created of clay like Adam, she rejected his supremacy, ran off and became a demon, obsessed with sex and stealing babies. Both dark moons are interpreted as malevolent and relating to betrayal, obsession, stillbirth and abortion.

)))➤ *Apogee, Hypothetical Planets*

DATA

Information needed to cast a chart. Data refers to the time, date and place used. Unreliable data that cannot be verified by official sources is known as 'dirty data'. Data is classified by its reliability according the Rodden system, established by data collector and

astrologer Lois Rodden. In this system AA is accurate as recorded, A accurate from person or close associate, B biography or autobiography, C no source, DD conflicting information given, X no time, XX no confirmed date. This is now the international guide to data quality used by all astrologers.

DAY

Measurement of time. What is normally referred to as a day is the period of light between sunrise and sunset, the period of daylight or sunshine. The interval of time between two successive passages of a star over the meridian is a sidereal day. A lunar day is the day of the full Moon.

)))➤ *Sidereal Time*

ABOVE: The dark moon is also called Lilith, after Adam's first wife in Rabbinic mythology. This terracotta relief of her dates from c. 2000 BC
ABOVE LEFT: The cycle of the zodiac, with its solstices and equinoxes.

DAYLIGHT SAVING TIME

Also called 'summer time' in the UK, this originated in England in 1916. It consists of setting ahead the clock by one hour, shifting all the day's activities an hour earlier, ending the workday sooner and leaving an hour more of daylight. In the US, where the term is most commonly used, it usually commences at 2 a.m. of the Sunday following the third Saturday in April, and ends on the Sunday after the first Saturday in October.

)))▶ *Summer Time*

DEBILITY

Measure of planet's strength. A planet is said to be debilitated when it appears in certain signs and houses which are considered to be incompatible with the energy or characteristics of the planet. It is weakened by an adverse aspect, being in the sign of its detriment or fall, or by being in a cadent (third, sixth, ninth, twelfth) house. Being retrograde is also a debility. Often the term is simply used to refer to a planet in the sign opposite that of its rulership (detriment) or exaltation (fall). The Sun is in detriment in Aquarius, fall in Libra; the Moon is in detriment in Capricorn, fall in Scorpio; Mercury is in detriment in Sagittarius and Pisces, fall in Pisces; Venus is in detriment in Aries and Scorpio, fall in Virgo, Mars is in detriment in Taurus and Libra, fall in Cancer, Jupiter is in detriment in Gemini and Virgo, fall in Capricorn; Saturn is in detriment in Cancer and Leo, fall in Aries. The outer planets – Uranus, Neptune and Pluto – are not part of this traditional system and therefore cannot be said to be debilitated.

)))▶ *Detriment, Dignity, Fall, Retrograde*

DECANATE

Division of signs; also known as decan. The root of the word *decanate* is the Greek for '10 days apart'. This concept was borrowed from the Egyptians, who had a 360-day calendar. Each sign of the zodiac occupies 30 degrees. Every sign is further sub-divided into three 10-

ABOVE: The signs of the zodiac each occupy 30 degrees of a full circle, and a decanate is a 10-degree sub-division of these segments.

his contemporaries, who regarded the quintiles as an artificial, sinful and useless addition to the natural order as expressed by the classic major aspects. Like the quintile, the decile is an aspect of subtle influence. It confers insight into the workings of natural forces combined with mental resourcefulness and creative talent, and is also associated with occult interests. In some instances it may resemble a Uranian influence and indicate working with groups. The innate talent, however, needs to be consciously developed by the individual.

))))➡ *Aspect, Minor Aspects, Semi-Quintile*

DECLINATION

Astronomical measurement. Declination is the equivalent of latitude in the sky. It reports how far a star is from the celestial equator. To find the declination of a star, follow an hour circle straight down from the star to the celestial equator. The angle from the star to the celestial equator along the hour circle is the star's declination. It is the angular measurement of a celestial object north or south of the celestial equator, the Earth's equator extended into space. Zero degrees of Aries and Libra have no declination as they are on the equator. Declination is measured in degrees.

))))➡ *Latitude*

degree segments called decanates, ruled by the three signs of the same element. For example, the first segment of Aries is sub-ruled by the planetary rulers of Aries, the second by Leo and the third by Sagittarius. An alternative system of decanates gives planetary rulers to each section of the signs in the order of Mars, Sun, Venus, Mercury, Moon, Saturn, Jupiter. The term is also used to mean 'face', although face is only five degrees in size, rather than 10. Each decanate may be further broken down into two-and-a-half degree segments called 'dwads'.

DECILE

Minor aspect. The decile is an aspect of 36 degrees and is generally allowed an orb of one degree or, if the lights are involved, two degrees. It is also known as 'semi-quintile' and belongs to a series of aspects introduced by seventeenth-century astrologer Johannes Kepler, who based these aspects on the division of the circle into five segments. Kepler was much criticized by

RIGHT: Johannes Kepler introduced the decile, also called the semi-quintile.
ABOVE: A medieval astronomer puzzles over some measurements. Declination is a way of measuring a star's distance freom the celestial equator.

DECREASING IN LIGHT

During the period that the Moon is going from full to new, it is said to be decreasing in light. Although generally applied to the Moon, the term is also applicable to any planet passing from an opposition to conjunction with the Sun.

))))▶ *Conjunction, Increasing in Light, Lunation, Opposition*

DECUMBITURE

Medical diagnosis by astrology. The name *decumbiture* comes from the Latin word *decumbo*, meaning 'to lie down' or 'to fall'. In this traditional form of astrology, a chart is cast for the moment that a patient falls ill or goes to bed. It was used in times when herbal physicians such as Nicholas Culpeper made their diagnoses, prognoses and choice of herbs. There are a number of possible moments on which to base a decumbiture. Firstly, the moment when the patient feels so overcome by their illness that they have to lie down. This is the truest moment in time to judge a decumbiture; however, not everyone takes to their bed when unwell, even if they would like to. Alternatively, if a disease starts suddenly following an accident or some other specific event, this moment in time can also be used. In the past a chart was often cast for the moment that the physician/astrologer received a urine sample from the patient. This form of astrology is rarely used today.

))))▶ *Medical Astrology*

ABOVE: A urine analysis plate. Astrologers used to provide decumbiture charts for the moment that they received a patient's urine sample.

DEE, JOHN

Astrologer. Born in 1527, Dee studied mathematics and astronomy at Cambridge and took his MA in 1548. He had to leave England after accusations of being a conjurer. On his return he was already well known as an astrologer and was granted a pension by King Edward. On the accession of Mary he was imprisoned and charged with using enchantments against the Queen's life. When Elizabeth I took the throne he elected a date for the coronation and became a court astrologer. In 1581 he came into contact with Edward Kelly and their lives became completely entwined. Kelly was an Irishman who had lost his ears for forgery. He was reputed to be able to summon spirits. He was killed in 1595 while attempting to escape from prison in the Hague. They involved themselves in alchemical research and necromancy. For eight years they travelled abroad together before quarrelling and separating. When Dee returned to England in 1594 he stopped dabbling in spiritualism and alchemy. James I ejected Dee from his sinecures and he retired to his small estate in Mortlake, Surrey, where he died at the age of eighty-one. Dee's interests were wide but he focused primarily on astrology. He has now gained almost legendary status.

))))▶ *Earth Zodiac*

DEGREE

Astronomical measurement derived from Babylonian astronomy. The 360th part of a circle.

ancient and probably based on the interpretation of fixed stars, such as the Theban calendar or the so-called Angelus Degrees described by the sixteenth-century astrologer Johannes Angelus. Hellenistic astrology used the monomoira, a system in which each zodiac degree was assigned to a specific planet. Scottish astrologer Wemyss constructed a system of degree symbols that includes the meanings of hypothetical planets. Other systems of degree symbols have been devised by psychic methods. The 'Sabian Symbols', first published by Marc Edmund Jones and later re-interpreted by Dane Rudhyar in his famous work *An Astrological Mandala*, are the most popular system of degree symbols today.

))))➤ *Degree, Hellenistic Astrology, Sabian Symbol*

The entire sky spans 360 degrees. Up to about 180 degrees of sky is visible from any given point on Earth with an unobstructed horizon. The degree is used to make measurements of distance or position.

DEGREE SYMBOL

Zodiac degree classification. A system of degree symbols assumes that each zodiac degree has a special meaning, which is expressed by the symbol assigned to it. There is a vast number of such systems, some of them

ABOVE RIGHT: John Dee, occultist, astrologer and magician.
ABOVE: Elizabeth I, for whom Dee worked as court astrologer after electing the date of her coronation.

DERIVED HOUSES

Interpretation technique. Derived houses are usually used in horary astrology, although some people apply the technique to natal astrology. It is a method whereby the astrologer turns the chart and uses another house as the first house. For example, if there is a question about a spouse, the person asking the question is represented by the first house and their spouse by the seventh. If the question is about the spouse's employer, the seventh house is used as the first and the employer is represented by the tenth house from the first, or in other words, the fourth house of the chart.

))))➤ *Horary Astrology, Houses*

DESCENDANT

Cusp of the seventh house; also referred to as the setting sign. The western angle or cusp of the seventh house represents our relationships with those around us and what we project on to others. Calculated for the time, date and place of birth, the descendant moves about one degree every four minutes. The sign on the descendant shows how we relate to other people as individuals. Because the descendant is one of the four angles of the chart, any planet in conjunction with it is regarded as having a strong influence in the chart. Planets that make an aspect to the descendant have an influence on relationships. As the seventh house rules partnership and marriage, the descendant may be taken to describe the marriage partner. The descendant is one of the main points to consider in synastry and if your partner's ascendant is in the same sign as your descendant it shows an exceptionally close bond. It is also a significant point in relation to contracts, buying and selling, and competition.

)))➧ *Angles, Angular, Ascendant, Seventh House, Synastry*

DETRIMENT

Measure of a planet's strength. The detriment of a planet is in the sign that is opposite to the one that it rules. Being in detriment weakens a planet and is considered a debility. A person represented by a planet in detriment may feel outclassed or obliged to work. A planet in detriment may also indicate loss or difficulty. The planet generally functions at a disadvantage. It cannot operate at full strength and may indicate a need to adhere to rules. Describing a planet

---

LEFT: Partnerships, such as that of Adam and Eve (painted here by Van Eyck), are ruled by the seventh house, of which the descendent is the cusp.
ABOVE: Mars is in its detriment when in Taurus, the Bull.

as being in detriment is not a moral judgement of the value of the planet, or the individual whose chart it is, but is rather an aid to balancing the differing factors of the horoscope. The Sun is in detriment in Aquarius, Moon in Capricorn, Mercury in Sagittarius and Pisces (Jupiter-ruled signs), Venus in Aries and Scorpio (Mars-ruled signs), Mars in Taurus and Libra (Venus-ruled signs), Jupiter in Gemini and Virgo (Mercury-ruled signs) and Saturn in Cancer and Leo (Moon-ruled signs).

))))➡ *Debility, Dignity, Fall*

DEXTER

Dexter means 'on the right-hand side' and is a direction of an aspect. A dexter aspect is one in which the faster planet is waxing, or increasing in light with respect to the slower one. The faster planet is casting its rays to the right because the slower planet is on the right side of the applying planet when viewed from the Earth. It goes against the direction of the signs. A dexter aspect is more potent than a sinister aspect (one that falls to the left).

))))➡ *Sinister*

DIGNITY

Measure of a planet's strength. There are two kinds of dignity – essential and accidental. Essential dignity refers to a planet being in a degree of the zodiac where it is in a strengthened position. The essential dignities are those of rulership, exaltation, triplicity, term and face. A planet in its rulership is completely comfortable there, as if it were at home and can set its own agenda. A planet in its exaltation is like a welcomed guest - things are done for them. In its triplicity it is comfortable as a neighbour popping around for coffee would be and is considered fortunate. In its term it is an acquaintance invited indoors and in its face it is accepted. The precise zodiac degrees where planets are in dignity can vary depending on the system used. A list of the commonly used dignities appears in the introduction. An accidental dignity occurs when a planet is placed in the first, seventh, tenth, fourth or eleventh house, is moving quickly or is within seventeen minutes of the Sun's position (cazimi). Other positions can also give accidental dignity. A planet may have essential or accidental dignity, both or neither. The more dignity a planet has, the stronger it is, and essential dignity is always stronger than accidental dignity. The opposite to dignity is debility.

))))➡ *Debility, Exaltation, Face, Rulership, Term, Triplicity*

DIRECTION

Prediction method. The term direction refers to numerous different ways of moving the planets in the chart and judging their new positions in relation to their birth chart. Generally, the term direction is used to describe a method whereby a special measure is added to the position of all planets, related to a period of life. There are a number of forecasting methods that can be called directions. Primary directions are based on the idea that one year of life can be represented by four minutes. Secondary progressions are based on the actual movements of the planets but symbolically related to a time period or cycle in life. A day is held to represent one year. Tertiary progressions operate on the same basis but a day is held to represent a month or week of life. Transits are based on the actual motion of the planets at any given time.

))))➡ *Primary Directions, Progression, Secondary Progression, Tertiary Progressions, Transit*

DISPOSITOR

A planet disposing of another. The ruler of the sign in which a planet finds itself disposes of, or is the dispositor of that planet. For example, if Venus is in Aries, Aries is ruled by Mars, and Mars is the dispositor of Venus. The disposing planet has influence over the planet being disposed of. A chart may have a 'final dispositor'; in this case the planet concerned acts almost like a chart ruler. According to other authorities the ruler of the sign on the cusp of a house is the dispositor of a planet that is placed in that house.

ABOVE: The direction method refers to the ways of moving the planets in a chart, as the planets move around the zodiacal system and change our fortunes.

DISSOCIATE

Type of aspect. A dissociate is an aspect in which the planets involved are not in the expected signs. For example, when in opposition they are not actually in opposite signs. In older texts this term was used as an alternative name for the quincunx aspect, as this always involves incompatible signs. Whatever the aspect, the term describes an uncomfortable combination.

))))➤ *Quincunx*

DIURNAL

Term meaning 'of daytime'. Refers to a chart when the Sun is in the top half and the individual is born in daylight hours. It can also refer to the daily motion of a planet. It is often used to describe the motion of any planet from midnight to midnight along the ecliptic.

))))➤ *Nocturnal*

DOUBLE-BODIED SIGNS

See Bi-Corporeal signs

DRYNESS

Aristotelian principle. Dryness is one of the four principles formulated by Aristotle and regarded as underlying all phenomena. Ptolemy's classification of signs and planets is also used in traditional astrology to describe their essential nature. The fire signs – Aries, Leo and Sagittarius – are hot and dry; the earth signs – Taurus, Virgo and Capricorn – are considered to be cold and dry. Of the planets, the Sun and Mars are classified as hot and dry, while Mercury and Saturn are regarded as dry and cold. These descriptions are used in medical astrology and are also taken quite literally when pertaining to locations.

))))➤ *Aristotle, Moisture, Ptolemy*

EARTH

Planet and central focus of astrology. Astrology is still based on an Earth-centred (geocentric) model of the Universe because psychologically and practically speaking the geocentric model still works for the purposes of astrology. In the past the Earth was believed to lie at the centre of the Universe with the planets and stars rotating

ABOVE: The pre-Copernican system of the universe. Earth is at the centre, orbited by the other planets, including the sun, and surrounded by stars.

around it. The entire system was set up and put in motion by God, and it was by His will that the planets influenced life on Earth in a regular way. The planets (the Moon, Mercury, Venus, the Sun, Mars, Jupiter and Saturn), the stars and the heavenly regions rotated around Earth (and man). The Earth in the birth chart is always 180 degrees from the natal

position of the Sun. Thus, if the Sun is at one degree Scorpio, the Earth will be found at one degree of Taurus. The Earth is the esoteric ruler of Sagittarius and represents the physical location of a person's spiritual path.

))))➡ *Nicolas Copernicus, Planet, Universe*

EARTH SIGNS

Signs of the earth triplicity. The signs expressing the earth element are Taurus, Virgo and Capricorn, ruled by Venus, Mercury and Saturn respectively. They represent the realm of matter, which has given them the reputation of being purely materialistic. Taurus represents fertile plains, Virgo symbolizes valleys, which can hold shadows of sadness, while Capricorn is associated with majestic mountain peaks. Taurus, the fixed earth sign, is said to stay in one place and to secure the rhythmic repetition of daily life. Virgo, the mutable earth sign, deals with the organization of everyday occurrences and finds fulfilment in service to others. Capricorn is associated with a slow but steady climb on the social ladder and the arrival at the top of the social hierarchy. Psychological astrology regards the earth signs as representing the different facets of the perceptive type, who focuses on the perceptions of the five physical senses. Because of this concentration on physical phenomena, self-expression is difficult and can often only be achieved through an act of will.

))))➡ *Air Signs, Element, Fire Signs, Water Signs*

EARTH ZODIAC

Natural zodiac. In the past, vast tracts of land were laid out so that they might be explored using maps of the constellations; these are known as the terrestrial or earth zodiacs. So far a total of 13 have been discovered in Britain including the zodiacs at the Lizard, Bodmin Moor, Ffarmers in Wales, Glastonbury, Althorp Park, Kingston-on-Thames, Cambridge and Hebden Bridge. They have as their centre the stone circle at Arbor Low, Derbyshire. The most famous is the Glastonbury zodiac, a great landscape configuration 10 miles across. The 12 zodiac signs appear in their right order, formed by hills, outlined by roads and rivers. Katherine Maltwood, who rediscovered this great circle in 1925, claimed it as the original Round Table of legendary Avalon. In the sixteenth century John Dee had mentioned the existence of a zodiac in or around Glastonbury, but his descriptions are vague and there is no evidence that this corresponds to the Glastonbury zodiac.

))))➡ *John Dee*

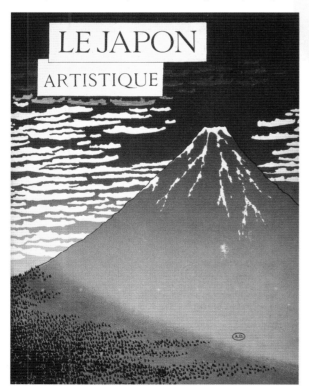

ABOVE: A mid-nineteenth century representation of the planet Earth, esoteric ruler of Sagittarius.

LEFT: The sign of Capricorn is associated with majestic mountain peaks.

EAST POINT

Astrological chart point. The east point is a symbolic point showing where the ascendant would be if we were born at the equator. It lies directly opposite the point where the ecliptic intersects the prime vertical. This point is known as the vertex. The east point is therefore also known as the vertex and the anti-vertex (opposite to vertex) is known as the west point.

))))➤ *Equator, Prime Vertical, Vertex, West Point*

EBERTIN, REINHOLD

Twentieth-century astrologer. Members of the Ebertin family – Elsbeth (Reinhold's mother), Reinhold himself, and his son Baldur – have been a major force in both German and international astrology since the early years of the twentieth century. Ebertin was born in 1901 in Goerlitz, Germany, and was initially a student of the Witte System, but he later abandoned the Trans-Neptunian (hypothetical) planets. Throughout the 1920s he researched and developed a streamlined version which focused on the midpoints and which he named cosmobiology. The system was taught around the world and he wrote 60 books on the subject. He published his first book, *Into the Horoscope*, in 1927 and *Transits* in 1928. The best known of these is *Combination of Stellar Influences*. Ebertin advocated a scientific approach, throwing out many of the time-honoured techniques of traditional astrology and concentrating on planetary and angular relationships. House systems were discarded in this system as they were not considered sufficiently reliable. Together with his wife he formed the publishing house known as the Ebertin-Verlag. He died in 1988.

))))➤ *Cosmobiology, Hamburg School, Midpoint, Midpoint Tree*

ECLIPSE

The concealing of one celestial body by another. An eclipse occurs when one celestial body obscures another; the term is generally used to refer to the relationship between the Sun and the Moon. A lunar eclipse occurs when the Moon passes into the Earth's shadow, and is visible over the whole night hemisphere of the Earth, lasting up to two hours. During a total lunar eclipse the Moon takes on a dark red colour. When the Moon shadows the Sun's light as viewed from the Earth, or passes through

ABOVE: Antoine Caron's Astronomers Observing an Eclipse. *An eclipse occurs when one celestial body obscures another.*

TAB. VII. *ad A.* 1682.
pag 109.

Eclipsis lunæ totalis cum mora
Anno 1682 *die* 21 *Febr.*
observata

GEDANI
à
Joh. Hevelio.

Fig. 1.

Phases decrescentis ad totalem.
obscurationem usq.
21 febr. vesp.

Initium Eclips.

Total. obscur.

Fig. 2.

Phases Crescentis à recuperatione
luminis ad finem Eclips.
22 febr. mane

Recuper. Lum

Finis Eclips.

the shadow cast by the Earth, it is known as a solar eclipse. Eclipses may be total, partial or annular (a ring of the Sun is left around the Moon). In a total eclipse the surface of the is completely blocked by the Moon, in a partial eclipse it is only partially blocked, and in an annular eclipse it is partial, but the apparent diameter of the Moon can be seen completely against the apparent diameter of the Sun. A solar eclipse may be all three of the above for different observers.

)))➤ *Occultation*

ECLIPTIC

Circle of the Sun's path. The ecliptic is so named because eclipses can only occur when the Moon crosses this great circle. It describes the centre line of the zodiac, which extends about eight degrees above and below the ecliptic. The ecliptic is the plane of the Earth's orbit around the Sun. From the Earth we seem to see the Sun moving along the ecliptic rather than the Earth. As we look into the heavens, the Sun appears to follow its path through the

centre of the zodiac. In reality we are following our cyclic path around the Sun.

)))➤ *Celestial Sphere*

EGRESS

Description of planetary orbit. From the Latin *egressus* (from egredi 'to go out'), in astronomy egress means to exit from behind a second body or its shadow. Both ingress and egress are used to describe the times when, for example, the Moon enters and leaves the Earth's shadow during a lunar eclipse. Astronomically, this is the point at which a body leaves a constellation. In astrology, the term is used slightly differently, referring to the point at which a planetary body or luminary leaves a sign.

)))➤ *Ingress*

TOP: *The phases of a lunar eclipse.*
ABOVE: *The sun's place in the ecliptic. Eclipses can only occur when the moon crosses this circle.*

EGYPTIAN ASTROLOGY

Ancient astrology. After the fall of Babylon in 538 BC, astrology experienced a decline. At this time in Egypt a system of magic had been developed which included telling the future through dreams and it continued to grow. Between the second and first centuries BC two occult works were developed. The first was an astrological work attributed to the pharaoh Nachepso and his priest Petosiris. *The Revelations of Nechepso and Petosiris* were supposed to have been the secrets revealed after studying the stars. There also appeared the books known as the work of Hermes Trismegistus. These writings were a compendium built up from the library at Alexandria. Claudius Ptolemy next drew together elements of astrological theory in one logical whole. Much of our understanding of Egyptian astrology is contained within the Cairo Calendar, which consists of a listing of all the days of an Egyptian year. The listings within the calendar are broken up into favourable and unfavourable. Many Egyptian astrologers followed Ptolemy, including Paul of Alexandria, Hephaestion of Thebes and Palchus.

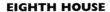 *Ptolemy*

EIGHTH HOUSE

Sector of chart. In modern astrology this is often known as the house of other people's values. It describes that which is shared, how we unite with others and sex. It is the house of death, inheritance, any activities concerned with the dead, executors of wills and the finances of your spouse. Financial obligations, debts, taxes, losses and loans are also represented by this house. Traditionally, it is related to crisis, hidden matters and deadly fears. Psychological astrology regards it as a house of inner transformation and growth. In political astrology it represents the national debt, collector of taxes, danger through war or national disasters, the resources of the enemy and financial relations with other countries. It is also associated with public mortality and the death rate. In conflicts and legal matters it represents the friends and assistants of the defendant. In medical astrology it is associated with the sex organs, haemorrhoids, gallstones, bladder and poisons generally. It is associated with the colours green and black and is a feminine, succedent house. It represents the direction west-south-west. It is associated with Scorpio and

ABOVE: Ceiling decorated with astronomical scenes in tomb of Ramses VI, 20th dynasty Egyptian pharoah.

Saturn. It is also known as epicataphora (casting down), abodes of typhoon (sedes typhonis) and the house of death.

)))➤ *Scorpio, Saturn*

ELECTIONAL ASTROLOGY

The astrology of electing, or choosing, the best time to go ahead with a project or activity. There are two types of electional charts – universal and particular. Universal elections do not use a specific nativity, while

particular elections do. Universal election can be used, for example, to elect a time for building structures, planting crops or moving to a new location. Particular election examples are undergoing surgery, marriage, going on a journey or purchasing property of any kind. The rules of electional astrology are broadly similar to those of horary, and it is another traditional form of astrology that does not require a birth time. To cast an electional chart it is decided what needs to be achieved and what planets and houses are associated with the event. With practical considerations taken into account, the astrologer examines the positions of the planets and chart points over a given period and seeks to cast a chart that gives the most auspicious moment for the event to take place.

)))➤ *Horary Astrology*

ELEMENT

Division of the zodiac by triplicity. Western and Vedic astrology divide the zodiac into four elements: fire, earth, air and water. Because each of the elements contains three signs, they are also referred to as 'triplicities'. Each element symbolizes a specific way of manifestation or a manner of perception. The active fire element, consisting of Aries, Leo and Sagittarius, is concerned with the initial spark of inspiration, creativity and future vision. The

LEFT: The eighth house is also known as the house of death.
BELOW: The four elements, zodiac signs and alchemical symbols, from a seventeenth century publication.

receptive earth element, containing Taurus, Virgo and Capricorn, concerns itself with maintaining, organizing and regulating the material aspects of life. The active air element collects and logically analyses information and develops a theoretical understanding in Gemini, Libra and Aquarius; while the receptive water element experiences, maintains and expresses the emotional, nurturing and caring component of life. Modern astrology often equates the elements with the four psychological types described by Carl Jung: fire = intuition, earth = perception, air = thinking, water = feeling. Esoteric astrology follows

Aristotle, by assuming that there is a fifth element, called 'quintessence' or 'ether', which is the binding medium for all the other elements.

)))➤ *Air Signs, Earth Signs, Fire Signs, Mode, Vedic Astrology, Water Signs*

ELEVATION

Astronomical measurement. Elevation is equivalent to altitude, as it measures the distance of a planet or body above the horizon. Elevation of the pole is equivalent to latitude. If a planet has more latitude than another, it is said to be in elevation by latitude. If they have the same, the one with most declination is the most elevated. In astrology it refers to a planet close to the midheaven. It is one of the accidental dignities.

)))**➤** *Declination, Latitude*

ELEVENTH HOUSE

Chart division. In modern astrology the eleventh house is associated with friends, friendship, larger groups and networking. It is the house of ideals and social

BELOW: Crocus-picking for the production of saffron, which is associated with the eleventh house.

reform. Traditionally known as the house of good fortune, it is related to supporters, benefactors, hope, trust, praise, comfort, goals and ambitions. In horary astrology it refers to the friends of the person asking the question, stepchildren and the profit or income from a professional endeavour. In political astrology it is associated with Parliament, especially the House of Commons, Senates and other major political bodies, town and country councils and friends and allies of a nation. It represents the hopes of a nation. Places of comfort and relief are also represented here. In medical astrology it represents the legs to the ankles. It is associated with the colour yellow or saffron, and is a masculine and succedent house. Traditionally, it was regarded as a powerful house, considered equal in some sources to the fourth and seventh houses. Its direction is south-south-east, and it is associated with the Sun and Aquarius. Jupiter has joy – is happy in – this house. It is also known as bona fortuna (good fortune), good daemon and the house of friends.

)))**➤** *Houses*

ELONGATION

Astronomical measurement. Elongation is the angle between a planet (or moon or other object) and the Sun, as seen from the Earth. In standard ephemerides, this is usually denoted by the Greek letter epsilon (e). A celestial object's (an object within the Solar System) phase angle is the elongation of the Earth from the Sun, as would be seen by an observer. It is, however, not a term in general use in astrology.

)))**➤** *Ephemeris*

EPHEMERIS

A set of tables listing the 'ephemeral', or rapidly changing positions, which each solar-system body will occupy on each day of the year; their longitude, latitude, declination and similar astronomical phenomena. An astrologer's ephemeris lists these positions in relation to the Earth. An ephemeris for the year of birth is essential to calculate a horoscope. Before 1925 the astronomical day began at noon, so positions in older ephemerides were always given for that time. Nowadays they may be given for midnight or noon.

EQUAL HOUSE SYSTEM

Method of chart division. The Equal house system is the oldest system in use, dating from the first century BC. In this system, each house is exactly 30 degrees, starting with the ascendant as the cusp of the first house. In most cases, this means that the midheaven will not be the cusp of the tenth house, but a separate point instead. The cusp of the tenth house, also called the nonagesimal, is exactly 90 degrees from the ascendant, as measured along the ecliptic. Many astrologers in the United Kingdom and India use this house system, largely because astrological schools in those countries have promoted this system. It is commonly held

that this is the house system advocated by Ptolemy in his *Tetrabiblos.* However, it is now believed that attribution of Equal houses is a misunderstanding of the text and that what is in fact referred to is whole-sign houses, in which the whole of the sign that the ascendant falls in is counted as the first house, the following as the second house, and so on.

➠ *Ecliptic, House System*

LEFT: The title page of Parker's Ephemeris, which gave celestial information for the preparation of horoscopes.
BELOW: Ptolemy, who advocated the Equal house system.

EQUATOR

Astronomical and geographical coordinate. The equator is the line of latitude which passes through the centre of a planet at the greatest distance from its rotational axis, splitting the planet into northern and southern hemispheres. It is one of the most significant imaginary lines running across the surface of the Earth. The equator is the longest line of latitude on Earth, the line where the Earth is widest in an east-west direction. The equator runs through Indonesia, Ecuador, northern Brazil, the Democratic Republic of the Congo, and Kenya, among other countries. It is 40,075.16 km (24,901.55 miles) long.

))))**➤** *Latitude*

EQUINOCTIAL SIGNS

Equinoctial or solstice signs refer to Aries and Libra. When the Sun is at zero degrees of Aries (approximately the twenty-first of March), it is the time of the spring or vernal equinox, the first day of spring, and day and night are of equal length all around the Earth. From this date the hours of daylight are longer than the hours of night. Consequently when the Sun is at zero degrees of Libra (approximately the twenty-first of

ABOVE: The equator is a line of latitude which spans the centre of the planet. BELOW: The Sun, whose position in relation to the celestial equator determines the two annual equinoxes.

September) it is the autumn equinox. Day and night are of equal length again, but from this date the hours of daylight gradually become less than the hours of night.

))))**➤** *Aries, Ecliptic, Equinox, Libra*

EQUINOX

Seasonal measurement. There are two equinoxes annually. Although it originally referred to the time of year when night and day are of equal length, the modern definition is when the Sun's centre crosses declination 0. Day and night are not quite the same length on the equinoxes. The vernal, or spring equinox (near 21 March) occurs when the Sun crosses the celestial equator moving northwards. It was originally in Aries. It now occurs when the Sun is in Pisces. In astrology it is still counted as when the Sun enters Aries. The autumn equinox (near 23 September) occurs when the Sun crosses the celestial equator, moving southwards. Astrologically this is when the Sun enters Libra.

ESOTERIC ASTROLOGY

Esoteric astrology is a system that is used to analyse spiritual factors in someone's life. It reveals the soul's intention and indicates how the soul seeks to

express itself in one's outer life for the purpose of service to others. This form of astrology was developed out of the Theosophical Society, formed by Helena Blavatsky in the late nineteenth century. It correlates the theosophical seven rays with the planets and signs. According to this system, each person has certain rays predominant in their

personal chart. These rays correspond to the chakras or energy centres. Esoteric astrologers also use the Earth and a hypothetical planet, Vulcan, as objects in the chart. The astrologer Alan Leo began to popularize this form of astrology in the late nineteenth century. From 1936 the theosophist Alice A. Bailey wrote a series of books entitled *Esoteric Astrology* and these form the main texts in this field. This type of astrology reached the general public with popular works such as Alan Oken's *Spiritual Astrology*.

))))➤ *Ray*

EXALTATION

Exaltation is one of the five essential dignities. A planet in its own exaltation acts as if it was a welcomed guest, having things done for it but not having complete control over the situation. The strength of the planet is augmented and its virtues are magnified. It is only slightly less favourably placed than when it is in its own sign. The opposite sign to the sign of exaltation is that of fall, taking the opposite meaning. Exaltation is a traditional technique that may be used in any form of astrology but is primarily used in electional and horary. The Sun is exalted in Aries, especially at 19 degrees; the Moon in Taurus, especially at three degrees; Mercury in Virgo, especially at 15 degrees; Venus in Pisces, especially at 27 degrees; Mars in Capricorn, especially at 28 degrees; Jupiter in Cancer, especially at 15 degrees and Saturn in Libra, especially at 21 degrees. The modern planets, Uranus, Neptune and Pluto, are not included in the scheme as they were undiscovered when the system was devised.

))))➤ *Dignity, Electional Astrology, Fall, Horary Astrology, Rulership*

FACE

Face is one of the five essential dignities. A planet in its own face is slightly fortunate. Face is little used in modern astrology, although with the re-establishment of horary astrology it has become more popular in recent years. The division of the 360-degree circle into units of 10 degrees was developed by the Egyptians and then adopted by other civilizations. Beginning with zero degrees of Aries, the first 10 degrees are assigned to Mars, its ruler. From there each face ruler in sequence is in Chaldean order: Mars, Sun, Venus, Mercury, Moon, Saturn, Jupiter. Thus, up to 10 degrees of Aries is ruled by Mars, from 10 to 20 by the Sun, from 20 to 30 by Venus; the first 10 degrees of Taurus by Mercury and so on. In the past, faces were used extensively in weather forecasting. The faces represent worry or concern about matters related to the planet in question. Some authorities have assigned fear to the faces.

))))➤ *Chaldean Order, Decanate, Dignity, Horary Astrology.*

LEFT: Helena Blavatsky, whose Theosophical Society developed esoteric astrology – a form of astrology which analyzes the soul.

FALL

Fall is one of the five debilities. A planet in fall is opposite the sign of its exaltation. It is believed to be severely weakened because the sign's characteristics are inimical to the natural expression of the planetary energy. It refers to a situation where the planet concerned drops out of sight, not allowing the issue to be perceived properly. In an horary chart a significator (a planet that symbolizes the matter or person in question) in its fall may indicate an unfortunate, helpless, insolvent or cruel person. It may refer to a person who has fallen, been disgraced or suffered some kind of limitation. In charts about a missing object, it may have fallen down from where it was originally. The Sun is in its fall in Libra, the Moon in Scorpio, Mercury in Pisces, Venus in Virgo, Mars in Cancer, Jupiter in Capricorn and Saturn in Aries. There are no specific degrees of fall. The modern planets, Uranus, Neptune and Pluto, are not included in the scheme as they were undiscovered when the system was devised.

))» *Debility, Exaltation.*

FATE

Philosophy applied to astrology. The word *fate* is derived from the Latin *fatum*, meaning 'prophecy' or 'doom'; *fatum* is derived from *fari*, meaning 'to speak'. It is the supposed force, principle or power that predetermines incidents and the inevitable events predestined by this force. It describes, therefore, a final result or consequence – an outcome. Fate is seen as something ordained by the gods, our destiny. It describes circumstances against which it is useless to struggle and it has been common to talk of fate as if it were a power superior even to the gods. Christian theology places God above the laws of nature, ordaining things to His will. To accept a fatalistic view of the Universe, therefore, is in direct opposition to Christian – and indeed many other – belief

systems. Astrology has long struggled with this issue and answers the conflict of whether or not it is fatalistic by the statement that the stars impel, not compel. Therefore, an element of choice remains and all is not ordained.

FEMININE

Division of the zodiac and the planets. The feminine signs of the zodiac are Taurus, Cancer, Virgo, Scorpio, Capricorn and Pisces – all of the earth or water element. They are sometimes labelled as 'negative' signs, perpetuating the misconception that everything feminine is negative. The terms 'feminine' and 'negative' rather refer to the basic receptive mode of these signs, comparable to

TOP: The fate of the newly-created Earth is considered, on the one hand by God and his angels, and on the other by demons.

ABOVE: Eastern tradition represents feminine and masculine as Yin and Yan.

the 'Yin' of the eastern tradition. The feminine earth signs first need to be presented with factual circumstances or material necessities in order to function and develop their practical talents. The feminine signs of the water triplicity need an initial impulse from outside before they can react with a feeling which will lead them to a judgement of their experience and induce them to unfold or withdraw their caring and nurturing capabilities. The feminine planets are the Moon and Venus. Here, the term does not only refer to the receptive and reflective basic attitude. Modern and traditional astrology alike associate these planets with feminine qualities and with actual women in the native's life.

))))➤ *Masculine, Mode*

VENERE

ABOVE: Venus, who is happily placed in the fifth house, rides her dove-drawn chariot through the clouds.

FERAL SIGNS

One of the divisions of the zodiac, used in traditional and ancient astrology. It refers to the signs Leo and Sagittarius. Both signs are bestial signs, represented by four-footed creatures, but they have the added description of being feral or wild beasts. This pertains to the nature or characteristics of Leo and Sagittarius as partaking of unpredictable and uncontrollable qualities as opposed to those creatures of a domesticated nature.

))))➤ *Leo, Sagittarius*

FIFTH HOUSE

Sector of the chart. In modern astrology the fifth house represents creative expression, sports and recreation, gambling and speculation, and any hobbies. It is associated with activities that make us feel good about ourselves. Romance and sexual expression also fall under the fifth house, and it is the house of children and pregnancy. Conception, promiscuity, scandal and over-indulgence are shown by this house. Places of entertainment are also included here, including pubs, theatres and parks. In horary astrology the fifth represents the children of the person asking the question and the sex of the unborn child. In mundane astrology it represents ambassadors and diplomats as well as all public places of enjoyment and recreation, and social issues related to children. In medical astrology it represents the stomach, liver, heart and back, the back of the shoulders and sides of the body. It is also related to medical problems during pregnancy and the bearing of children. It is associated with the colours black, white and honey. It is a masculine and succedent house. It represents the direction north-north-west. It is the joy of Venus, which means that Venus is happily placed there, and it is also associated with Leo. The fifth house is also known as good fortune and house of pleasure.

))))➤ *Houses*

FINANCIAL ASTROLOGY

Financial astrology has been around for centuries. Traders in grains and precious metals in ancient India used it to set trading times in the markets. Aristotle

recorded the story of Thales of Miletus (699–635 BC), who used his knowledge of heavenly cycles to predict a bumper olive crop, and turned a handsome profit. Financial astrology can refer to the practice of predicting cycles on the stock markets by allying them with planetary cycles or by casting a horoscope for a person's financial institution and analysing it in terms of finances. Many of the theories used today are based on the work of W. D. Gann, who developed a reputation for using astrology successfully to predict market trends and was said to have calculated exact price movements in correlation with planetary movements. The banker J. P. Morgan, who consulted astrologer Evangeline Adams in timing some of his most important business and investment moves, is often quoted in support of using astrology for trading: 'Millionaires don't use astrology; billionaires do!'

))))▶ *Aristotle, Evangeline Adams*

ABOVE: Aristotle, who recorded the story of Thales of Miletus, a man who used his knowledge of the heavens to make money.
RIGHT: Leo the lion, an example of a fire sign.

FINGER OF FATE

Aspect pattern. The finger of fate, also known as the finger of God or Yod, is a triangular aspect pattern, in which two planets connected by sextile (60 degrees) are each forming quincunx aspect (150 degrees) with a third planet. The planet in the apex of the triangle is often referred to as the 'action point'. The planets involved in the quincunx aspects are operating from signs of an incompatible element background, while the planets forming the sextile are operating from a compatible element background. This contradiction characterizes the workings of the whole aspect pattern. While the quincunx aspects continuously confront the native with the necessity of choice, the sextile provides the ability to use favourable circumstances to their advantage or the opportunity of creating them. Therefore, the finger of fate is often linked to a special life purpose and the strong inner drive to accomplish something very important.

))))▶ *Kite, Mystic Rectangle, Yod*

FIRE SIGNS

Signs of the fire triplicity. The signs expressing the element fire are Aries, Leo and Sagittarius, ruled by Mars, the Sun and Jupiter respectively. The active fire element lends these signs the primal force of creative expression and the force of spirit. In the case of Aries, the cardinal fire sign, the energy

that this element brings is channelled into the act of initiating activity, manifesting thought in action and the individualizing of the self from the rest of humanity. Leo is the fixed fire sign and channels the fiery nature into acts of creation; there is a desire to remain in a central position from where they can shine outwards with passion, love and magnanimity. Sagittarius, the mutable fire sign, is a double-bodied sign, and, as such, has two expressions of fire – the higher ideals of spirit and civilization (which meets the aspirations of the soul) and the lower primal nature (which meets the desires of the body) – endeavouring to meld the two into a united whole. Modern astrology associates the fire signs with the animating force of the spirit, which is focused on self-assertion and creativity. This can sometime lead to burnout if not enough care is taken to contain the energy, or re-stock the fuel.

)))➤ *Air Signs, Earth Signs, Element, Triplicity, Water Signs*

FIRST HOUSE

Sector of the chart. The first house is that which begins with the ascendant and it is therefore an angular house. In modern astrology the first house represents the personality and its expression. It is associated with the appearance, general behaviour and general tendencies in relationships with others. It can also indicate

ABOVE: Mercury, who is said to have joy in the first house, rides his chariot over citizens practicing the arts and sciences.

the level of personal vitality and strength. The first house is the house of the individual. In a horary chart it represents the person who is asking the question. In mundane astrology it represents the common people or the general state of a nation, the country as a whole. In a chart for a lawsuit or conflict it represents the person who initiates the action. In a chart for an event it represents whoever makes the first move. In medical astrology it represents the head and face. It is associated with pale colours and white. It is diurnal, masculine and cardinal. It represents the direction east. Mercury is said to have joy, or be happily placed, in the first house. Saturn and Aries are traditionally associated with the first house. It may also be called the eastern angle, ascendant, horoscope, anatole and house of life.

)))➤ *Ascendant, Diurnal, Houses*

FIRST POINT OF ARIES

Specific zodiac degree. The first point (degree) of Aries is actually located at 0 degrees Aries. It is the beginning point of zodiacal measurement; all planetary positions can be referred back to this point. The first point also marks the spring equinox and thereby the beginning of the astrological year.

)))➤ *Cardinal Points, Degree, Equinox*

FIXED

The signs of the zodiac are divided into three categories, each of which describes the functioning of that sign: cardinal, fixed and mutable. The fixed signs are Taurus, Leo, Scorpio and Aquarius; the fixed or succedent houses are the second, fifth, eighth and eleventh. The term originates in the fact that the season to which each of the fixed signs belongs is firmly established by the time the Sun enters into them. Accordingly, matters signified by these signs and houses in horary charts tend to be of a lasting nature, and new undertakings will be a long time developing. Psychological astrology equates the fixed quality with the introverted type of Jungian description. People with an emphasis on fixed signs or houses are focused on inner impulses rather than the demands of their environment. Fixed types will only act on their own accord and tend to stay with decisions once made, even if proven wrong. Consequently, they are said to be slow but determined, stubborn but dependable and persevering. Negatively, inflexibility may lead to isolation.

)))➡ *Cardinal, Mode, Mutable, Quadruplicity, Quality*

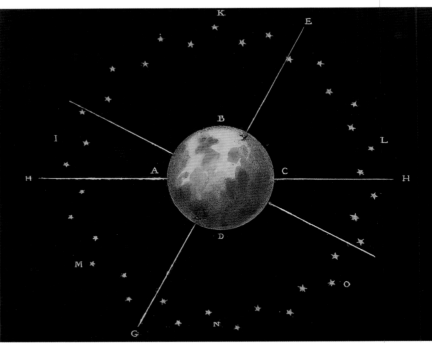

FIXED STARS

The fixed stars were so called to distinguish them from the planets, or wanderers. Fixed stars are those that appear to be stationary relative to the Earth, although they do advance at the rate of less than one minute a year, moving one degree in 72 years. They do not move across the ecliptic as the planets do. Those near the ecliptic and of significant magnitude have consider-

ABOVE: The fixed stars, which appear to be stationary from the Earth, but which in fact advance, albeit extremely slowly.

able influence. Fixed stars do not lie within the zodiac; they are all beyond it in the constellations, whereas planets move within the zodiac. Fixed stars have an influence when making a major aspect to a planet or significant point in the chart. They are particularly important when near the ascendant or angles, or when near the Sun or Moon. Because they move so slowly they have to be within one degree of an aspect of a chart point or body to have a relationship with it. Many astrologers only use fixed stars when in conjunction, with the body or point being considered.

)))➡ *Aldebaran, Antares, Caput Algol*

FLAT CHART

Chart created when no birth time is available. As birth times are not commonly recorded in the UK – with the exception of Scotland and for the birth of twins – many people do not know their birth times. In this case a horoscope is erected for an arbitrary time, often noon or sunrise, and the chart is described either by the substitute time used or as a flat chart. The angles and houses are ignored on such charts.

)))➡ *Sunrise Chart*

FOURTH HOUSE

Chart division. The fourth house is that which begins with the Immum Coeli and it is therefore an angular house. In modern astrology the fourth shows our roots and past. It represents the influence of our family of origin and a parental figure. In modern astrology it is usually held to represent the father (although some sources give it to the mother). In traditional astrology it always represented the mother. It also represents grandfathers, hidden treasure, land and property. In horary astrology it represents the father of the person asking the question, property for sale, lease agreements, boundaries and gardens. In political astrology it represents land, the workers on it, crops and produce as well as the farming and mining industry. In a war chart it represents a place under besiegement. A planet representing a lost object in this house suggests that it will be found. In medical astrology it represents the breast or lung area. It is an angular, feminine and nocturnal house. The fourth house is associated with Saturn as well as Cancer and the Sun. It is also called the Northern angle, angle of the earth, Immum Coeli (lower midheaven), ypogeon (below the earth and the house of parents.

))))➡ *Houses, Immum Coeli*

FORTITUDE

An ancient term indicating a quality or strength possessed by a planet when it is in its own sign or in the sign of its exaltation. It is often used to describe how dignified or debilitated a planet is. A high degree of fortitude means that the planet concerned is heavily dignified. The term is generally applied to essential dignity only, not accidental dignity.

FORTUNE

Name for Jupiter or Venus. The fortunes are the benefic planets; Jupiter is classed as the greater fortune and Venus as the lesser. The Sun and Mercury (or according to some authorities, the Moon and Mercury) are also classed as fortunes when well placed and aspected, especially if by Jupiter or Venus.

))))➡ *Infortune*

LEFT: Fortitude, from Ambrogio Lorenzetti's Allegory of Good Government. *BELOW: Jupiter, also known as the greater fortune, carries thunderbolts as he rides in his chariot.*

FREE WILL

Free will refers to the ability or discretion of human beings to make a free choice and the power of making free choices that are unconstrained by external circumstances or by an agency such as fate or divine will. It implies that there is no coercion or restraint on taking action borne of necessity or of a physical nature. The concept of predestination clashed with that of free will in ancient Greek culture as much as in Christian theology. Caught up between the idea of blind and merciless fate and the belief that humanity was responsible for its own actions meant that the Greeks threw the burden back on to the shoulders of the Fates. One astrologer to grapple with the problem of free will was Abumassar, who made a distinction between the influence of the planets and of the fixed stars; the former controlled – or could control – the details of everyday life and the latter affected only the grand design of the Universe in a way that was so slow it was scarcely visible to the human eye.

)))➤ *Abumassar, Fate*

LEFT: Cosmic fatality depicted on a seventeenth century Tarot card. The notion of free will challenged the idea that fate was responsible for the destiny of men. Abumassar tried to explain this in terms of planets and fixed stars.

FRIENDS AND ENEMIES

Matter of the seventh, eleventh or twelfth house. In analogy with the seventh sign Libra, allies and associates are described by the seventh house. However, since this chart area is just concerned with the principle of relating, a malefic in this house or its afflicted ruler may signify an open enemy, for example; in a lawsuit. The eleventh house relates to one's hopes and dreams, which can only be fulfilled through the co-operation of like-minded people, hence its connection with friendships. The twelfth house signifies secret enemies, often in the sense of a person being their own worst enemy.

))))➤ *Eleventh House, Seventh House, Twelfth House*

FRUITFUL SIGNS

A division of the zodiac, used in traditional or ancient astrology. This term is rarely used in modern astrology; however, in the judging of a horary chart, when a fruitful sign appears of the ascendant or fifth house cusp, it suggests that further action invested in the matter will produce worthwhile results. The fruitful signs are the three water signs, Cancer, Scorpio and Pisces – water being the universal element necessary to nurture life and promote growth.

))))➤ *Cancer, Horary Astrology, Pisces, Scorpio, Water Signs*

TOP: *Libra is associated with the twelfth house, along with allies, associates and open enemies*

ABOVE: *The full Moon, which is thought to provoke unpredictable behaviour in people.*

FRUSTRATION

Planetary combination preventing another planetary combination. Frustration means that a faster planet is travelling towards a slower one, but before they join in a conjunction the slow one joins up with a different planet. The first two planets are held to signify an event in horary or electional astrology. The third planet produces an abscission of light that frustrates the promised effect of the slower-moving aspect; meaning that what is promised cannot take place. At the least the matter will be delayed in a way that is related to the house of which the planet that frustrates is the ruler.

))))➤ *Abscission of Light, Electional Astrology, Horary Astrology*

FULL MOON

One of the phases of the Moon. The Moon is full when its lighted side faces the Earth. This means that the Earth, Sun and Moon are nearly in a straight line, with the Earth in the middle. The Moon that we see is very bright from the sunlight reflecting off it. In astrology the full Moon represents a pinnacle point, taking things to extremes. It was commonly believed that during the full Moon people could act in an unpredictable manner, giving birth to the word 'lunacy'. The flow of blood is believed to increase around the time of a full Moon, so traditionally this is a bad time to undergo surgery. The two-and-a-half week period after the full Moon is the best time to consolidate, organize and complete that which you began earlier.

))))➤ *Moon*

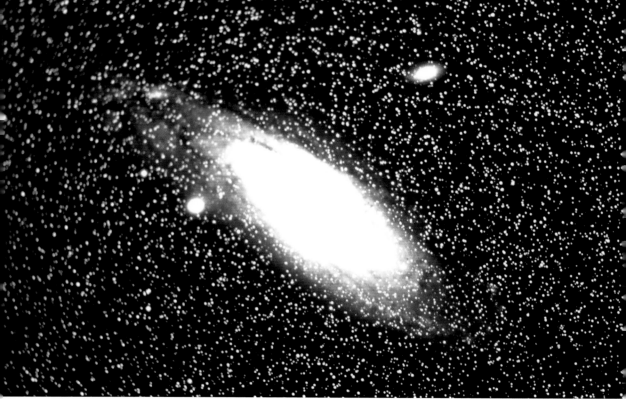

GALACTIC CENTRE

The gravitational centre around which the Sun revolves in the Milky Way, or the point in our Galaxy around which the Solar System revolves in a 225-million-year period known as a cosmic year. It is currently around 26 degrees Sagittarius. The Sun and stars in the Milky Way all revolve around this point. In the birth chart a planet or chart point near the galactic centre is said to indicate someone who is likely to do something on a large scale. When examining this point in the birth chart only the conjunction and opposition are used.

))))➤ *Galaxy*

GALAXY

Group of stars. A galaxy is a star cluster, or group of stars, dust and gas, held together by the gravitational attraction between its components. The Sun and its system are contained within the Milky Way galaxy, which moves around a gravitational hub called the galactic

ABOVE: The Great Galaxy in Andromeda. A galaxy is a group of stars, dust and gas held together by gravity.

centre. From long-exposure images made with large ground-based and space telescopes, we know today that the Milky Way is similar to countless other galaxies and we now recognize that galaxies are the major structural units of the Universe. Our galaxy was originally called the Milky Way because it was believed to have been formed from a luminous celestial fluid. Galaxies are usually classified as elliptical, spiral or irregular in shape. Elliptical galaxies appear like ellipsoidal clouds of stars, with very little internal structure apart from (in some cases) a denser nucleus. Spiral galaxies are flat disc-shaped collections of stars with prominent spiral arms. Irregular galaxies have no apparent structure or shape. Only three galaxies outside the Milky Way can be seen from Earth.

))))➤ *Galactic Centre, Solar System, Universe*

GAUQUELIN, MICHEL

Twentieth-century astrologer. Michel Gauquelin (1928–91) was born in Paris, France. Originally a statistician, Gauquelin attempted to repeat work done by previous researchers in an attempt to establish the relationship between certain planets and types of profession.

He began with a test list of 576 physicians, finding that Mars and Saturn appeared in the horoscope in a manner that could not be dismissed as chance. Extending his work gave equally positive results. With his wife, Françoise, Gauquelin conducted research over 30 years, demonstrating that certain astrological principles held true to a high degree of statistical validity. The most striking example was the Mars Effect – in which they found that the charts of sports champions tended to have Mars within 10 degrees of one of the four angles of the chart. The results inflamed the scientific community, who went to great lengths to disprove the results and in one case falsified data to achieve the results they wanted. After the couple divorced in 1982 they continued to research separately. He died in 1991.

ABOVE: A spiral galaxy.
LEFT: Mars, commonly found to be near one of the angles in the charts of sports champions – Michel Gauquelin's so-called Mars Effect.

GEMINI

Gemini is the third sign of the zodiac, a member of the mutable triplicity, masculine and of the air element. A human sign, the symbol for Gemini is the heavenly twins and its ruling planet is Mercury. The Sun enters the sign of Gemini around 21 May and exits around 21 June. People whose birthdays fall between these dates are said to be Sun-sign Gemini. This is the third month of spring, and the nature and qualities of Gemini are closely associated with this time of year as the days lengthen towards that longest day of the year – the summer solstice. More light is being shed on the world so that it can be seen, contemplated and understood in its myriad expressions of life.

In physical terms, Gemini rules the hands and arms, which it likes to use in conjunction with the mind to explore one idea after another. Because of the bi-corporeal nature of the sign it is also true to say of Gemini that sometimes the left hand does not know what the right hand is doing. As Gemini also rules much of the body's nervous system, this sign reacts to almost every form of stimulation in its immediate environment; Gemini is eager for excitement and experience, a thrill-seeker. This can lead to restlessness and fickleness in the direction that energy is channelled, occasionally resulting in a dissatisfaction that lasts only long enough until the next mental interest is stimulated.

Gemini represents a search for self through the mental process and understanding the dualistic nature of what is observed and experienced. Gemini is able to see that there is more than one side to any story, the observer and the observed, action and reaction. The Gemini mind is constantly examining the many sides of any situation in order to discover all aspects to gain greater understanding.

Gemini is an intellectual, experimenting with ideas, analysing data, systemizing information and drawing conclusions. There is an imperative to

reason through every thought and experience, which then must be communicated to those in the immediate environment. Gemini is perpetually shifting from one perspective to another, at each stage rationalizing that position before switching to the next. This contributes to Gemini's reputation for being changeable, fickle and tricky, but also versatile and adaptable.

There is an insatiable curiosity and a passion for

RIGHT: Gemini, the twins, tends to be changeable, resulting in a fickle, yet adaptable personality.

seeking knowledge. Gemini is not content to sit in one place for long but must be out and about gathering more information, more mental stimulus, making connections with others who can help feed the hungry mind. Gemini is a social butterfly, alighting here one minute to gather information, then flying off to alight somewhere else the next, cross-fertilizing as they gather more and move on again.

Gemini is the sign of the teacher, writer, traveller and graphic artist; as long as there is plenty of scope in daily life to take in information and pass it on, Gemini is fulfilling the innate talents and skills of the sign. The communication skills of Gemini are enormous; an excellent memory, clever mind and delightful wit combine to make a brilliant raconteur. On the flip side this mental trickiness has a tendency to tie themselves and others up in mental knots, as Gemini can rationalize and talk themselves into anything they want to believe.

Relationships, friendships and associations are important to Gemini as they provide exchange of thoughts and ideas; it is often easy to find an immediate rapport that is light, entertaining and full of excitement. However, due to the airy nature of the sign, the connection with Gemini is always mental and rarely does it carry any depth of emotion. Although Gemini has feelings like any other sign, emotions are processed through the intellect and can occasionally remain unexpressed unless there is a logical framework through which to understand them. There is a flirtatious manner about Gemini that is sometimes perceived as indiscriminate and insincere. This makes it difficult for Gemini to form permanent close attachments. The questing need for freedom of thought requires a partner that will not clip the butterfly's wings.

Any planet in a horoscope found in this sign will operate through the energies connected with it. Mars in Gemini, for example, suggests a keen understanding of strategy, a strong passion for ideas, and a need to express them forcefully, perhaps even aggressively. Uranus in Gemini would operate as an innovative and inventive mind, a sympathy for scientific method and occasional flashes of inspiration.

Whatever part of the horoscope that Gemini is found is the arena of life in which there will be a concern for rationalization on the mental level. Gemini on the ninth house cusp, for example, indicates a curiosity in matters of a philosophical and spiritual nature as well as an interest in foreign cultures and ideas.

In its most positive expression, Gemini's value lies in a clever intellect, versatility, a light-hearted, fun-loving nature, and the ability to look at life from many different perspectives. In its negative expression, Gemini is a dilettante, nervous, unemotional, fickle and silly, unable to find a unifying strength of purpose.

))➤ *Air Signs, Bi-corporeal Signs, Human Signs, Masculine, Mercury, Mutable, Sun-signs*

TOP: Gemini's behaviour in society can be likened to a butterfly; perhaps it was the sign of this lady from an early Georges Melies film.
ABOVE: A crater on the surface of the planet Mercury, ruler of Gemini.

GEOCENTRIC

Having the Earth for a centre. It was originally believed that the Earth lay at the centre of the Universe. Our modern view of astronomy in which the Earth rotates on its axis and revolves around the Sun evolved in the sixteenth and seventeenth centuries, largely from the works of Copernicus, although it had been postulated much earlier. Geocentric theory appears to have originated with the Greeks or Egyptians prior to 300 BC. It was summarized by Claudius Ptolemy. Astrology relies on a geocentric view of the Universe, although astrologers are perfectly aware that the Earth orbits the Sun.

))))➤ *Heliocentric*

GEODETIC

Prediction method. The theory of geodetic equivalents was first put forward by the astrologer Sepharial. His work showed how to calculate charts for any place on earth and how eclipses can trigger events at these locations. An eclipse falling on the meridian geodetic equivalent of any place is seen as highly significant. Geodetic equivalents is a house system structure into which you can place any chart. It can be used to observe political or geophysical activity, the formation of weather patterns and as a relocation assessment. A geodetic chart has zero Aries rising if cast for zero degrees of latitude.

GIBBOUS MOON

One of the phases of the Moon. The waxing gibbous Moon can be seen after the first quarter Moon and before the full Moon. It grows larger each day. The waning gibbous Moon can be seen after the full Moon, but before the last quarter Moon and grows smaller each day.

))))➤ *Moon*

GLYPH

Astrological symbols. The symbols used to represent the planets, signs and aspects in astrology are designated glyphs. They are of ancient origin and have meanings derived from the combination of circles, crescents, crosses and straight lines. The glyphs that represent signs are representative of the images used for the signs.

GRAND CROSS

Aspect pattern. The 'grand cross' is a combination of four or more planets involved in two oppositions which are separated by square aspects. They are thus forming a cross of planets in each sign of the relevant quadruplicity (i.e. cardinal, fixed or mutable). Due to the tense nature of both, the opposition and the square, the

TOP: A plan of a geocentric universe.

ABOVE: Glyphs are astronomical symbols used to represent the signs and planets, as shown in this circle of the zodiac.

grand cross implicates a lot of tension and conflict, in the individual's life as well as in the situation described by a mundane horoscope; conflicting impulses and points of view provide a constant source of irritation and demand continuous effort to solve the arising difficulties. The emphasized quadruplicity may provide a clue as to the source of some of the problems. The cardinal cross may be too commanding and dominating, the fixed cross tends towards rigidity, inflexibility and procrastination, while the mutable cross may be spreading itself too thin and thereby try to avoid problem-solving. The positive aspect of the grand cross lies in its creative approach and in the opportunities for learning and accomplishment it provides.

))))➤ *Aspect, Opposition, Quadruplicity, Square*

ABOVE: Sepheriel's geodetic prediction method found that eclipses, as in this work by Giulio Ferrario, had a particular significance on earthly events.

GRAND TRINE

 Aspect pattern. The grand trine is a triangular aspect pattern involving three or more planets separated by an angle of 120 degrees ('trine') each. The relevant planets are situated in signs of the same triplicity and, due to the harmonious nature of the trine aspect, cooperate in an easy flowing manner. The grand trine is regarded as an extremely fortunate asset, implicating special talents, favourable circumstances and good opportunities. Because of the lack of tension the pattern may also denote laziness or inertia. Since everything goes well, there is no reason for action and hence no opportunity to stimulate growth.

))))➤ *Aspect, Kite, Trine*

GREENWICH MEAN TIME

The times of various events, particularly astronomical and weather phenomena, are often given in Universal Time (UT), often referred to as Greenwich Mean Time (GMT). The two terms are often used to refer to time kept on the Greenwich meridian (longitude zero). It is the basis for the worldwide system of civil times, and times that vary from Greenwich Mean Time are expressed plus or minus a specific number of hours. It was adopted in 1884 at the International Meridian Conference as the single meridian to replace the numerous ones then in existence. It is civil time in the UK in winter.

))))➤ *Summer Time, Universal Time*

GUARDIANS OF HEAVEN

Fixed stars. The Guardians of Heaven, also known as The Four Watchers or the Royal Stars, are four fixed stars individually named Aldebaran, Regulus, Antares and Fomalhaut. Their astronomical positions in the constellations of Taurus, Leo, Scorpio and Pisces form a cross; therefore one of them appears above the horizon every six hours approximately. Persian astrologers used them, instead of cardinal points, to mark the four quarters of the heavens as early as 3000 BC.

))))➤ *Cardinal Points, Fixed Stars*

HAMBURG SCHOOL

Modern astrological system. The astrology promoted by Alfred Witte started the trend in the 1920s in Germany and evolved into what was to be known as the Hamburg School. Witte spent his life investigating the interpretation of symmetries and patterns of relationships using a moveable dial. He was a surveyor by profession and was employed by the city of Hamburg, where he was responsible for laying out the municipal airport, amongst other achievements. Through the examination of thousands of charts, Witte was able to predict many precisely timed events, for example, the moment of artillery barrages and explosions on the Western Front. In 1928 he published a summary of his findings in their major systematized dictionary *Rules for Planetary Pictures*. Despite Witte's desire to simplify and rationalize astrological interpretation and to bring astrology into the twentieth century, his ideas appeared too radical and too technical for the mainstream traditionalists. His work was ignored by most students until well after World War II and his concepts only really began to penetrate the astrological establishment in the 1950s and 1960s.

HARMONICS

Although the use of harmonics is generally attributed to the publication of John Addey's book *Harmonics in Astrology* in 1976, similar techniques have been used in Vedic astrology for many centuries and were also used by Hellenistic astrologers around the time of Ptolemy. Harmonics is a method for investigating specific themes within the horoscope. They are a universal way of describing the shape and form of a wave, or of talking about the various kinds of energies that blend together to

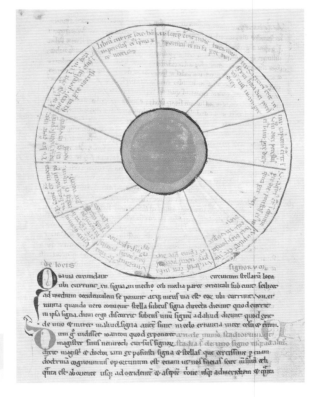

ABOVE: Alfred Witte of the Hamburg School predicted the precise moments of explosions on the Western Front.

RIGHT: The solar sphere; heliacal refers to Sun-related events.

form that wave. In astrology, these harmonics correspond to the common idea of aspects, the various ways that planets can combine their energies, even though they lie in different parts of the zodiac. A harmonic chart is calculated by multiplying the positions of the planets by the number of the harmonic. A fifth harmonic chart, which is associated with creativity, is derived by multiplying the positions by five and drawing the new positions in the chart. The signs simply act as reference points and the angular relationships between the planets are interpreted.

))))➤ *Aspect, Hellenistic Astrology, Ptolemy, Vedic Astrology*

ABOVE: *A heliocentric universe, in which the Earth circles the Sun, which illuminates different parts of the globe according to the season and time of day.*

HAYZ

From the Arabic *hayiz*, a planet in hayz is a masculine, diurnal planet that is above the Earth in a day chart or a feminine nocturnal planet below the Earth in a night chart. This is a form of accidental dignity that fell out of use during the Renaissance but has been recently revived. The Arabs did not consider a planet in hayz unless the masculine planet was in a masculine sign and the feminine in a feminine sign. The feminine, nocturnal planets are Moon and Venus. The masculine, diurnal planets are Sun, Jupiter and Saturn. Mars is masculine but nocturnal.

))))➤ *Dignity*

HELIACAL

Of, or relating to, the Sun, especially that which rises and sets with the Sun. From the Greek *helios*, meaning 'Sun'. It refers to the rising of a celestial object late in the morning twilight, just before the rising of the Sun. Venus has its heliacal rising when it is moving retrograde, and in ancient times it was considered to be destructive during this period. The Babylonians were particularly interested in heliacal risings and settings of planets and stars, and gave the dates and positions of these in their ephemerides. In ancient Egypt the seasons were determined not by the solar equinox or solstice, but by the heliacal rising of the star Sirius.

))))➤ *Matutine, Vespertine*

HELIOCENTRIC

Centred around the Sun. The Greek Aristarchus of Samos (c. 310–230 BC) developed a heliocentric model of the Universe, in which he proposed that all the planets, including Earth, revolved around the Sun, and that the Earth rotated on its axis once a day. His ideas did not gain widespread acceptance during his lifetime. The sun-centred model was later revived by Nicolas Copernicus, around 1500. He was dissatisfied with the complexity of the geocentric model but was later to have trouble with the Church for his ideas. Some parts of his model have been modified – the planetary orbits are elliptical, not circular, and the Sun rotates on its axis, for example, but his ideas nonetheless revolutionized astronomical thought.

))))➤ *Geocentric*

HELLENISTIC ASTROLOGY

Astrology arrived on the Greek peninsula with the second wave of Greek civilization – that of classical Greece. Pythagoras produced a system of religion and science that was to be the basis of European thought until the seventeenth century, and is still the basis of the philosophy of astrology. The founder of Greek astronomy is generally considered to be Thales, who founded the Ionian school. He was followed by Anaximander, who believed that the Universe was contained within the rim of a wheel filled with fire. Early Greek philosophers were astronomers rather than astrologers, but they gradually built up the intellectual structure that was combined with Babylonian divination to form modern astrology. It has been argued that astrology became the most popular method of divination in the western world because it inherited the intellectual depths of Greek philosophy. The names of the planets as we now know them, and the myths associated with them, are inherited directly from classical Greece. In recent years new translations of Hellenistic texts have become available, and their techniques are slowly coming into our reach.

ABOVE: The Eastern and Western hemispheres, which focus on the self and a search for identity, respectively.

HEMISPHERE EMPHASIS

A strong emphasis on any of the hemispheres gives a chart a basic theme. Eastern hemisphere: focusing on the self, exerting control and shaping one's own destiny. Western hemisphere: search for identity and meaning, dependency on approval from others, difficulty to effect inner change. Upper hemisphere: socially and success-oriented, searching for the meaning of all experience, treating others as 'objects'. Lower hemisphere: focusing on personal experience, subjective approach, experiencing relation-ships as obstructive.

HERBALISM

Medical system and astrology. The ancient Chinese, Indians, Egyptians and Babylonians were all herbalists, as were the ancient Greeks and Romans. Throughout the Middle Ages, herbalism was preserved in the monasteries of Britain and mainland Europe. Each physician gardener who wrote a new herbal sought to standardize the use of plants. Theophrastus Bombastus von Hohnenheim (1493–1541), better known as Paracelsus, emphasized the importance of experience with patients and railed against blind faith. Although he distrusted traditional herbalism he revived the first-century 'doctrine of signatures'. According to this, each herb has its own 'sign'; the appearance of the plant, its colour, scent or living environment governed its use. A century later Nicholas from a speculative emphasis to that of experimentation, herbalism began to separate from medical science. The birth of botany saw the end of traditional herbalism as a mainstream medical treatment.

)))➤ *Nicholas Culpeper*

HERSCHEL, WILLIAM

Astronomer and discover of the planet Uranus. Born in Hanover, Herschel (1738–1822) was a successful musician. An amateur astronomer, on 13 March 1781 he observed an unusual object presenting an extended disk-like shape and thought he had discovered a comet. Continuing his observations, however, he discovered the orbit lay beyond that of Saturn and was fairly circular. This was no comet – it was a new planet. Different names were suggested, including his own. He wanted to call it 'Georgium Sidus', after his patron, George III, but the name did not find favour with the astronomical community. It was eventually named Uranus, after the mythological god of the skies. Herschel was granted a pension of £200 a year, knighted and made King's Astronomer. As a full-time astronomer he made numerous discoveries. He observed sunspots and confirmed the gaseous nature of the Sun. He discovered not only the planet Uranus, but two of its moons, and two of Jupiter's. His principal works were on stars. He discovered nearly 1,000 double stars.

Culpeper revitalized astrology and herbalism. Astrological herbalists connected herbs to different planets and used astrological affinities to decide which herb to prescribe. Culpeper broke with other herbalists, as he believed they were only guessing. With the transformation of science

---

ABOVE: Salvia or Sage, from a fourteenth century treatise on the use of herbs for medicinal purposes.
ABOVE RIGHT: William Herschel, who discovered Uranus in 1781.

HOME LIFE

Matter of the fourth house and the Moon. Questions concerning a person's home life are answered by planets in the fourth house, position and aspects of its ruler and by the position and aspects of the Moon. The fourth house is traditionally connected to the father but has become the modern domain of the mother, because of its Cancerian undertones. In either case it describes early family experiences, which shape the subject's domestic behaviour as an adult. The Moon provides information about the individual's caring qualities and emotional needs, which are likely to express themselves in the intimacy of the home.

))))➤ *Cancer, Fourth House, Moon*

HORARY ASTROLOGY

Horary astrology is the name given to the branch of astrology that casts a chart for the moment that a question is asked and provides an answer for that question by examining the chart. The rulerships of the planets, signs and houses are taken into consideration. Only those parts of the chart that have direct relevance to the question in hand are studied. With its strict rules, horary astrology can be a very speedy way of using astrology for someone who is adept at it. It is unnecessary to know the birth time of the person asking the question as the chart is cast for the question alone. The practice reached its height in the seventeenth century, but fell out of popularity until it has almost disappeared by the beginning of the twentieth century. The republication of William Lilly's *Christian Astrology* in 1985 resulted in renewed interest in this area and it continues to gain in popularity. Horary astrology is more closely akin to divination than any other form of astrology.

))))➤ *Electional Astrology, William Lilly*

HORIZON

Astronomical measurement. The circle around the Earth that separates the visible and invisible hemispheres or an extension of the plane of the observer. The astronomical horizon, called the rational horizon, is obtained by drawing a line from the Earth's centre parallel

to the horizon. The terms 'visible' or 'physical horizon' describe the line that terminates our vision where the celestial bodies appear and disappear. In astrology the eastern horizon is the degree rising in the chart.

))))➤ *Ascendant*

HOROSCOPE

Birth chart. The word horoscope is derived from the Greek *horoscopos* meaning 'I watch the rising', which is the ascending point or sign rising over the eastern horizon at the time. It was originally taken to simply mean 'ascendant'. As generally used nowadays, it indicates the map of the heavens drawn for a given date, location and time by an astrologer for judging character

ABOVE: The Moon, shown here complete with man inside, is the ruler of domestic life and behaviour.

Magnifico Smokentissimo Custardissimo Astrologissim Zuthingmanussimo Rabbinissimo Viro IACKO ADAMS le Clarkenwell Greeno hanc lovelissiman sui Picturam

Hobbodeboody pinxit et ✗ ✗ ⌐ scratchabat

and making predictions. Also often simply called a 'chart'. It is a diagram that depicts the position of the planets in relation to the Earth. An astrologer interprets the positions of the planets and their relation to the 12 signs of the zodiac. A horoscope can be cast for an event or question, as well as a person. It has also been termed the radix, figure, scheme or nativity in the past. In popular usage it refers to the columns that appear in the press based on the sign the Sun appears in on the date of birth. Astrologers refer to these as Sun-sign columns.

HOUR ANGLE

◼ Astronomical measurement. The hour angle is the angle between the great circle that passes through the North and South Poles and bisects a specific point in the heavens. It is expressed in hours as indicating an interval of time before or after it passes over the meridian at the rate of 15 degrees an hour. If the vernal equinox is at the observer's local meridian and sidereal time is 0H, the hour angle is equivalent to local sidereal time.

))))▶ *Sidereal Time*

LEFT: Astrologer Jack Adams prepares a horoscope for a woman ('the Queen of Sluts'), whose mother wonders if she is a princess.
BELOW: The signs of the zodiac, which appear in Sun-sign columns.

HOUSES

📖 Chart division. Houses are one of the four essential tools of astrology, along with planets, signs and aspects. Their 12-fold division is one of the fundamentals of astrological interpretation. Although there is a tendency amongst modern astrology to ally the house meanings with the signs – the first house being similar to Aries, for example – houses and signs were originally completely separate concepts. The earliest text to describe the meaning of houses is the *Astronomica* by Manilius, dating from about AD 10. A method is chosen whereby the chart is divided into 12 sectors. Depending on how this is done, the sectors may be of equal or unequal size. Each sector has a meaning. Planets placed in the sector, or house, are effective in the area of life described by that house. The planet that rules the sign that falls on the cusp, or beginning, of the house, also has a relationship to that house. The quality of any angular relationships between the planets are again coloured by the houses that they fall in.

))))▶ *House System*

HOUSE SYSTEM

A house system is the method used whereby the horoscope is divided into 12 sectors, each representing a different area of life. The earliest astrologers have provided us a wide mixture of house systems from which to choose today. Each house system is different, so the house a planet is in for any given chart depends on the house system used in constructing the chart. Some astrologers favour a single house system, whereas others argue that different systems suit particular purposes, and may use one system for natal charts and another for predictive work. The mathematics of calculating the houses is divided into three types: the ecliptic systems, where the ecliptic is divided to determine the house cusps; the space systems, where another great circle such as the celestial equator, the horizon or the prime vertical is divided to determine the house cusps and projected onto the ecliptic; and the time systems, where the time taken for the ascendant or midheaven to travel an arc of the celestial sphere is equally divided to determine the house cusps.

)))▶ *Houses*

HUMAN SIGNS

One of the manifold divisions of the zodiac used in traditional and ancient astrology. It refers to the zodiac signs Gemini, Leo, Libra and Aquarius and pertains to the qualities of these signs as partaking of a manly, humane or courteous nature. Each sign represents aspects of human behaviour and a concern with energy that actively promotes the furthering of human ideals through the use of intellectual abilities and creativity of a progressive nature.

)))▶ *Aquarius, Gemini, Leo, Libra*

ABOVE: An astrologer charting a horoscope, a process which requires the use of a house system.

LEFT: *The cycles of the Sun and Moon, two of the five hylegs.*
BELOW: *This seventeenth century quack doctor's cures would be located, astrologically speaking, in the tenth house.*

plane. There are about 35 hypothetical planets actually being used by some astrologers. Although some of them have been given ephemerides and certain astrological meanings, the matter remains confused, because some of the hypotheticals bear names of existing asteroids. Attempts to ascertain the effectiveness of hypothetical planets statistically have hitherto only had negative results.

One exception is the planet Pluto: intuited, named and assigned to Scorpio by the theosophist Isabelle Pagan in 1911, it was discovered in 1930 and is by now fully integrated in modern astrology.

)))➤ *Esoteric Astrology, Pluto*

HYLEG

Used to determine length of life; it means 'the giver of life' and it refers to a planet that is located so as to have influence on longevity. The five traditional hylegs are the Sun, Moon, ascendant, midheaven and Pars Fortuna. The hyleg to be used is chosen based on how dignified it is. Some astrologers also use the new or full Moon immediately prior to birth. The Sun is most commonly used for day births and the Moon for night.

)))➤ *Alcocoden, Alpheta, Anareta*

HYPOTHETICAL PLANETS

Planets postulated but not proven to exist. As the term suggests, 'hypothetical planets' are undiscovered bodies which are believed to be a part of the Solar System. The term summarizes different varieties of this exotic category. Some astrologers claim the existence of more than a thousand of so-called 'Aromal planets', most of which have been 'discovered' by such uncertain means as intuition and clairvoyance. Esoteric astrology, as taught by Helena Blavatsky and Alice Bailey, claims that there are six 'ethereal planets', which only exist on a non material

ILLNESS

Matter of the sixth house. The basic theme of the sixth house is service, and because the body is seen as serving the soul, it also describes the subject's health. Planets in this area and the condition of its ruler are factors to be considered when assessing the basic health disposition. Afflictions, which may possibly result in illness, can be triggered by transit or progression. Traditional astrology also considers the ascendant, its ruler and first-house planets as indicators of illness or health, since they describe the physical manifestation of the native. In a horary chart concerning an illness, the ninth house gives information about its outcome, while the cure is to be found in the tenth house. Transits of the Moon over critical degrees mark turning-points in the course of an illness. Long and chronic illnesses are ruled by Saturn. A connection between the sixth and the twelfth house may indicate illness as a result of self-destructive behaviour or hospitalization. The modern planet Pluto appears to be connected with major surgery

)))➤ *Body, Critical Degree, Transit*

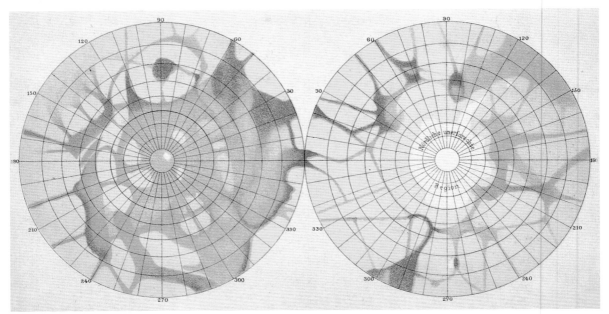

IMMUM COELI

Cardinal point in a chart. The immum coeli, or IC, is the cusp of the fourth house in the chart and one of the four angles opposite the midheaven. The term means 'the lowest heaven' as it lies at the base of the chart. It is the north angle of the chart. It is one of the four cardinal points in the horoscope and the third most powerful following the ascendant and midheaven. A planet placed near it is extremely potent negatively or positively, depending on the nature of the planet and the aspects it makes in the chart. It is a highly personal point as it is calculated according to date, place and time of birth. In predictive work it may be moved forward, or directed, to describe what is likely to happen in the area of life it relates to. It is most closely associated with issues relating to the home, past, family and domestic concerns. In horary astrology it indicates the end of the matter in question.

))))➤ *Angles, Fourth House, Horary Astrology, Midheaven*

IMPEDITED

Term used to describe a planet that is badly aspected, particularly by the malefics, Mars and Saturn; also termed impeded. It also describes the Moon when it is moving to a conjunction, square or opposition to the Sun, Mars or Saturn. In modern astrology a planet is also counted as impeded when aspecting Neptune, Uranus and Pluto, although the term is not generally used except in traditional forms of astrology, such as horary. The Moon impedited by the Sun at birth was traditionally associated with a blemish in or near the eye.

))))➤ *Aspect, Conjunction, Horary Astrology, Malefic, Opposition, Square*

ABOVE: The two hemispheres of Mars, one of the malefics which can be responsible for an impedited planet.

LEFT: Domastic concerns are associated with cardinal point Immum Coeli.

INCONJUNCT

Minor aspect. In traditional astrology, the term may sometimes indicate the sextile and is at times wromgly used instead of 'disjunct', pertaining to an unaspected planet. Commonly though, the inconjunct, also known as 'quincunx', is an aspect of 150 degrees, with an orb of three degrees. It frequently manifests itself as a crisis, in which several urgent and contradicting demands are placed upon the individual, who is forced to set priorities and to choose between desire and necessity. When approached positively, this may lead to a redefinition of the individual's goals or to a reassessment and improvement of working methods. Negatively, the individual may be tempted to use occult methods or public resources with selfish motives, which will result in even more problems in the areas indicated by the relevant planets, their position by the houses they rule. The inconjunct is also part of the significant aspect figure called 'Yod'.

)))▶ *Aspect, Minor Aspects, Quincunx, Yod*

ABOVE: An inconjunct aspect may have incited these witches to experiment with occult practices.

INCREASING IN LIGHT

Due to the visibility of the Sun by day, a planet in conjunction with the Sun is invisible in the sky. It is said to increase in light as it becomes visible, after the conjunction has been completed. For example, after the new Moon, the waxing Moon increases in light.

INCREASING IN MOTION

The term, increasing in motion, relates to the daily movement of a planet, which increases when the planet is in its apogee (closest to earth); at the end of a period of retrograde motion, having passed through the stationary period, a planet picks up speed, i.e. increases in motion.

)))▶ *Apogee, Retrograde, Swift in Motion*

INFERIOR CONJUNCTION

Joining of planets. The conjunction of an inferior planet (one which orbits between the orbit of the Earth and the Sun) – Mercury or Venus – with the Sun is an inferior conjunction when that planet is between the Earth and the Sun. It is a superior conjunction when the Earth is between the Sun and the planet.

)))▶ *Conjunction, Inferior Planet, Superior Conjunction*

INFERIOR PLANET

A planet that has an orbit between the Earth and the Sun: Mercury and Venus. A superior planet is one that has its orbit around the Sun, outside the Earth's orbit. The superior planets are Mars, Jupiter, Saturn, Uranus, Neptune and Pluto.

))))▶ *Superior Planet*

INFORTUNE

The malefic planets, Mars or Saturn. Saturn is classed as the greater infortune and Mars as the lesser. Other planets may be counted as infortunes if they make difficult aspects to either Saturn or Mars. A traditional term rarely used in modern astrology.

))))▶ *Fortune*

INGRESS

Meaning 'to disappear behind', in astronomy ingress means that a body has just passed behind a second body or its shadow. In astrology, an ingress is when any planet enters a new sign and is 00 degrees 00 minutes of that sign. For example, when Venus enters Virgo, Venus is at the ingress of Virgo and therefore 00Virgo00. Ingresses are used extensively in Sun-sign astrology.

))))▶ *Egress*

INTERCEPTION

Describes a sign that is wholly in one house but is not contained on the cusps of that house. The house cusps are of the preceding and subsequent sign. For example if the cusp of the second house is in Cancer and the third house is in Virgo the sign Leo is said to be intercepted. Although it is referred to as an intercepted sign, it is more correct to consider it as an intercepting sign, as it is the house that is being intercepted.

INTERPRETATION

Assessment and description of the horoscope. There are as many ways to interpret a chart as there are astrologers, but there are also very clear rules pertaining to the interpretation of different kinds of horoscopes. In a natal chart, the astrologer has to integrate all factors if (s)he wants to arrive at a detailed analysis,

ABOVE: This chart, showing the details of Mr George Witchell, astronomer at the Royal Academy, Portsmouth, could be interpreted in a number of ways.

RIGHT: The planet Venus is said to have joy when in the fifth house.
BELOW: The term 'judicial astronomy' was used to separate the work of astrologers from that of astronomers, such as the ones shown here from a Sanskrit treatise on the Zodiac.

WILLS'S CIGARETTES.

DIRECTION OF SUN

ORBIT OF VENUS

SUNLIT SIDE OF VENUS.

even while trying to assess one specific area in the life of the individual. In a horary chart, only the factors pertaining directly to the question are looked at. In synastry, which compares two natal charts to analyse the compatibility of their owners, all factors of the natives' personalities must be considered, but the emphasis lies on the overlays and connections between the horoscopes. Composites and relationship charts are to be interpreted with two people in mind, but as a description of their relationship as a third entity. Above all, however, the astrologer has to learn to apply the many rules of the art without bending or stretching them before applying his/her intuition and creativity to the interpretation.

))))▶ **Synthesis**

JOY

Term used in older texts to describe an affinity between certain planets and signs, not necessarily of the nature of dignities. A planet is said to be 'in joy' when although in debility, another planet with which it shares some similarity is placed in one of its dignities. At a later date the idea of planets having joy in certain houses developed. Saturn is considered to have joy in the twelfth, Jupiter the eleventh, Mars the sixth, Venus the fifth, Mercury the first, Sun the tenth and the Moon in the third.

))))▶ *Dignity*

JUDICIAL ASTROLOGY

Old-fashioned term used to differentiate between astrology and astronomy. The expression is often used interchangeably with mundane astrology; however, it actually refers to the use of judgement of a chart, and was often applied to what we now call natal astrology – the interpretation of the horoscopes of individuals. It was used as a term to differentiate the art from natural astrology, or what we today call astronomy. Although the terms astrology and astronomy were often used interchangeably, the influence of the planets on the actions of humans was a subject of considerable debate. Pope Paul IV issued the *Index Expurgatorius* in 1559 as a blacklist of forbidden books and studies; he also forbade the practice of judicial astrology along with other forms of divination. These actions were followed by a papal bull in 1586. Although condemned as unchristian superstition, astrology did not completely disappear. Any form of astrology that can be used to make predictions may be termed judicial – the results of the interpretation being reliant on the astrologer's analysis.

))))▶ *Astrology, Astronomy*

JULIAN DAY

International dating method. On 1 January 1925 the astronomical day was superseded by the Julian day, numbered consecutively, beginning from 4713 BC. To avoid confusion in the comparison of ancient and modern dates, the Julian day was made to begin at noon, 12 hours later than the civil day. Julian days are given in ephemerides. Knowledge of the Julian day enables conversion of dates between different types of calendars and eliminates confusion when working with different calendars in chart calculation.

))))➤ *Calendar*

JUNG, CARL

Dr Carl Jung (1875–1961) was born in Kesswil, Switzerland. He studied medicine and became assistant professor at a psychiatric clinic in Zurich. He remained there for nine years, at the end of which he was created instructor of psychiatry. During this time he

became increasingly interested in Freud's methods of psychoanalysis. After meeting Freud in 1907 the two became firm friends. Jung set up in private practice in 1909. By 1911 the relationship between Freud and Jung was under strain because of Jung's interest in astrology. In a letter to Freud in 1911, he wrote: 'My evenings are taken up largely with astrology. I make horoscopic calculations in order to find a clue to the core of psychological truth. Some remarkable things have turned up which will certainly appear incredible to you… I dare say that we shall one day discover in astrology a good deal of knowledge that has been intuitively projected into the heavens.' The friendship was broken in 1913. In 1948 the C. G. Jung Institute opened.

ABOVE: Carl Gustav Jung, Swiss psychgologist, in 1912.
ABOVE RIGHT: Jupiter, fifth planet from the sun and ruler of Pisces, influences the activities of merchants.

JUPITER

Fifth planet from the Sun, ruler of Sagittarius. Jupiter orbits the Sun between Mars and Saturn, in a rotational cycle of approximately 12 years. It is the biggest planet in our Solar System, which is possibly why it is traditionally labelled as the 'great good fortune'. Jupiter was the traditional ruler of Sagittarius by day and Pisces by night before the discovery of Neptune, which has been assigned to Pisces by modern astrology. Jupiter is exalted in Cancer and in its fall in Capricorn; its nature is masculine, hot and moist. Jupiter is seen as a benefic and has key words like generosity, popularity, expansion, success, optimism, happiness, wisdom, thoughtfulness, spirituality, honesty and justice attached to it. Jupiter describes judges, lawyers, teachers, healers, philosophers, religious leaders, seekers of knowledge and truth, industrialists and members of government. An afflicted Jupiter can signify an inability to accept limitations and may thus indicate reck-lessness, over-optimism, vanity or self-indulgence. The physical appearance of a Jupiterian person is traditionally described as dark-haired with a good complexion and a high forehead, a well formed, large and healthy body with a tendency to plumpness or obesity in later life. The body parts ruled by Jupiter are the thighs and the liver.

))))➤ *Affliction, Dignity, Pisces, Ruler, Sagittarius*

ABOVE: The Hindu god Krishna in a garden. Hinduism is one of the religions that believes in the effects of Karma.

JUPITER RETURN

Type of chart. Jupiter's orbit is 11.86 years and after that time it will return to the same zodiacal position that it held at the time that the chart was cast. This is referred to as the Jupiter return, and a chart is cast for this moment, using the location of the subject at that time. Return charts may be cast for any planet. It is used as a stand-alone chart representing the end of one Jupiter cycle and the beginning of another, as well as in comparison to the birth chart. It provides information about forthcoming opportunities and areas of growth.

))))➤ *Jupiter*

KARMA

Philosophy applied to astrology. A number of meanings have been attributed to the term 'karma'. Derived from Sanskrit, the word is used in Buddhism and Hinduism; it refers to the total effect of a person's actions and conduct during the successive phases of existence, and is regarded as determining destiny in the next incarnation. Reincarnation is implicit in karma. Often it is used inter-changeably with fate or destiny, although correctly it implies a person's responsibility for their own actions. The term became popularized in the West through the writings of Helena Blavatsky and the ensuing interest in eastern religions from the late-nineteenth century onwards. Blavatsky and her fellow theosophists saw karma and the doctrine of fate as inflexible cause and effect, a theory of inevitable consequence. Within astrology the term is used when discussing past lives as shown by the chart, or when referring to a person's spiritual path. In this context the Moon's nodes and the planet Saturn are the most important chart points to consider.

KEPLER, JOHANNES

Astrologer and astronomer. The German astrologer Johannes Kepler (1571–1630) was born in Wiel, in Wartemberg, and joined Tycho Brahe in Prague in his early adulthood. At Graz, in 1594, he took up a post of teacher of mathematics and astronomy. During this tenure he produced four almanacs. In the first of these he prophesied very cold weather and an invasion by the Turks. Both occurred and for the rest of his life he was to some extent considered a professional astrologer. In the introduction to *Tertius interveniens* he warned readers that while justly rejecting the stargazers' superstitions, they should not dismiss the true value of astrology. Kepler was convinced that mundane events could be predicted using this science. He discovered a harmonic, musical relationship between the planets and musical scale. Many of the minor aspects used by astrologers are also attributed to Kepler. Although claims have been made against his belief in astrology, he clearly made use of it. Though appointed Imperial Astronomer, he could hardly keep his family from starvation and died from a fever worsened by disappointment and exhaustion.

ABOVE: Johannes Kepler, German mathematician, astrologer.
ABOVE RIGHT: Kepler's House of Astronomy – the Temple of Urania with various astronomers.

KEY WORDS

Teaching method. A method of teaching astrology developed by Margaret Hone. One of the founding members of the Faculty of Astrological Studies, Hone wrote *The Modern Textbook of Astrology*, which contained a few brief keywords for each sign, planet and house that are modified according to aspects. Students begin interpreting a chart by listing factor by factor in a particular order. The phrases are then changed to proper sentences. For example, Venus in the sixth house could use the keywords 'relating (Venus) through service (sixth house).' If Venus were in square to Saturn, it would be amended to 'relating through service with challenge (square) of fulfilling responsibilities and duties (Saturn).' Over fifty years later, the Faculty continue to use this method, and it has become generally accepted as the main way to teach modern astrology.

KITE

Aspect pattern. The 'kite' is an aspect pattern used in natal astrology. It is based on three planets forming a grand trine, one of which is opposed by a fourth planet, which is in sextile with the two remaining points of the grand trine. The pattern implies the sensitivity and creativity of the grand trine, but also contains the inner tension of the opposition and the restlessness frequently accompanying the sextile. Whereas the grand trine often denotes a person with talent but little drive to develop and make use of it, the opposition that is part of this pattern indicates the tension needed to overcome laziness and to focus the creative forces in a productive way. The sextiles signify advantageous circumstances presenting themselves. The whole pattern is regarded as an indication of an integrated personality and of success in the area described by the planet on top of the 'kite'.

)))➤ *Aspect, Finger of Fate, Grand Trine, Mystic Rectangle, Yod*

KOCH HOUSE SYSTEM

Method of chart division. The Koch, or birthplace system, was introduced by the German astrologer Dr Walter Koch in the 1960s and first published in 1971. It is based on dividing the quarters of the chart formed by the ascendant and midheaven axes into three equal time segments. This results in individual calculation of the intermediate house cusps for the birth location, using the ecliptic, the ascendant and place of birth as reference points. It has been described as a variation on the Alcabitius System. The specific 'Tables of Houses' was only ever calculated to 60 degrees latitude, as the system did not work in polar regions. For example, there can be a difference of almost a complete sign between Koch and Placidus cusp calculations in high latitudes. This system is reasonably popular, especially in Europe. Some practitioners claim that the intermediate cusps in this system are powerful points that respond to transits and progressions. This system is popular with technical astrologers.

)))➤ *Alcabitius House System, Ascendant, Ecliptic, House System, Midheaven*

ABOVE RIGHT: The Sun, shown here on a Tarot card, can have no latitude as it is on the ecliptic.

LATITUDE

Astronomical and geographical coordinate. Astronomical latitude is the angle between a line downwards from the plane of the equator and that plane itself. It is measured in degrees north or south of the ecliptic. There are three types of celestial latitude. The one that parallels the horizon is called altitude; the one that parallels the equator is called declination; and the one that parallels the ecliptic is called latitude. As the path of the Sun forms the ecliptic, the Sun can have no latitude. In geography it is the angular distance north or south of the equator.

)))➤ *Declination, Ecliptic, Longitude*

LEAP YEAR

Leap years occur every four years, except years ending in 00, unless that year is divisible by 400. Leap day (29 February) only occurs during a leap year. The Julian calendar assumed that the year had 365 1/4 days, with a 366-day leap year added every fourth year. The accumulated error of one day every 128 years led to the use of the Gregorian calendar. To make future adjustments for the error of about three days every 400 years, it was decided that years ending in 00 would be common years rather than leap years – except those divisible by 400.

)))➤ *Calendar*

LEO

Leo is the fifth sign of the zodiac, a member of the fixed triplicity, masculine and of the fire element. A feral sign, the symbol for Leo is the Lion, and its ruling planet is the Sun. The Sun enters Leo around 23 July and exits around 22 August. People whose birthdays fall between these dates are said to be Sun-sign Leo. This is the second month of summer and the nature and qualities of Leo are closely associated with the time of year, when the heat of the Sun is ripening the fruits of the Earth as brought forth during the nurturing time of Cancer. It is a time of abundant growth and glorious warmth.

In physical terms, Leo rules the heart, connecting the sign to the virtues of man such as courage, love, loyalty and generosity. Leo responds to life's stimuli with an enthusiastic but steady spirit, offering a constant strength to any pursuit. Leo exudes a natural nobility and inner confidence which inspires trust, devotion and loyalty.

Leo represents the search for self through the creative urge and a desire to affect the immediate environment so that it reflects favourably the individual identity of the ego. Leo demands to be seen as a benefic leader, a stable centre around which others revolve, much like the sign's ruling planet the Sun. There is a tendency to occasionally lie back and lazily bask in the glory that Leo feels is his due, like the symbol for the sign, the lion, stretched out under a tree in the savannah while the lionesses hunt for his supper. There is a robust and handsome element, and a pride in appearance; however, this pride can easily turn to vanity and a capricious need for attention, making Leo easily won over by flattery and the

manipulations of others. But Leo offers much in return for the attention and adulation sought: to those members of the inner circle, Leo is open, loving, warm and generous. Leo is passionate about love and intensely romantic. Possessive, territorial and completely loyal, the power of the emotions that Leo feels for their partner is tremendous. Nothing is too good for Leo's loved ones; extravagance and opulence are hallmarks of the manner in which Leo bestows bounty, never resenting the effort or counting the cost. There is no limit to the ardent desire and affection that Leo likes to give and receive.

Equally, there is no holding back with enemies. With a roar and claws bared, Leo attacks with a ruthless determi-

LEFT: Leo, the lion, from a sixteenth century Turkish treatise on Astrology.
ABOVE: The Sun, shown here as a solid body with mountains and other features, is Leo's ruler.

nation to put anyone who questions the lion's authority, or dares to invade their territory, firmly back in their place.

The sign is closely connected with creativity and individual creative ideas are developed by Leo; they become the children, the work of art or the pet project to be played with, explored, and lead through the paces that encourage maximum expression of innate potential. Leo has an exceptional talent for the dramatic, is keenly aware of the importance of making a favourable – even sensational – impact in every situation. The lion is a consummate actor and performer who seeks to be admired as a star, and in this way Leo remains a little apart from the crowd, keeping a distance from any threat that may damage the well-protected ego. This is where Leo is vulnerable, the delicate but large ego is unable to suffer criticism or embarrassment, Leo rarely forgets a betrayal or a slur to their character, so high is the regard in which they expect to be held.

The creative arts are an area where the Lion can fulfil not only the inherent talent of the sign, but also achieve the fame and admiration so important to them. Whatever the chosen career, Leo must be free to put an individual stamp or brand on the final product. It is important that there is enough scope for Leo to be congratulated and appreciated for the effort that is put into any pursuit.

Any planet in a horoscope found in this sign will operate through the energies connected with it. The Moon in Leo, for example, suggests a strong emotional need to be liked, and an appreciation of drama, ostentation and glamour in everyday affairs. Mars in Leo would express itself as a powerful and energetic creative urge as well as an inclination towards taking risks and gambling with life.

Whatever part of the horoscope in which Leo is found,

is the arena of life in which there will be a concern for individual creative expression; for example, Leo on the second house cusp suggests an ability to be creative in the manner of acquiring wealth, as well as a desire to show off possessions as status symbols.

In its most positive expression, Leo is confident, warm and generous, with an artistic flair and a refined manner, affectionate, romantic and loving, with a happy disposition. In its negative expression, Leo can be a vain show-off, egotistical and demanding, overly extravagant and hedonistic, an attention-seeking dictator.

))⏵ *Feral Signs, Fire Signs, Fixed, Masculine, Sun, Sun-sign*

LEO, ALAN

Nineteenth - century astrologer (1860 –1917). Born in 1860, Leo (born William Allen) is thought of as the father of modern astrology. Brought up by his mother, a member of the Plymouth Brethren, Leo began life as a commercial traveller. Whilst managing a grocer's shop in Manchester, he began studying astrology. With Frederick Lacey he launched the *Astrologers Magazine* in 1889. This was later to become *Modern Astrology*, one of the longest running astrological journals ever published in English. From 1898 it was edited by his wife Bessie when Leo became a professional astrologer. Business was so good that he employed a staff of nine and developed a system of facsimile horoscopes, the forerunners of computerized horoscopes. A member of the Theosophical Society, he twice visited India. In 1914 he was prosecuted for fortune - telling but was acquitted. A later case in 1917 saw him fined £25. He wrote numerous textbooks and ran a correspondence course in astrology. His highly simplified books have remained in print and his approach was the forerunner of psychological astrology. He died on 30 August 1917.

))⏵ *Almanac, Zadkiel*

LIBRA

Libra is the seventh sign of the zodiac, a member of the cardinal triplicity, masculine and of the air element. A human sign, the symbol for Libra is the scales; its ruling planet is Venus. The Sun enters Libra around 23 September and exits around the 22 October. People whose birthdays fall between these dates are said to be Sun-sign Libra. This is the first month of autumn, following the autumn equinox when the hours of daylight become

shorter than the hours of night. The nature and qualities of Libra reflect this time of year, when the leaves begin to turn and put on a magnificent display of colour, in readiness to drop and re-enrich the earth to balance that which has been taken in harvest.

In physical terms, Libra is linked to the skin and the organs that regulate and filter the intake of the body, such as the kidneys and liver. Like its symbol the scales, Libra is immediately aware of imbalance and channels its energy to bring about the balance and harmony needed for any situation to operate smoothly.

Libra represents the search for self through active cooperation with another; relationship is sought in order to gain self-knowledge by having a reflection from which an objective point of view is acquired. This is a strong motivating force and promotes a charming and pleasing countenance so that the experience of the reflection is positive.

Libra is unlikely to be cruel or to deliberately injure another; the innate sense of justice understands the dynamic of giving and receiving, getting back what is put in. Libra learns and grows by paying attention to the quality of the experience received in relationship with others, continually adjusting behaviour in order to create a more harmonious environment for all concerned. This can mean that there is an inability to deal with intense emotions and an avoidance of the darker and more unpleasant aspects of a relationship in an effort to keep everything light and flowing, which can ultimately lead to the very imbalance that Libra finds so destabilizing. When Libra does feel out of balance, it is possible that in order to achieve equilibrium again, Libra will deliberately effect the destabilization of the other person in the situation so that all is fair and equal. Justice and equality are of paramount importance to Libra, which is why the sign has a reputation for excelling in any form of partnership or cooperative venture. Libra, as a cardinal sign, is active in achieving their own ambitions, but uses the talent of diplomacy and gentle persuasion to implement their wants and desires. Libra has a natural ability to spot and promote the talent of others, and will seize any opportunity to do so for mutual benefit. Libra is sociable and adept at analysing the psychological make-up of the society that surrounds them, with a keen interest in what makes others tick. Libra makes a good counsellor, negotiator and mediator, due to a strong sense of democracy and the ability to see value in both sides of any argument; however, this also highlights the difficulty that Libra has in making decisions, as every aspect needs to be

ABOVE: Libra, the scales, and treading grapes from a French mid-fifteenth century Calendar and Book of Hours.

measured and weighed before the passing of judgement. It can sometimes take so much time for Libra to make up their mind that the opportunity has been lost; the fear of making a wrong decision means that they don't make any in time.

As an air sign ruled by Venus, the mental facilities of Libra are intellectual, imaginative and artistic, with a predisposition towards romance and beauty. By keeping these as goals of the mind, Libra endeavours to promote them in each sphere of life in which they participate. The need for

TRANSIT OF VENUS OVER THE SUNS DISC.

harmony and balance is displayed in Libra's personal domain by creating an aesthetically pleasing space that calms the senses. Libra dislikes crude, sloppy and unsophisticated behaviour, and is perceived by others as refined, orderly and elegant.

Any planet in a horoscope found in this sign will operate through the energies connected with it. The Moon in Libra, for example, might suggest an intuitive and emotional imperative towards making close connections with another or an inability to display intense feelings for fear of reprisal from outside. Saturn in Libra could operate as cautious and conservative approach to relationships and a dispassionate need to affect a sense of justice in all dealings with others.

Whatever part of the horoscope that Libra is found, is the arena of life in which there will be a concern for co-operation and operating in partnership with another; for example, Libra on the second house cusp might suggest that possessions, luxury and wealth are acquired through, or by working in close connection with, a marriage or business partner.

In its most positive expression, Libra is loving and romantic, charming, pleasant and cooperative with a

ABOVE LEFT: The transit of Venus, Libra's ruler, over the Sun's disc.
ABOVE: Psyche Receives First Kiss From Cupid *by Francois Gerard. Being ruled by Venus, Libra is predisposed towards romance and beauty.*

natural artistic flair and sense of fair play. Libra is highly intelligent and an excellent listener and communicator. In its negative expression, Libra can be incapable of making a decision, superficial and insincere, a manipulative seeker of relationships for personal gain.

))))▶ *Air Signs, Cardinal, Human Signs, Masculine, Sun-sign, Venus*

LONGITUDE

Astronomical and geographical coordinate. Geographical longitude is the distance of any point on the Earth's surface measured east or west of Greenwich. Celestial longitude is the distance between the first point of Aries and any celestial body, measured along the ecliptic. Both are measured in degrees. Geocentric longitude figured from the Earth as the centre is used by astrologers to express the zodiacal positions of the planets, but is rarely used by astronomers. The search for longitude originally began with navigation and it was a number of years before a reliable system was defined for its use.

)))) *Latitude*

LORD OF CHART

Strongest planet on a chart. The lord of the chart, also known as almuten in Arabic astrology, has special significance in that it is said to 'colour', i.e. determine, the whole chart. It is found by weighing the strength of all planets by sign, house, triplicity, term and face. Traditionally, the lord of a chart was the strongest planet by house position, while the most emphasized planet by sign and aspect was known as the ruler of the horoscope. In a rather simplistic fashion, modern astrologers often refer to the ruler of the ascendant as both – 'chart ruler' or 'lord of chart'. A feminine planet such as Moon or Venus may be referred to as 'lady of chart'.

)))) *Almuten, Ruler*

LOVE

Even beginners in astrology would agree that feelings of love are symbolized by Venus or, in the case of motherly love, by the Moon, but there are as many differentiations concerning the significator of this human condition as there are forms of love. Traditionally, love matters are described by planets in the seventh house and the position and aspects of its ruler. Infatuations and mainly physical romantic adventures belong to the fifth house. While love is generally perceived as positive, even malefic planets rule certain forms of love: Saturn rules love of the body and of property.

)))) *Fifth House, Marriage, Moon, Seventh House, Venus*

LUMINARY

The Sun and Moon; a term used to indicate their particular importance. The term 'light of the time' refers to the Sun during the day or in a daytime horoscope and to the Moon during the night or in a night-time horoscope.

)))) *Lights*

LUNAR MANIONS

Chart division. A series of 28 divisions of the Moon's travel through one complete circuit of 360 degrees, each mansion representing one day's average travel – roughly 13 degrees – beginning at zero degrees Aries. Lunar mansions were originally sidereal, based on the movement of the Moon relative to certain stars. In Vedic astrology they are called asterisms or nakshastras. Only 27 are used in Vedic astrology – the twenty second is omitted. Lunar mansions were used in Arabic, Chinese and Indian

ABOVE: *The Sun and Moon, shown here in a fifteenth century Discourse on Alchemy, are also known as luminaries.*

LEFT: These Arabic astrologers observing the sky from the Galata tower in Constantinople, would have made use of Lunar Mansions.
BELOW: Ptolemy, who catalogued the stars according to their magnitude.

birthday. In interpreting this chart attention is paid to the house that the Moon falls in in the natal chart as well as the aspects (angular relationships) made. It gives a snapshot of monthly activity. A study of this chart focuses on emotional issues and how you will feel emotionally during the following month. The lunar return is for short-term prediction and to focus in more strongly on a smaller time span than offered by other return charts.

))))⯈ **Planetary Return, Solar Return**

LUNATION

Complete cycle between two new Moons; also known as a synodic month and a syzygy. Lunations average 29 days, 12 hours and 44 minutes. The new Moon falling on sensitive points in the chart is significant of coming events in the next month. The term is often used interchangeably with new Moon. New Moons fall in the same degree and sign only once every 19 years. A sidereal lunation is the period between two passages of the Moon over the same degree. An embolismic lunation is an intercalary month.

))))⯈ **New Moon, Syzygy**

astrology. It is not known exactly how they were used but it is clear that great importance was attached to them. The cusps of the mansions were known as crucial or critical degrees and the days on which the Moon formed inharmonious aspects to the Sun – seventh, fourteenth, twenty-first and twenty-eighth days – were said to be critical days, coinciding with the cusps of the first, eighth, fifteenth and twenty-second mansions.

))))⯈ **Critical Degree, Vedic Astrology**

LUNAR RETURN

Prediction method. A lunar return chart is one constructed for any particular month when the transiting (current) Moon returns to the exact position it held in the birth chart. A chart is drawn up for this moment and examined as a chart in its own right as well as in comparison to the original birth chart. It occurs thirteen times a year and can be seen as a kind of monthly

MAGNITUDE

In astronomy, the measure of the brightness of a star or other celestial object. The stars catalogued by Ptolemy in the second century AD – all visible with the unaided eye – were ranked on a scale of brightness such that the brightest stars were of 1st magnitude and the dimmest stars were of 6th magnitude. The modern magnitude scale was placed on a precise basis by N. R. Pogson in 1856. The modern magnitude scale permits a precise expression of a star's relative brightness and extends to both extremely bright and very dim objects. Thus, an object 2.512 times as bright as a 1st-magnitude star is of 0 magnitude; brighter objects have negative magnitudes. The sun's magnitude, for example, is –26.8.

))))⯈ **Fixed Stars**

MAJOR ASPECTS

 Angular planetary relationships. The major aspects form a group of specific angular planetary relationships, defined by Ptolemy and also known as 'Ptolemaic aspects'. They include the conjunction (0 degrees), sextile (60 degrees), square (90 degrees), trine (120 degrees) and opposition (180 degrees). Their interpretation is based on the relationship between the elements or qualities of the occupied signs. For example, planets in signs of the same element are in trine, i.e. considered to be in a harmonious relationship, whereas planets in signs of the same quality are squaring each other, i.e. functioning at cross-purposes.

))))➤ *Aspect, Minor Aspects*

MALEFIC

Traditional classification. The term 'malefic' (Latin for 'evil-doer') is applied to certain planets and aspects by traditional astrology. Mars and Saturn are regarded as malefics because their manifestations are often opposed to everything humans regard as constructive, positive and fun. Saturn – also called the 'greater infortune' – symbolizes rigidity and obstruction, while Mars – the 'lesser infortune' – is seen as the creator of quarrel and strife. The aspects classified as malefic are the square and the semi-square, which involve planets operating from conflicting elements or opposing modes. Modern astrology has a slightly different view on the positive potential of the malefics.

))))➤ *Benefic, Element, Mars, Mode, Saturn, Semi-Square, Square*

MANILIUS, MARCUS

Ancient astrologer. Little is known of Marcus Manilius's life. He is likely to have been a Chaldean by birth and was a Roman poet, who followed the style of Lucretius, Virgil and Ovid in his work. He wrote the first Roman work on astrology, dedicated to the Emperor Augustus. This, the unfinished *Astronomica*, was written about 45 BC, according to the book's dedication, although there is also evidence that this work was written around AD 14. In five books this poem gives an outline of astrology, beginning with an account of celestial phenomena and including instructions for calculating the ascendant and details of decans, zodiacal geography and other technical matters. The work was rediscovered in the fifteenth century and published in various editions, including three important ones edited by Joseph Scaliger in 1579, 1590 and 1600. Manilius's work had an enormous influence in the Middle Ages and ranks alongside Ptolemy's work as the most classic of astrological texts.

))))➤ *Ptolemy*

MARRIAGE

Subject of the seventh house. Marriage matters are generally described by planets in the seventh house and its ruler by position and aspect. Since these astrological rules were first laid out, our attitude towards traditional marriage has drastically changed, so nowadays relationships

ABOVE: The poet Virgil, whose work, along with that of Ovid, inspired Roman astrologer Marcus Manilius.

LE PETIT JOURNAL ILLUSTRÉ

UNE JEUNE MARIÉE QUI PREND PEUR

resembling marriage are also included. Traditional astrology assigns Libra and the Moon as cosignificators of this subject, because Libra is the sign of relating and the Moon rules emotional matters and domestic affairs. Planets in the seventh house describe the psychological tools we bring into the partnership or the expectations we project on to our partner; they therefore give an indication of the type of partner we will choose or how the marriage is going to develop. For example, the planet Jupiter in this house shows a generous attitude towards others and the choice of an equally generous partner; hence a marriage will be prosperous, provided that the planet and the ruler of the seventh house are both in good shape. Since the seventh house also represents public enemies and lawsuits, afflictions may still end in divorce.

))))➤ **Cosignificator, Love**

MARS

Fourth planet from the Sun; ruler of Aries. The red planet Mars, named after the Roman god of war, circles the Sun between Earth and Jupiter with a rotational cycle of roughly two years. Before the discovery of Pluto, the modern ruler of Scorpio, it was the traditional ruler of that sign. Mars is exalted in Capricorn, in its fall in Cancer, and its nature is masculine, hot and dry. Modern astrology interprets Mars as the inner drive for action, self-manifestation and both positive and negative aggression, as well as the male sex drive. A dignified Mars indicates courage, pride, physical strength, decisiveness, healthy sexual appetites and a sense of fair competition. An afflicted Mars may

LEFT: Matters of marriage, such as a bride fleeing the altar, are governed by the seventh house.
BELOW: The planet Mars overlooks a battle scene.

signify rashness, uncontrolled anger, violence, egocentricity, tyranny, ruthlessness, obscenity, dishonesty or rebelliousness. Mars rules all matters, objects and people connected with warfare, bloodshed, conquest and destruction, as well as all sharp, pointy and metallic objects and those who handle them, such as surgeons, butchers, cooks, barbers, tailors or carpenters. Sports people, chemists, pharmacists and physicians are Mars-ruled as well. Physically, Mars rules the primary sexual organs. The Martian person is said to be of medium stature, fair to red-haired and of a ruddy complexion.

))))➤ **Affliction, Aries, Dignity, Ruler, Scorpio**

MASCULINE

Division of the zodiac and the planets. The masculine signs of the zodiac are Aries, Gemini, Leo, Libra, Sagittarius and Aquarius – all of the fire or air element. They are also called 'positive' signs, but both terms rather refer to the basic active, enterprising mode in which these signs tend to approach the world, comparable to the 'Yang' of eastern philosophy. The masculine fire signs, Aries, Leo and Sagittarius, actively strive for future visions, creative endeavours and a synthesized philosophical view. The masculine air signs, Gemini, Libra and Aquarius, actively collect, analyse and distribute information and pursue the construction of a theoretical framework for the understanding of life's processes. The planets regarded as masculine by ancient astrology are Mars, Jupiter and Saturn, to which traditional astrology added the Sun as representative of the masculine principle. This strict division still plays an important part in horary astrology. Less well-known ancient rules state that planets of either the eastern or upper hemisphere are masculine, while certain ascendant degrees are said to bestow a 'masculine appearance' on feminine individuals.

)))) *Feminine, Mode*

MATUTINE

Term used to describe a planet that rises in the morning in the east before the sun. This used to refer to Mercury, the Moon and Venus when they appeared in the morning. When a star or planet rises before the Sun, it is called matutine until it reaches its first station or appears to stop moving, before it becomes retrograde or appears to move backwards.

)))) *Heliacal, Vespertine*

MEAN NODE

Method of calculation for the point where the Moon's orbit crosses the ecliptic (the apparent path of the Sun). The nodes do not move at a predictable speed and vary from day to day. The mean node is the position based on average speed. With the assistance of computer software it is now easy to calculate the position of the true node (the actual position).

)))) *North Node, South Node*

MEDICAL ASTROLOGY

Medical astrology deals with the workings of the human body. The astrologer analyses the person's birth chart and determines bodily strengths and weaknesses, proneness to various disease states, and nutritional deficiencies. In the event of illness or disease, a medical astrologer will use predictive methods to try to determine the severity and duration of the disease. Sometimes a medical astrologer can help determine the course of a disease by the use of a chart called a decumbiture – one that is cast for the time of the onset of the illness. Medical astrology is also used in choosing the best time for surgery. The practice has very ancient roots, but it reached its peak in Europe in the late medieval and early modern periods, about 1450–1700. Astrologers assigned signs of the zodiac to rule over parts of the body, planets to rule over organs, diseases and drugs. There continue to be some practitioners of medical astrology, although in many places it is illegal to give medical advice in this way.

)))) *Decumbiture*

ABOVE: The celestial influx acting on the body of a woman, one of the main ideas behind medical astrology.

MEDIEVAL ASTROLOGY

Astrological history. The medieval period is generally defined as the years between 1000 and 1450 AD. After several hundred years of being in its heyday, astrology in the West, although never totally dying out, became very quiet during the Middle Ages. Although there was doubt about astrology's use on a personal level, it continued to be used in meteorology and agriculture, and most scholars took the view that it was an important part of general knowledge. Boethius' sixth century book *The Consolation of Philosophy* was influential in reinforcing what astrological knowledge remained in Britain in the tenth century. One area where astrology was particularly powerful was that of medicine. Throughout the medieval period and until the eighteenth century, it would be impossible to qualify as a doctor without passing an examination in astrology at some universities. Arabian astrology flourished from about the tenth century and was to have an incredible influence on the west. One of the most notable of English scholars, Adelard of Bath, was born in the eleventh century and translated several Arabic astrological works. Through his work, as well as that of other writers, many Arabic texts found their way into Europe.

MERCURY

Nearest planet to the Sun, ruler of Gemini and Virgo. Mercury, named after the Roman messenger of the gods, has a rotational cycle of around 88 days. Apart from Venus, it is the only planet which rules two zodiac signs. Its nature is traditionally described as cold and dry. Mercury is neither feminine nor masculine, but takes on the nature of the planet(s) with which it is connected. Its

ABOVE: A medieval astrologer contemplates some diagrams.
ABOVE RIGHT: Messenger of the gods Mercury in his chariot, below Virgo, the sign which he rules.

exaltation in Aquarius and fall in Leo are not accepted by all astrologers. The key words for Mercury are movement and communication. Astrology generally equates Mercury with the ability to analyse and communicate, also with the ability to make connections between people, objects, facts and events. Therefore, Mercury rules thought, written and spoken language, telephones, newspapers, traffic, logistics, transport, shops, offices and commerce; it describes teachers, messengers, salesmen, secretaries, journalists, travel agents, etc. A dignified Mercury indicates a quick logical mind, wit, humour, eloquence, good memory, organizational talent, craftsmanship and adaptability. An afflicted Mercury may indicate learning difficulties, nervousness, fickleness, speech impediments, lying, cunning or craftiness. Traditionally, Mercury rules the hands, shoulders and lungs; some modern medical astrologers connect it with the nervous system and blood circulation as well.

)))➡ ***Affliction, Dignity, Gemini, Virgo***

MERIDIAN

Circle of longitude that passes through the south point of the horizon, through the zenith, to the north point of the horizon. It coincides with geographical longitude. Each point on Earth has its own meridian which passes through its zenith. The point in the heavens where the projection of this circle intersects the ecliptic marks the midheaven in the horoscope. The Sun is at the meridian at noon. It is often used interchangeably as a term for the midheaven, although the two points are different. Occasionally it is used to describe the tenth house.

))))➤ *Horizon, Midheaven, Tenth House, Zenith*

METALS

Apart from the general rule that all metallic objects come under the rulership of Mars, traditional astrology differentiates between various kinds of metal. This was important in horary astrology at a time when many natural resources were undisclosed. Traditionally, the Sun rules gold, the Moon silver, Mercury corresponds with the element of the same name, Venus rules copper and brass, tin

BELOW: The midheaven is one of the points used in a birth chart, such as this one calculated by Dr John Butler, using the details of Jesus of Nazereth.
BELOW LEFT: The Sun is the traditional ruler of gold.

is assigned to Jupiter, Mars rules iron and Saturn presides over lead, as well as the rubble and slag left over from metal production.

))))➤ *Rulership*

METONIC CYCLE

Lunar cycle. The metonic cycle is named after the Greek astronomer Meton, who, in about 432 BC, discovered the Moon's 19-year period, at the end of which the new Moon occured on the same day of the year. Based on this information, Meton corrected the lunar calendar. His calculations were two hours off the correct figure. The period had been discovered in Babylon 50 years previously, so it seems likely that he learned of it through Babylonian sources. Four metonic cycles are known as a callipic cycle, named after Callipus, who proposed it as an improvement.

))))➤ *Saros Cycle, Syzygy*

MIDHEAVEN

Cardinal point in a chart; also known as medium coeli or the southern angle and south point. The midheaven is the cusp of the tenth house in the chart, and one of the four angles opposite the midheaven. It is the point where the Sun is at midday at the time and place you were born. It is one of the four cardinal points in the horoscope and the second most powerful following the ascendant. A planet placed near it is extremely potent negatively or positively, depending on the nature of the planet and the aspects it makes in the chart. It is a highly personal point, calculated according to date, place and time of birth. In predictive work it may be moved forward, or directed, to describe what is likely to happen. It is most closely associated with career, status and public image. This point represents the public persona, and differs from the ascendant in that it's not exactly about the way a person is initially perceived, but more about how their career and social standing reflects upon their place in the world.

MIDPOINT

Chart analysis technique. The use of midpoints dates back to Ptolemy's work where he stressed them as helping to locate places of power in a chart. Midpoints were also used before and after the Middle Ages, the most popular form being that of Arabic Parts. Early in the twentieth century, midpoints as a technique were re-invented by a group of astrologers living in Hamburg, Germany. Planetary pictures are a form of midpoints activating midpoints. The midpoint of two planets is the exact halfway point between them. There are two midpoints for each pairing, one of long arc and one of short. It is the midpoint of shorter arc that is usually referred to. The meaning is based of the combination of meanings of the planets involved. Midpoints are written with / between the planets concerned, for example, Sun/Jup, for the Sun, Jupiter midpoint. If that point makes an aspect to a planet or chart point, it is followed by =. So Sun/Jupiter = Ascendant means that the Sun Jupiter midpoint is aspected by the ascendant.

))))➤ *Cosmobiology, Reinhold Ebertin, Hamburg School, Midpoint tree, Uranian Astrology*

MIDPOINT TREE

Chart analysis technique. Midpoint trees display, in diagrammatical form, the list of midpoints connected, by aspect, to a planet within a selected orb. The midpoint, planet or chart point under consideration is written at the top and a vertical line drawn downwards. Horizontal lines are then drawn across this vertical line. Any two factors that give a midpoint that makes an aspect to the chart point being considered are listed on these horizontal lines, placed on the right and left respectively. The closest

RIGHT: Minutes shown on an ornate clock, which once belonged to Louis Pasteur's great uncle.

aspect is listed first. This allows the astrologer to see all factors involved in the pattern at one time.

))))➤ *Cosmobiology, Reinhold Ebertin, Hamburg school, Midpoint, Uranian Astrology*

MINOR ASPECTS

Angular planetary relationships. The group of specific planetary relationships defined as 'minor aspects' contains aspects of various backgrounds. Some of them are mathematically derived from the original 'major' aspects, like the semi-sextile or the semi-square. Their interpretation is often intimately linked with that of the 'major' original and simply provided with the adjective 'weaker', although in case of the sesquiquadrate, which originates from the square, the affixed adjectives could be 'stronger' or 'more intense'. In the seventeenth century, Johannes Kepler introduced a whole range of aspects based on the division of the zodiac into five segments. This group, known as 'Keplerian aspects' includes quintile, bi-quintile, decile, semi-decile, quindecile and quincunx. Some of these, especially the quincunx and the quindecile, have caught the attention of modern astrologers in recent times and have been demonstrated to be of almost major significance. Other minor aspects based on an abstract division of the zodiacal circle are the septile, bi-septile, tri-septile and the novile. This last group of aspects is disregarded by most astrologers.

))))➤ *Aspect, Johannes Kepler, Major Aspects*

MINUTE

Unit of measurement. The sixtieth part of one hour or degree. The Babylonians performed astronomical calculation in the sexagesimal (base 60) system. This was convenient for simplifying time division, since 60 is divisible by 2, 3, 4, 5, 6, and 10. A minute derives from the first fractional sexagesimal place.

))))➤ *Hour Angle, Second*

MIXED RECEPTION

Planetary placement. This occurs when two planets are in dignities assigned to the other, but the nature of the dignities are different. For example, Mars is in Cancer, ruled by the Moon, and the Moon is in Capricorn where Mars is exalted. It is stronger if the two planets concerned are also making an aspect to each other. It gives a bond between the two planets and they can be read as if they had changed places in the chart. Only rulership and exaltation tend to be used, although technically any of the five dignities may be applied.

)))■▶ *Aspect, Dignity, Exaltation, Mutual Reception, Rulership*

MODE

Classification of zodiac signs. The term mode originates from the Latin word *modus* ('way of') and refers to the different modes of operation and temperament that charac-terize each sign. Confusingly though, astrological language uses it in three different ways. The first meaning refers to the division of the signs by quality, e.g. cardinal, fixed and mutable. These 'modes' or 'qualities' are also known as 'quadruplicities' and categorize the different manners of expression of each element. The second meaning refers to the Aristotelian principles 'hot', 'dry', 'cold', and 'moist' in combination with the astrological elements fire, earth, air and water, respectively. These modes are linked with the ancient classification of bodily fluids and temperaments (choleric, melancholic, sanguine and phlegmatic) which is highly important in medical astrology. The third meaning of the word 'mode' refers to the division of the signs into 'feminine' and 'masculine'. The signs of the masculine mode are said to be of an active nature, while the signs of the feminine mode are regarded as operating in a re-active way.

)))■▶ *Cardinal, Dryness, Element, Feminine, Fixed, Masculine, Moisture, Mutable, Triplicity, Quadruplicity*

MOIETY

Traditional astrology considers every planet to be surrounded by an orb of light which defines its sphere of influence. Half the diameter of this orb is called the moiety of the planet. To determine the orb of aspects between two planets, their orbs are added up and then divided by two. In other words, the moieties determine when the faster planet starts applying to the slower. Al-Biruni made the first recorded list of planetary orbs, which was slightly altered by William Lilly. Still, contrary to modern practice, the use of moieties defined aspect orbs rather precisely.

)))■▶ *Al-Biruni, Aspect, William Lilly, Orb*

MOISTURE

One of the four principles formulated by Aristotle and regarded as underlying all phenomena. Ptolemy's classification of the signs and planets to describe their essential characteris-tics is also used by traditional astrology. The air signs, Gemini, Libra and Aquarius are regarded as hot and moist, while the water signs, Cancer, Scorpio and Pisces, are classified as cold and moist. Of the planets, Venus and the Moon are regarded as cold and moist, while Jupiter combines moisture with heat. These descriptions are quite important in the horary judgement of illnesses and can also literally apply to locations.

)))■▶ *Aristotle, Dryness, Ptolemy*

ABOVE: Modes are a way of classifying the zodiac signs, which appear on this carving from Ancient Gaul, representing the god Mithras.

MOON

Luminary, ruler of Cancer. Although the Moon is not a planet, but the Earth's satellite, it is the second most important celestial body in astrology. It rules zodiacal Cancer, is exalted in Taurus, its fall in Scorpio and has a rotational cycle of 27 days 7 hours 43 minutes. Its nature is feminine, cold and moist. The Moon rules women, fertility, marriage, motherhood, emotions, the family, the home and cyclic or routine activities. It also rules the growth cycles of plants, food, all natural bodies of water and matters pertaining to them, history, the past and the general public. In the natal chart, the Moon describes the imaginative, reflective side of the individual, unconscious impulses, emotional reactions, childhood experiences, the mother–child relationship and the native's need for

ABOVE: Page from an old Arab manuscript depicting Cinnamon, Balsam, Nard and Valerian, the growth cycles of which are ruled by the Moon.
ABOVE RIGHT: A 1920s Tarot card showing the Moon.

emotional comfort. A dignified Moon indicates a highly sensitive, caring and compassionate nature, the ability to give shape to one's ideas and plans, public success, artistic talents or paranormal abilities. An afflicted Moon often indicates emotional or material instability, self-absorbance, over-sensitivity, weakness, confusion, fear or the failure of one's plans. In the body, the Moon traditionally rules the breast, but is also connected to the womb, the digestive system and glandular secretions by some.

▶ *Affliction, Cancer, Children, Dignity, Lights, Luminary, Marriage, Ruler*

MOORE, FRANCIS

Seventeenth-century astrologer. Dr Francis Moore was a physician at the court of Charles II, and his original broadsheet combined herbal recipes and remedies

with favourable astrological times for taking them. He died in 1715 and the title was bought by the London Liveried Stationers Company, who sold it to its present publisher, Foulshams, in the nineteenth century. His name was adopted by Henry Andrews in the late 1770s. During Andrews' time as compiler of the tables sales rose from 100,000 to 500,000 per year. He received the same remuneration throughout his 43 years' association

with *Old Moore's* – £25 per annum. *Old Moore's* became a more esoteric publication in the years following Andrews' death. It still sells by the million and at one time could be purchased from street hawkers. It became an assortment of advertisements for the sale of mystic objects, household hints and astrological forecasts concerned with national celebrities and the rise and fall of nations. Since Andrews' death innumerable astrologers have been 'Old Moore'.

MOTION

Planetary movements. The term 'motion' literally means 'movement'. In astrology, it refers to the movements of the planets through the zodiac, which are the foundation of any astrological method of prediction. Until the sixteenth century, the planets were thought to move around the earth. Trying to improve Ptolemy's planetary system, Copernicus discovered the earth's

movement around the sun. His assistant Kepler revolutionized astronomy by introducing the heliocentric system in his *Three Laws of Planetary Motion*.

))))➤ *Nicolas Copernicus, Johannes Kepler*

MUNDANE ASTROLOGY

Mundane astrology is the application of astrology to world affairs, taking its name from the Latin *mundus*, meaning 'the world'. In the Middle Ages it was more commonly known as the study of revolutions, meaning the study of the revolutions of the planets in their apparent orbits around the Earth. This is the origin of the idea of the political revolution – the rise and fall of states in line with celestial revolutions. Mundane astrology was used to explain history and predict the future. Originally developed in Babylon, the fundamentals were laid down by Claudius Ptolemy. In the ninth and tenth centuries Arabic astrologers added many more techniques.

ABOVE: Charles II, at whose court Franceis Moore was a physician.
RIGHT: Mundane astology was based upon the apparent orbits of the planets around the Earth, in what was then considered to be a geocentric universe.

The twentieth century saw techniques based on the use of planetary cycles rather than the interpretation of individual horoscopes. In 1951 Charles Carter wrote a book called *Introduction to Political Astrology*. He used the term political astrology to differentiate from the traditional practice of mundane astrology, although the terms are often used interchangeably. Mundane astrology is used extensively with a whole range of techniques.

MUSIC OF THE SPHERES

Pythagoras discovered that the pitch of a musical note depends on the length of the string that produces it. He was able then to correlate the intervals of the musical scale with simple numerical ratios. The Pythagoreans thought that earthly music was no more than an echo of the 'harmony of the spheres'. In ancient cosmology, the planetary spheres ascended from Earth to Heaven like the rungs of a ladder. Each sphere corresponded to a different note of a musical scale. The tones emitted by the planets depended upon the ratios of their orbits. The doctrine was transmitted to medieval Europe where it found expression in the architecture of abbeys and cathedrals designed to conform to the proportions of musical and geometric harmony. Kepler found that the angular velocities of all the planets closely correspond to musical intervals. When he compared the extremes for combined pairs of planets, they yielded the intervals of a complete scale. The Kepler scholar Francis Warrain found that the angular velocities of Uranus, Neptune and Pluto also correspond to harmonic ratios. The dynamics of the solar system are seen as directly analogous to the laws of musical harmony.

))➤ *Johannes Kepler*

ABOVE: According to the Pythagoreans, the music made by this lyre-playing Israelite would have been simply an echo of the harmony of the spheres.

MUTABLE

The signs of the zodiac are divided into three categories which describe their mode of expression: cardinal, fixed and mutable. The mutable signs are Gemini, Virgo, Sagittarius and Pisces; the corresponding mutable or 'cadent' houses are the third, sixth, ninth and twelfth. Traditional astrology also refers to the mutables as 'common signs', not only because they are situated between the fixed and cardinal signs, but also because their mode of operation combines the characteristics of both. In horary astrology, the common signs denote connection, mediation and diversity, but also change and instability. Modern astrology regards the 'mutable type', i.e. someone with a strong emphasis on mutable signs or houses in their chart, as a 'mixed type'. Such a person is described as mobile and versatile, an open-minded mediator between impatient initiators and rigid maintainers, who has both modes at his disposal, but can be highly unstable under pressure. Instead of being a blessing, the ability to oscilate between extroversion and introversion is only used to avoid conflicts.

))➤ *Cardinal, Fixed, Mode, Quadruplicity, Quality*

MUTE SIGNS

One of the divisions of the zodiac used in traditional and ancient astrology; also known as signs of slow voice. In the judging of a horary chart, when a mute sign appears on the ascendant, it suggests that there will be little or no further news pertaining to the matter questioned, or that any news will be slow in arriving. The Mute signs are the three water signs, Cancer, Scorpio and Pisces.

))➤ *Aspect, Cancer, Horary Astrology, Mercury, Pisces, Saturn, Scorpio, Water Signs*

MUTUAL RECEPTION

This occurs when two planets are in each other's dignity. For example, Mars in Gemini and Mercury in Aries are in mutual reception because Mars rules Aries and Mercury rules Gemini. Mutual reception by ruling sign is the strongest. In order of strength, there can be reception by sign, exaltation, triplicity, term or face. Only rulership and exaltation tend to be used, although technically any of the five dignities may be applied. It is stronger if the planets concerned are in aspect to each other. Each planet can be read as though they had exchanged places.

))))➤ *Aspect, Dignity, Exaltation, Mixed Reception, Rulership*

MYSTIC RECTANGLE

Aspect pattern containing four or more planets connected by two trines and two sextiles, with oppositions running between all four corners of the figure. This pattern has been defined in recent times and apparently gained its name from the fact that Helena Blavatsky, founder of the Theosophical Society, was born with such a figure in her natal chart. The mystic rectangle does not necessarily imply mystical abilities in the

individual, but the characteristics associated with it could make such tendencies possible. The trines facilitate creativity with their inherent ability to understand, while the sextiles add some restlessness and the opportunity to be productive. The oppositions promote awareness through conflicting impulses which demand integration. Thus the mystic rectangle denotes an individual with an extraordinary ability to make use of his abilities and to sustain his productive efforts over a prolonged period of time.

))))➤ *Finger of Fate, Kite, Yod*

NADIR

The lowest point below the Earth, or the opposite point to the zenith. Often confused with the immum coeli, and the two terms tend to be used interchangeably, although they are not the same. The nadir is the lower point on the circle that passes through the east and west points of the horizon (prime vertical). The IC is the lower meridian, the lower point on the circle on the Earth's surface that runs perpendicular to the equator and passes through the north and south poles. Because the term is often used for IC, any interpretations of this point are intended to be those applying to the IC.

))))➤ *Immum coeli, Midheaven, Zenith*

ABOVE: The moment of birth, and the planetary arrangements at that time, form the basis for natal astrology..

LEFT: Helena Blavatsky was born with a mystic rectangle in her chart.

NAIBOD

 Prediction method. Naibod refers to a table of times for calculating an arc of direction. Named after Valentine Naibod, a sixteenth-century professor of mathematics who wrote a number of books on astrology, Naibod tables are used to calculate primary directions, a form of forecasting. Primary directions are a calculation based on the number of four-minute intervals during which a given planet will move from its birth position to the place where it joins or aspects a sensitive degree. To use them the right ascension (the distance measured along the celestial equator eastwards from the spring equinox) of the body concerned is calculated and subtracted from its longitude. This is then reduced to time, counting each degree as one year, five days and eight hours, and each minute to six days and four hours. Naibod tables save hours of tedious calculation when working with this predictive method. However, as primary directions such as these have fallen out of fashion, few people nowadays use the method. With better computer software, directions are gaining in popularity once more.

))))➤ *Direction*

ABOVE: *The astrological calculations based on the nativities of Louis XVI and Marie Antoinette reveal their tragic destiny.*

NATAL ASTROLOGY

Natal astrology is the study of the personal characteristics, traits, strengths, weaknesses and talents that an individual is given at birth, based on the planetary patterns at the time, date, and place of birth; in this way it is highly individualized. This is what most people think of as serious astrology. The ancient Greeks are given the credit for developing natal astrology and it has been studied and practised since 250 BC. The primary use of natal astrology is to show facets of a person's character, strengths and weaknesses, who they are and how they are likely to react to certain situations. In this way it is used as a tool for self-development. Applying forecasting techniques to the natal chart enables the astrologer to offer guidelines on what is likely to happen and in what way a person is likely to cope. Although there are many fields of application for astrology, natal astrology remains the most popular.

NATIVE

Subject of the horoscope. The birth chart was, until relatively recent times, known as a nativity – a reflection of the birth moment. The person for whom the chart was cast was therefore known as the native. Curiously, the field of astrology now known as natal was commonly called 'genethliacal' or 'pertaining to birth' when the term 'native' was in common use. There is no single term in general use today.

))))▶ *Horoscope*

NAYLOR, R. H.

Twentieth-century astrologer. R. H. Naylor (1889–1952) was the assistant of Cheiro (William John Warner, who also went by the name of Count Louis Hamon) – the biggest name in astrology in the 1920s. Because of Cheiro's unavailability, Naylor was asked by the editor of the *Sunday Express* to cast the horoscope of the newly born Princess Margaret Rose, daughter of the future King George VI. He did so, and its popularity led to the newspaper's editor inviting Naylor to contribute the following week. In this horoscope, Naylor suggested that

ABOVE RIGHT: Elizabeth, wife of George VI, with baby Princess Margaret Rose, for whom R H Naylor cast a horoscope.

TOP: Mythological Neptune with his chariot and winged horses.

British aircraft might be in danger. On the day of publication, the airship R-101 crashed in northern France. The newspaper gave Naylor massive publicity, and he became famous overnight. It was also Naylor who invented the Sun-sign column on 31 August 1930. He had to find a way of writing so that each reader could feel involved, and chose to divide his essays into 12 paragraphs, one for each person born when the Sun was passing through a particular zodiac sign.

))))▶ *Sun-Sign Astrology*

NEPTUNE

Second Trans-Saturnian planet, modern ruler of Pisces. First observed in 1795, but mistaken for a star, Neptune was officially discovered in 1846. This planet orbits the Sun between Uranus and Pluto with a rotational cycle of 164.75 years. Mythological Neptune is the Roman equivalent of the Greek god Poseidon, ruler of the sea and brother of Zeus (Roman: Jupiter). In modern astrology, the planet Neptune rules Pisces, the traditional domain of Jupiter. Like the other Trans-Saturnian planets, Neptune is said to be connected to the collective mind and to human evolution. Astrologically, Neptune's main characteristics are unlimitedness and the dissolution of clearly defined outlines, e.g. the border between consciousness and unconscious, between individuals, between truth and illusion, etc. Positively, Neptune may indicate great sensitivity, empathy, compassion, altruism, high ideals, self-sacrifice, spirituality, psychism, clairvoyance, telepathy, a rich dream life, altered states of consciousness, artistic inspiration or musical talent. Its negative manifestations include over idealization, delusion, deception, alcoholism, drug abuse, apathy, neediness, disappointment, irrational fear and identification with the role of the victim. On a mundane level, Neptune rules anything to do with the sea, floods, actors, movies, fashion, chemicals, gasses, mass movements, chaos and hidden or secretly undermining activities or influences.

))))➤ *Pisces, Ruler, Trans-Saturnian Planets*

NEW MOON

One of the phases of the Moon. The new Moon is the phase of the Moon when it is not visible from Earth, because the side of the Moon that is facing us is not being lit by the Sun. This means that the Sun, Earth, and Moon are almost in a straight line, with the Moon between the Sun and the Earth. The Moon that we see looks very dark. At the time of the new Moon, the Moon rises at about the same time as the Sun, and it sets at about the same time as the Sun. In astrology a new Moon heralds a time for new beginnings, as it adds a new infusion of potential. It opens fresh, new possibilities and is the perfect time to write down what you want to manifest in your life, to set goals and start new projects

))))➤ *Full Moon*

NINTH HOUSE

Sector of chart. In modern astrology, the ninth house is known as the house of the higher mind. It is associated with religious and philosophical issues and

ABOVE: Monks at their work, along with other religious and philosophical matters, are ruled by the ninth house.

religion in general. It is the house of in-laws, higher education and long journeys, foreigners and foreign interests, law and lawyers. In traditional astrology it is associated with dreams, divination, mysticism and belief. In horary astrology, it also represents the spouse's brothers and sisters as well as grandchildren. In political astrology, the ninth house describes the Church, other religious institutions and all institutions of higher learning. It also represents foreign affairs and the foreign office, international law and the United Nations. Shipping, airlines and anything connected with long journeys as well as the publishing industry; universities and scientific organizations are also represented by this house. In legal matters it represents lawyers who serve the prosecution and writs or communications that affect the defendant. In medical astrology it represents the buttocks, hips and thighs. It is associated with the colours green and white, and is a cadent and masculine house. Its direction is south-southwest. The Sun joys, or is happy, in the ninth, and it is associated with Sagittarius and Jupiter. It is also known as deus (God) and the house of religion.

))))➤ *Houses*

NOCTURNAL

A way of referring to a chart for someone born during the night with the Sun in the lower half of the chart. In traditional astrology planets are classified as nocturnal or diurnal, no matter where they are located in the chart.

))))▶ *Diurnal*

NODE

From Latin *nodus* ('knot'); the node of any planet is where the orbit of a planet satellite intersects the orbital plane of a planet. Mercury and Venus occasionally transit (pass in front of) the Sun and can be seen as a black dot on the Sun's face. This will occur if an inferior conjunction occurs within a day or two of the date at which the planet crosses the ecliptic – when it crosses a node. Transits of Venus (or Mercury) happen only when the Sun, Venus (or Mercury) and Earth exactly line up.

NONAGESIMAL

Chart point. The nonagesimal is the ninetieth degree of the ecliptic, the middle or highest point which is at any given moment above the horizon. In other words, it is ninety degrees from the ascendant and, depending on latitude, may coincide with the midheaven. In the equal house system it is the cusp of the tenth house. The nonagesimal represents a more personal point of accomplishment than does the midheaven. Relating directly to the ascendant, it shows what we are willing to do to attain our personal goals. It is related to status in a similar way to the midheaven.

))))▶ *Ascendant, Equal House System, Midheaven*

NORTH NODE

Chart point; also called ascending node, caput draconis, dragon's head, katababazon and rahu. The Moon's nodes are points that indicate where the orbit of the Moon around the Earth crosses the ecliptic – the

ABOVE: The Flight of the Soul – a journey governed by the Moon's nodes – from Jean de Meung of Boethius' Consolation of Philosophy.

apparent path of the Sun through the zodiac. The nodes form an axis, rather than separate points being exactly opposite each other, although are generally interpreted separately. Often only the north node is entered on the chart. The ancients held that the Moon's north node partook of the nature of Venus and Jupiter. A planet in close conjunction to the north node at birth would bring honours or riches. In modern astrology the nodes are often taken to show the souls journey and provide information about past lives. Interpretation of the nodes varies widely.

))))▶ *Mean Node, True Node*

PORTRAIT
DE MICHEL NOSTRADAMUS,
Astronome célèbre.

LEFT: Astrologer and mystic Michel de Nostradamus.
BELOW: Pope Sixtus IV, whose significance was acknowledged by
Nostradamus when the Pope was still a humble monk.

mark by his successful treatment of plague victims. During his travels in Italy he discovered his faculty of seeing into the future. By now he was adept at astrology as well as being clairvoyant. The most famous story about him tells of how he met a young monk and fell to his knees before him. This young man was later to become Pope Sixtus IV. By 1550 Nostradamus had produced a yearly almanac and after 1554 *The Prognostications*. On 4 May 1555 the first edition of his *Centuries* was published. Widespread interest makes it clear that he was already known as a prophet. He came under the protection of Catherine de Medici as physician, drawing up horoscopes for the famous Italian family. He ended his life drawing up horoscopes and completing his prophecies.

NORTHERN SIGNS

The northern signs are also referred to as boreal or septentrional signs, and are so called because they decline from the equinoctial or celestial equator (the Earth's equator projected into space) in a northward direction. The northern signs are measured from zero degrees of Aries, the point where the Sun's path intersects the celestial equator at the spring equinox, and contain the first half of the zodiac; they are Aries, Taurus, Gemini, Cancer, Leo and Virgo.

))))➤ *Equinox*

NOSTRADAMUS

Sixteenth-century astrologer and mystic. Michel de Nostre-Dame (1503–66) was born in St Rémy de Provence, the son of Christianized Jewish parents. After studying law he went on to study medicine and developed an interest in astrology. He first made his

NOVILE

Minor aspect. The novile is one of the 'abstract' minor apects and involves two planets positioned at an angle of 40 degrees. The name refers to the division of the zodiac into nine segments, which lies at the base of this aspect. Astrological literature is remarkably quiet about the novile, therefore its allotted orb is as unclear as its meaning is in most cases. Those who attempt an interpretation nowadays, usually associate the novile with the ninth harmonic, which is closely linked to the navamsas in Vedic astrology and relates to the finding of one's true life purpose and connecting, as it were, to the higher octave of one's life. Accordingly, the factors involved in the novile are said to provide information as to the individual's unique earthly mission. The planets and their signs and houses indicate the key to self-realization and fulfilment through identification with one's spiritual purpose.

))))➤ *Aspect, Minor Aspects*

OBEYING SIGNS

Obeying Signs is one of the divisions of the zodiac used in traditional and ancient astrology. It refers to the final six signs of the zodiac – Libra, Scorpio, Sagittarius, Capricorn, Aquarius and Pisces – and describes the nature as being obeying due to the placement of these signs on the horoscope and their connection to the culminating stages of growth centred around the relationship of the self with others in the world and the fulfilment of joint needs.

))))➤ *Aquarius, Capricorn, Libra, Pisces, Sagittarius, Scorpio*

OBLIQUITY

Tilt of the Earth. Obliquity is the angle between the plane of a planet's orbit and that of the planet's equator. The apparent path of the Sun – the ecliptic – intersects the celestial equator at an angle of 23 degrees. The inclination of the ecliptic to the celestial equator is termed the obliquity of the ecliptic. The cause of the seasons is the obliquity of the Earth's rotational axis to its orbital plane. The hemisphere of the Earth that is tilted towards the Sun receives a greater flux of solar energy than the hemisphere tilted away, resulting in higher temperatures.

))))➤ *Ecliptic, Orbit*

OCCIDENTAL

In general, occidental means setting after the Sun, defining a planet as visible in the evening. It is considered better for planets between the Earth and the Sun to be occidental. In some systems Jupiter is classed as occidental as it can be visible in the

morning. Occidental planets are considered slower to take action. The Moon is occidental when moving from full to new. The Sun is considered occidental in the first, second, third, seventh, eighth and ninth house.

OCCULTATION

Celestial phenomenon. Occultations occur when a moving object, such as a planet or the Moon, blocks the light coming from a more distant object, such as a star. It describes when a smaller astronomical body passes behind a larger astronomical body. If the primary source of illumination of a reflecting body is cut off by the occultation, that phenomenon is also called an eclipse. When a large celestial body hides a small one from view (as when the Moon moves in front of a star or Jupiter over one of its moons), the event is usually termed occultation.

))))➤ *Eclipse*

ABOVE RIGHT: The final six signs of the zodiac, which appear on the lower half of this wheel, are called the obeying signs.
RIGHT: Waiters and service in general, including servants or employees, are matters ruled by the sixth house.

OCCUPATIONS

Matter of the sixth and tenth house. The planets, and the rulers of the signs on the cusps of the sixth and tenth houses, have special significance when considering occupations. Traditional astrology reserves the sixth house for one's 'servants' (i.e. employees) and looks at the tenth house and its ruler to find out about the most likely bread-winning activity. In modern astrology, the idea of 'service' as a basic theme of the sixth house remains intact, but is now connected with one's daily work and the circumstances under which this is carried out. Therefore, the factors connected with the sixth house may describe one's profession and give information about the working environment, colleagues, one's own attitude towards work, etc. The tenth house covers another area of the occupational theme. Psychologically, it describes what the subject identifies with and how he perceives his role in society. Factors of the tenth house describe the individual's ambitions, aspirations and, consequently, his most likely choice of career, as well as his chances of failure or success.

))))➡ *Planets, Sixth House, Tenth House,*

OPPOSITION

Major aspect. The opposition consists of two or more planets or horoscope points separated by an angle of 180 degrees, i.e. being positioned on opposite sides of the zodiac. As the name indicates, the opposition is mostly an aspect of conflict. In horary astrology, two opposing significators may indicate a negative answer to the question or an insurmountable obstacle to the matter at hand. In modern natal astrology, the relevant planets symbolize conflicting inner impulses activated simultaneously. The results are an underlying feeling of uneasiness, self-doubt and a difficulty in making decisions. A person with several natal oppositions is said to literally be in constant opposition in the areas occupied and ruled by the relevant planets. Action is taken after considering all arguments surrounding the matter, which is why the opposition is also attributed with promoting awareness. At the same time the signs which are occupied by the planets in opposition form an axis that deals with similar issues from different perspectives. Therefore, the opposition also offers opportunities for integration and personal growth.

))))➡ *Aspect, Major Aspects*

ABOVE: Winter, along with the other seasons, is a result of the obliquity of Earth's rotational axis to its orbital plane.

ORB

Traditional and modern term. The term 'orb' refers to a sphere of influence, within which an aspect is considered to be of effect, but it is used in quite different ways by modern and traditional astrology. Modern astrology attaches the word to the aspect itself and leaves the definition of specific orbs to the judgement of the individual astrologer, which is the source of much confusion for beginning students and experienced practitioners alike. In traditional astrology, the term 'orb' refers to a sphere of influence, literally a circle of light, which surrounds every planet. To determine whether the angular relationship between two planets is already or still effective, their specific orbs are added up and then divided by two. Thus the orb of an aspect is not determined by the angle, but by the planetary combination. Al-Biruni and William Lilly recorded two slightly varying lists with the following degree values: Sun 15/17, Moon 12/12.5, Mercury 7/7, Venus 7/8, Mar 8/7.5, Jupiter 9/12, Saturn 9/10.

))))➤ *Aspect, Moiety*

ORBIT

A regular, repeating path that an object in space takes around another. An object in an orbit is called a satellite. A satellite can be natural, like the Moon, or man-made. In our Solar System the Earth orbits the Sun, as do the other eight planets. They all travel on or near the orbital plane, an imaginary disc-shaped surface in space. All the orbits are circular or elliptical. In addition to the planets' orbits, many planets have moons in orbit around them. Orbits are the result of a perfect balance between the forward motion of a body in space, such as a planet or moon, and the pull of gravity on it from another body in space, such as a large planet or star. Comets are in an irregular orbit around the Sun. Most asteroids in our Solar System are orbiting the Sun in a band between Mars and Jupiter. Even our Sun is travelling around the centre of the Milky Way galaxy.

))))➤ *Motion, Solar System*

ORIENTAL

In general, oriental means rising before the Sun, defining a planet as visible in the morning. It is considered better for a planet outside the Earth's orbit to be oriental. This is because planets between the Earth and Sun must be slowing down in their orbit to be visible in the morning. The Moon is oriental when moving from new to full. The Sun is considered oriental in the fourth, fifth, sixth, tenth, eleventh and twelfth house.

))))➤ *Occidental*

PARALLEL

Alternative aspect type. In the tables of the ephemeris, the planetary positions are given in longitude (horizontal) and latitude (vertical) relative to the ecliptic. The longitude determines a planet's zodiacal position. Its latitude describes how far the planet in question is above or below, i.e. north or south of, the ecliptic. The angular relationships (aspects) between planets are usually measured by their position in the zodiac, i.e. their longitude. But if two planets are at the same vertical distance from the ecliptic and thus share the same degree of latitude, they are said to form a parallel or to be in parallel aspect. If these parallel planets are in an

BELOW: Halley's comet, which appears in Giotto's Adoration of the Magi, *is in an irregular orbit around the Sun.*

PARS FORTUNA (PART OF FORTUNE)

Chart point. An Arabian Part that bears the same relationship to the rising degree as the Moon does to the Sun. The Part of Fortune is derived from adding the longitude of the Moon to the ascendant and subtracting the longitude of the Sun (Moon + Asc – Sun). So if the Moon is at three degrees of Gemini (63 degrees of the circle), the ascendant at 22 Capricorn (292) and the Sun at 6 Libra (186) the Part of Fortune falls at 292 + 63 – 186 = 169 or 19 Virgo. The formula is reversed for night births. It is symbolized by a cross within a circle. It shows an area in the chart where benefit can be gained, and is most closely associated with indicating the area of life that will most readily contribute to your financial welfare. It is also judged by noting the ruler of the sign it falls in and analysing that planet's strengths and aspects (angular relationships). It can also be an indicator of friendship when used in synastry.

)))➠ *Arabian Part, Synastry*

angular relationship in the horoscope as well, this will be re-inforced by the parallel. But even if they are not forming a vertical aspect in the chart, the planets are considered to cooperate. The parallel planets are either on the same side, i.e. north or south, of the ecliptic (parallel) or one of them has a northern and the other a southern latitude (contra-parallel). Traditional astrology interprets both parallels as a conjunction, while modern astrology considers the contra-parallel to work like an opposition.

)))➠ *Aspect, Conjunction, Contra Parallel, Latitude, Longitude, Opposition*

ABOVE LEFT: A close-up of the Moon, which is said to be oriental when moving from new to full.
BELOW: Our Solar System, showing the planets orbiting the Sun.

PARTILE

 Exact aspect. The term, originating from the Greek reference to the degrees as 'parts', is applied to aspects formed by two or more planets from the same degree of their respective signs. Some astrologers use it only when the bodies are also forming an exact parallel. In horary astrology some practitioners work with the assumption that partiles with the nodes signal an intervention of fate according to the nature of the aspect in question.

))))➤ *Parallel, Plactic*

PEREGRINE

A planet is called peregrine ('wandering'), if it has no essential dignity in the horoscope. Essential dignity is given to a planet for being the ruler of the sign in question, day ruler of the triplicity in a daytime horoscope, or night ruler of the triplicity in a night-time horoscope; it is also given essential dignity if it rules the face or term it is situated in or if it occupies the degree of its exaltation. If none of these conditions apply, the planet is said to be weak and inclined to manifest its negative characteristics, even if it gains accidental dignity through angularity or reception. For example, the Sun in Cancer is always peregrine, because it does not rule the sign, the triplicity or any term or face. According to Lilly, the peregrine planet in horary charts concerning theft is the significator of the culprit, when angular or in the second house.

))))➤ *Angular, Dignity, Exaltation, Face, Horary Astrology, Reception, Term*

PERFECTION

Traditional term. The term perfection is used in two different ways. When an aspect becomes exact (two planets that are square to one another are precisely 90 degrees apart) the aspect concerned can be said to have perfected. In horary astrology, the term refers to a planetary combination that gives a positive answer to the question

ABOVE LEFT: The Sun is peregrine in Cancer, as it does not rule the sign.
ABOVE: Rudolf II's astrologer, shown here with the emperor at his court in Prague, would speak of perfection when he had reached an affirmative answer.

asked, and no other planet is involved in the configuration to interfere. An aspect that has not yet become exact but is approaching exactitude will give a positive answer, and the amount of degrees the planets are apart from an exact aspect can indicate when it will happen. For example, if there are three degrees between Venus and Jupiter in the chart and no other planet interferes, the event in question may occur within three days. Other factors, such as reception and dignity also need to be considered when deciding if a matter will come to perfection.

))))▶ *Horary Astrology, Significator*

PERIGEE

Perigee refers to a point in the Moon's orbit when it is at its closest to the Earth. The combined effects of orbital eccentricity and the Sun's tides result in a substantial difference in the apparent size, with the Moon looking much brighter at perigee.

))))▶ *Apogee*

PERIHELION

The point in its orbit where a planet is closest to the Sun; opposite of aphelion. The distance of the planets from the Sun can vary widely. Perihelion occurs around 4 July. Planets move more quickly at perihelion than they do at aphelion.

))))▶ *Aphelion*

PERSONAL PLANET

Planets from the Sun to Mars. Due to their fast motion through the zodiac, the Sun, the Moon, Mercury, Venus and Mars are also known as the personal planets. They are regarded as mainly describing personal characteristics and everyday activities as, for example, likes and dislikes or the subject's ways of thinking.

))))▶ *Transpersonal Planets*

ABOVE: The Moon at its perigee, when it is at its closest to the Earth – within 221, 500 miles.

PISCES

Pisces is the twelfth and last sign of the zodiac, a member of the mutable triplicity, feminine and of the water element. A fertile sign, the symbol for Pisces is the fish, its traditional ruling planet is Jupiter, particularly by night and its modern ruler Neptune, often both planets are used as co-rulers. The Sun enters Pisces around 19

BELOW: Planet Jupiter, ruler of Pisces, with its moons.
BELOW LEFT: Pisces is the final sign of the zodiac and embodies a mixture of all the emotions that have gone before.

February and exits around 20 March. People whose birthdays fall between these dates are said to be Sun-sign Pisces. This is the last month of winter and the nature and qualities of Pisces are closely associated with this fertile and receptive time of planting in anticipation of new growth in the coming spring.

In physical terms, Pisces rules the feet, which sustain the whole and connect it to the world; the feet also leap and dance and are able to carry the body to other realms. Pisces is a collection of all the energies that have gone before; there is an innate empathy and understanding of all the thoughts, actions, feelings and physical needs that have been expressed in the previous 11 signs of the zodiac.

Pisces represents a search for self through internal emotional activity that assimilates and processes all experience of the intuitive consciousness, affirming connection to the source of all life. This ability to receive, absorb and empathize with all views makes it difficult for Pisces to choose a specific path for individual self-expression.

A bi-corporeal sign, the symbol for Pisces is two fish swimming in opposite directions joined by the thread of consciousness; this illustrates the dualistic nature of the sign, and the two ways the energy is expressed. One fish swims towards Aquarius, representing the impetus towards sacrifice of the self for the sake of others, while the other fish swims toward Aries and the need to use all the resources gathered by others in order to attain personal goals. This is a constant battle and dilemma operating deep within the psyche of Pisces.

Pisces gathers information through feeling and instinct; rational mental constructs cannot contain the imaginative wanderings of the fish. The spiritual realm and the subconscious are no barrier to incursion from Pisces. Pisces is often referred to as the mystic of the zodiac, with a keen ability to develop the higher spiritual mind. There is a sensitivity to emotional vibrations and thought waves in the environment, so Pisces often exhibits talents as a medium or clairvoyant. Certainly Pisces perceives or knows more than they let on. Pisces feels a strong imperative to connect with and become absorbed into something bigger than themselves, beyond accepted reality. If this desire is not channelled constructively, Pisces may be prone to taking drugs and alcohol to free themselves from the limitations of the material world; this is one of the reasons Pisces is also referred to as the sign of self-undoing.

Pisces frequently exhibits the other energies of the sign, and is able to take advantage of the reservoir of intuitive, perceptive knowledge they contain and do well in the material world as artist, musician and actor. Even big business and politics can make good use of the Piscean talent for merging apparently disparate energies, and they make excellent administrators and powerful executives.

Others are drawn to Pisces because of the sympathetic, altruistic and non-judgemental qualities they exhibit. On the surface there is a feeling of delicate vulnerability and sensitive self-sacrifice, yet Pisces also exudes a feeling of quiet inner strength, which is fascinating and alluring to those with a desire for more than a superficial relationship. Pisces is incredibly romantic, and a little shy, with an otherworldly quality of magic and fantasy. They have a wonderful sense of humour, and are affectionate partners. When Pisces feels the threat of being pinned down or their freedom inhibited, they escape into the imaginative world and become elusive, perhaps even deceptive, avoiding direct confrontation but offering up a type of passive resistance by being impossible to reach.

Any planet in a horoscope found in this sign will operate through the energies connected with it. The Moon in Pisces, for example, suggests deep and constantly changing emotions and a truly empathic nature that identifies strongly with the feelings and pain of others. Saturn in Pisces might operate as an ability to channel intuitive and psychic energies into constructive pursuits such as art and music or as indolence, and giving up on activities that prove too demanding, where the end does not justify the means.

Whatever part of the horoscope Pisces is found is the arena of life in which there will be a concern for spiritual involvement and intuitive emotional understanding. Pisces on the third house cusp, for example, may operate as a talent for communicating spiritual ideals through the medium of poetry, literature or artistic images, it may also indicate a sacrifice of the self for the benefit of siblings and close relations.

In its most positive expression, Pisces is spiritual, romantic, imaginative and creative, unselfish, trusting and not in the least judgemental. In its negative expression, Pisces is dependent, gullible, deceptive, with a difficulty in keeping a grip on reality, and prone to temperamental escapism.

ABOVE : Pisces, prone to taking drugs and alcohol, is perhaps the Sun-sign of the people in this Scandinavian drinking scene.

 Bi-corporeal, Feminine, Jupiter, Mutable, Neptune, Sun-sign, Water Signs

PLACIDUS HOUSE SYSTEM

Method of chart division. The Placidus system is one of the most complex. This is a time-based system, based on trisections of arcs. The eleventh and twelfth house cusps are calculated by trisecting the time it takes any degree of the ecliptic to ascend from the ascendant to midheaven (or semi-diurnal arc). This provides the degrees for the opposite house cusps as well. Similarly, the time it takes for any degree to travel from the immum coeli to the ascendant (or semi-nocturnal arc) is trisected to produce the second and third house cusps. It is named after its assumed creator, the seventeenth-century astrologer monk Placidus di Tito but, according to some sources, his tutor, Giovanni Antonio Magini, invented it, and Placidus developed the mathematical method that made it easier to calculate the cusps. Another source states that he derived the system from the eighth-century Arabian astrologer ben Djabir. It has been the most popular house system for many years because its tables are readily available, but it cannot be used for high latitudes.

)))▶ *House System*

PLACTIC

Classic and traditional term. The term plactic or platick has two meanings. In Greek astrology, it referred to aspects by sign. For example, a planet in Libra would be in plactic trine with any planet in Gemini, regardless of the occupied degrees. In traditional astrology, a plactic is an inexact aspect within the allowed planetary orb. For example, an exact square has 90 degrees; an aspect of 89 or 92 degrees is a plactic square.

)))▶ *Moiety, Orb*

ABOVE: A diagram of the planets, from the thirteenth century work Breviary of Love, *by Ermengol de Béziers.*

PLANET

Astronomical and astrological term, derived from the Greek word for 'wanderer'. Astronomy applies the term to a celestial body of a certain size, circling a star and with no light of its own. Astrology applies the same term to the wandering stars of our Solar System, whose positions and interactions are believed to reflect life on Earth. Although not planets in the astronomical sense, the Sun and the Moon are included in this group and even given special importance as 'lights' or 'luminaries'. Each astrological planet has its own characteristics. Ancient, medieval and traditional astrology only recognized the planets visible to the naked eye, e.g. Saturn, Jupiter, Mars, the Sun, Venus, Mercury and the Moon, and divided them into benefics and malefics. They were believed to radiate their own light and to be floating in a multi-layered celestial sphere, which marked the gradual descent from spirit to matter. Modern astrology incorporates the newly discovered Trans-Saturnian planets, Uranus, Neptune and Pluto. Some modern astrologers also work with hypothetical planets and asteroids.

))))▶ *Asteroid, Benefic, Celestial Sphere, Horoscope, Hypothetical Planets, Lights, Luminary, Malefic*

PLANETARY HOUR

Astrological time measurement. In ancient times only seven planets were known of and each of them ruled one day of the week: Saturn (Saturday), Sun (Sunday), Moon (Monday), Mars (Tuesday), Mercury (Wednesday), Jupiter (Thursday), Venus (Friday). In rotation, each of the hours of the day was associated with a planet. If Saturn ruled the first hour, the second was ruled by the Sun and so on. The first hour of each day is ruled by the planet that rules that day. Under this system, an hour is not uniformly 60 minutes, but is one-twelfth of the interval between sunrise and sunset in the daytime, and sunset and sunrise at night.

))))▶ *Chaldean Order, Rulership*

PLANETARY PERIOD

Traditional tool of long-term prediction. In traditional astrology, the planetary periods, also known as 'alfridaria' or 'firdar', constitute a system of long-term prediction very similar to the dasas and bhuktis in Vedic astrology. All planets and the nodes are assigned rulership over a certain number of years corresponding to a person's age. Each of these

BELOW: In ancient times, the gods each ruled a day of the week. Venus, painted here by Sandro Botticelli, was the ruler of Friday.

planetary periods is divided into seven equal parts, which are assigned to planetary sub-rulers following the Chaldean order. These give further detailed information about the nature of events that can be expected. There are several such systems documented in Greek, Persian and Arabic literature.

))))▶ *Chaldean, Vedic Astrology*

PLANETARY RETURN

Prediction method. A return chart is constructed for when the transiting planet in question returns to the exact position it held in the birth chart. A chart is drawn up for then and examined as a chart in its own right as well as in comparison to the original birth chart. A return chart can be calculated for any of the planets, including the Sun and Moon. A solar return relates to the following year – the time it takes the Sun to move around the whole chart. A lunar return relates to one month, Mars return twenty-two months, Jupiter twelve years, Saturn return 29 and a half years. Because of retrograde motion, it takes a year for Mercury and Venus to travel around the chart. Each type of return chart refers to the issues relating to that planet. So a Venus return chart is primarily about relationships, as well as providing a picture for the following year. Only the solar and lunar return charts are commonly used except when a definite focus on an issue is needed.

))))▶ *Lunar return, Solar Return*

PLANETOID

Celestial body generally used in reference to larger asteroids; also known as minor planets. Planetoids are made up of much of the same material as planets, but they are smaller. In astrology the most commonly used planetoid is Chiron, although there are differences of opinion over the actual classification of this body (some claim it is a comet or an asteroid). It was first sighted in 1977 on its path between Saturn and Uranus. A new planetoid was discovered in October 2000. Officially named 2000 EB173, this measures about 640 km (400 miles) in diameter or about one-fourth the size of Pluto. Because of its small size, the new planet is known as a Plutino, meaning 'Little Pluto'. In the year 2000 there was much controversy about the classification of Pluto; many astronomers believe that it should be reclassified as a planetoid.

)))▶ *Asteroid*

PLUTO

Third Trans-Saturnian planet. Pluto was discovered in 1930 and was originally named after a cartoon character. The aphelion of Pluto's orbit lies outside and the perihelion inside Neptune's path. Pluto's maximum distance from the ecliptic is 17 degrees 8 minutes 34 s; it has a rotational cycle of 248.4 years. The long duration of its transit through one sign has made Pluto an indicator of the evolutionary development of man, for better or for worse. In its regenerating mode, it is linked to esoteric movements seeking redemption, the relentless elimination of outlived traditions and the positive transformation of lifestyles. Its eruptive, undermining and disturbing side is linked to plutonium, nuclear power, political or religious fanaticism, deadly

viruses and any means of mass destruction. As the modern ruler of Scorpio and the eighth house, Pluto is connected to death, hidden fears or talents, power, psychological insight, secrecy, sexuality and the unconscious. In its positive manifestation, Pluto's tremendous powers are generally used to heal and to regenerate with radical creativity; negatively expressed it may result in obsessive compulsive tendencies, often of a psychic nature. Any planet in aspect with Pluto tends to manifest in extremes.

)))▶ *Aphelion, Eighth House, Perihelion, Scorpio, Trans-Saturnian Planets*

ABOVE RIGHT: The planet Pluto rules all means of mass destruction, such as Mt Etna.
RIGHT: Pluto from Roman mythology, the ruler of the infernal regions.

PORPHYRY HOUSE SYSTEM

Method of chart division. The Porphyry system dates from the third century AD. It is named after the neo-Platonist Porphyry (AD 233–305), who wrote on Pythagoras, Plotinus and Ptolemy. It is possible that Porphyry derived this system from a little-known astrologer called Orion (*c.* AD 150 – 175). He reintroduced the system in his book *Introduction to Ptolemy's Tetrabiblos*, written in around AD 295. This makes it one of the earliest quadrant house systems. It is similar to the Equal house system but uses the midheaven as the tenth house cusp. The remaining houses are determined by trisecting each quadrant in thirds. This means that the ascendant does not form the first house cusp, and may not even fall into the first house, in a similar fashion to the midheaven in the Equal house system. The simplicity of this system makes it popular but it has never reached the levels of the Equal house system because its teaching is not so widespread.

))))➠ *Equal House System, House System*

POSITED

Planetary placement. The word literally means 'placed' and is used in older texts to describe the position occupied by a body in the heavens or in the signs and houses of a birth chart. It is usually used in reference to planets, but may also be used to describe the position of other chart points.

PRECESSION

Movement of equinoctial points. The precession of the equinoxes is the westward motion of the equinoxes along the ecliptic. Precession is caused by the slow movement of the Earth's axis that results in the celestial poles and equator appearing to move against the background of the stars. The equinoctial points move west at a rate of about 50 seconds a year, and in 25,800 years the Earth completes one precessional cycle. The Sun crosses the equator about 20 minutes earlier each year and 50 seconds of arc further west. This moving zodiac is known as the tropical zodiac. Because of precession there is now a discrepancy between the positions described by astrology and the actual astronomical positions in the zodiac belt; at present this is about 23 degrees. One of the foremost arguments against astrology is that its practitioners do not take note of precession in calculating charts. However, the tropical zodiac is directly related to the Sun's path and the seasons.

))))➠ *Equinox, Sidereal Astrology, Tropical Astrology*

1 Mercure . 2 Venus . 3 La Terre . 4 Mars . 5 Jupiter . 6 Saturne .

ABOVE: A posited can refer to the placement of a planet in the heavens. This is Fontenelle's understanding of the planetary arrangement.

PREDICTION

There are many different techniques that can be used for prediction, some of them based on the actual movements of the planets and others which are more symbolic. The issue of fate and free will is highlighted when prediction is considered, and it was this aspect of astrology that gave rise to opposition from the Church in the Middle Ages, and indeed still causes concern today. In traditional forms of astrology, definite and extremely specific predictions are made, often outlining events throughout a person's life. In the more modern forms of astrology, predictions take the form of outlining trends – good and bad periods – which the person can deal with as they see fit. It is often stated that while the stars may impel they do not compel. This implies that it is possible to exert conscious control over our lives and that nothing is completely inevitable. There is great disagreement about what an astrologer should attempt to predict. In the West it is rare for an astrologer to predict the date of death, whereas this is common practice in the East.

))) *Direction*

PRE-NATAL EPOCH

Method of rectifying a chart when the time of birth is unknown; also called the Trutine of Hermes. The theory, which dates back to the time of Ptolemy, states that at the time of conception the Moon should be in conjunction with, or in opposition to, the natal ascendant, and the ascendant in conjunction or opposition with the natal Moon. Pre-natal epoch theory allows for a symbolic chart to be calculated for nine months before birth, based

on the relationship between the Sun, Moon and ascendant in the horoscope. Taking this chart forward allows for the birth chart to be fine-tuned, giving an 'accurate' birth time. The astrological moment of conception is approximately nine months before birth, but not necessarily coinciding with the exact time of birth. The Moon's place on epoch day, or its opposite, becomes either the ascending or descending sign and degree at birth. It is a symbolic chart rather than a conception chart.

))) *Rectification*

PRIMARY DIRECTION

Prediction method. In general terms direction means any method of moving the planets and chart points forward so that predictions may be made. Usually the term is used to refer to primary directions. In this system a calculation of the four-minute intervals during which a given planet will move from its birth position to the place where it conjoins or aspects (makes an angular relationship to) a sensitive degree is made. As each four-minute arc represents a year of life, it is assumed that in a given year there will be in force a directed aspect between these two bodies. Primary directions are based on the first motion, the Primum Mobile of Aristotle, the apparent nightly trek of the planets across the sky from East to West. This means that calculations are made in Right Ascension along the

ABOVE: Dante and Beatrice meet Cacciaguida, who predicts Dante's exile.
ABOVE LEFT: A Tarot card which depicts the stars – linking two common means of prediction.

Equator, and that an error of four minutes in the actual birth moment makes a difference of one year in the timing of a prognosticated condition or event. Owing to difficulty in calculation they fell out of favour for many years.

))))➤ *Direction, Progression, Secondary Progression, Tertiary Progression, Transit*

PRIME VERTICAL

Astronomical coordinate. The prime vertical is the great circle that intersects the horizon at the east and west points, passing through the zenith at right angles to the meridian. All other vertical circles, which also pass through the zenith and nadir, do not pass through the east and west points of the horizon. The plane of the prime vertical corresponds to the points of the intersection of the horizon and equator.

))))➤ *Meridian, Zenith*

PRIMUM MOBILE

Ancient astrological theory. The term *primum mobile* means 'first mover'. The theory was expostulated by Aristotle to explain a pattern of westward flow in the oceans. The first mover, a theological being, was unmoved but acted on the circumference of the Universe, causing it to move. The shape of heaven is spherical and encloses successively smaller spheres down to the centre, i.e. Earth,

BELOW: The Primum Mobile theory separated the universe into concentric spheres. Here a medieval missionary finds a place where Earth touches Heaven.

with the motion of the outermost sphere being uniform and that of the inner spheres increasingly irregular as the centre is approached. Since the Sun and stars appeared to move west in an outer sphere, the first mover must be moving things in that direction.

PROFECTION

Method of prediction. This is the moving of a chart point or planet at the rate of one sign per year (in the case of annual profection), 13 signs in 12 months (monthly profection) or one sign every two-and-a-half days or one sign a day (depending on method used). This was a common method in ancient times and was used frequently by medieval astrologers, after which it fell out of favour. By the seventeenth century this ancient method of prediction had taken on the quality of a continuous rate of direction or progression. It has recently been revived.

))))➤ *Direction, Progression*

PROGRESSION

Prediction method. Progressions are based on the actual movements of the planets after birth, symbolically related to a time period or cycle of life. This method involves using the ephemeris for the year of birth and counting forward one day to represent a chosen time period. Usually a day is held to represent a year of life. In minor or tertiary progressions, one day can be held to represent a month or week of life. The rationale for secondary progressions is placed on an interpretation of a biblical passage, Ezekiel 4:6 '…I have appointed thee each day for a year…' As the planets from Saturn and beyond move comparatively slowly, only the planets from Mars inwards are progressed. House cusps, including the ascendant and midheaven, may also be progressed. Because this method only requires one set of tables for the whole of a person's life, it was popular as a technique for hundreds of years.

))))➤ *Direction, Primary Direction, Secondary Progression, Tertiary Progression, Transit*

PROHIBITION

Planetary combination preventing another combination. If two planets are travelling towards forming an angular relationship with one another, but before the aspect becomes exact another faster planet makes an aspect with one of them, this is a form of prohibition. In a horary chart it prevents the matter being questioned about occurring. For example, if the question was 'Will I get a job interview' it would show that an outside factor prevents it from happening so the answer would be no. If prohibition occurs by conjunction, it is referred to as 'bodily prohibition'. For example, if Venus is at five degrees of Cancer and moving towards Jupiter at 10 degrees of Cancer but before it gets there Mercury, which was at four degrees, passes Venus and reaches Jupiter first, there is prohibition.

))))➤ *Abcission of Light, Frustration,*

PROMITTOR

The planet to which another planet may be 'directed' or moved by a system in order to form an aspect (angular relationship) between it and the directed planet. The promittor is the planet in the birth chart that other planets are moved towards when predicting. The distance that the moved planet must travel to meet the promittor is called the arc of direction, and this is usually about the rate of one degree for a year and five minutes for a month, although systems vary slightly, giving differing results.

))))➤ *Direction, Primary Direction, Secondary Procession*

PROPER MOTION

Term used to describe the motion of any body in space, compared to apparent motion which results from the rotation of the Earth. Proper motion is loosely applied to the direct motion of a planet through the zodiac signs in distinction to the diurnal rising and setting caused by the Earth's rotation. A distinction between apparent and actual motion of a celestial body.

))))➤ *Apparent Motion*

PROPHECY

Prophecy means to speak by divine inspiration and a prophet is someone who speaks about a received

revelation. It happens spontaneously, and prophetic pronouncements are often very much like dreams and can be difficult to decipher. The traditional forms of astrology are forms of divination; both involve tapping into the unconscious mind, but divination involves using a technique as a focus and is more voluntary in nature. Many of the more famous prophets were also astrologers. Astrology is often defined as a science that utilizes the intuitive faculty in its interpretation.

))))➤ *Nostradamus*

PSYCHOLOGICAL ASTROLOGY

The study of the personality; one of the primary applications of astrology. Psychological astrology is carried out by examining the birth chart. Throughout the twentieth century astrology became more popular, reflecting the rise in popularity of psychology. German astrology from the 1920s led the field in using the horoscope to analyse character, rather than to predict.

ABOVE: The Green Book of Prophecies from 1912. Many of the more famous prophets were also astrologers.

RIGHT: Egyptian astrologer Ptolemy, holding globe and dividers.
BELOW: Ptolemy's understanding of the planetary system, which features the
Earth at the centre of the universe.

Psychoanalyst Carl Jung was interested in astrology and began to examine it in the context of his theories of synchronicity and the collective unconscious. Alongside this development, belief in human progress through technology and evolution made the predictive nature and supposed fatalism of astrology seem absurd. To adapt, some astrologers followed Jung's example and used his framework to explain the natal chart as a reflection of an individual's connection to archetypes in the collective unconscious. As the field of psychology split into different theoretical directions, such as psychoanalysis, behaviourism and humanism, so did astrology adopt different approaches to the practice. Psychological astrology remains hugely popular today although prediction is used within the field.

)))⯈ *Carl Jung*

PTOLEMAIC ASPECTS

Angular relationships between planets and chart points. The Ptolemaic aspects are those mentioned in Ptolemy's *Tetrabiblos*, a standard text for astrologers, which has been in common use since translations were made in the sixteenth century. The aspects are the opposition, trine, square and sextile. The conjunction is often included in this list, and it is certainly used in

Ptolemy's work, but it is more correctly termed a position as the word 'aspect' means 'to look at one another' and two planets in conjunction are placed side by side. Numerous other aspects have been added but these remain the primary ones.

)))⯈ *Aspect, Conjunction, Opposition, Ptolemy, Sextile, Square*

PTOLEMY, CLAUDIUS

Ancient astrologer. Little is known for certain about Ptolemy, except that he was not related to the Ptolemaic rulers. He was an Egyptian astronomer, mathematician and geographer who lived near Alexandria about AD 150. He was born in Upper Egypt and he is believed to have been head librarian at the famous library in Alexandria. He worked from the data of past astrologers to map over 1,000 stars. He compiled a list of 48 constellations and described the lines of latitude and longitude on the Earth. He believed Earth was the centre of the Universe and outlined his theories in his most famous work, the Almagest. These theories would remain the basis for all astronomical thought for more than 1,400 years. *Tetrabiblos* also proved to be one of the foundations of modern astrology. The four books of this work became familiar to Europeans, as Latin translations were available from 1434.

)))⯈ *Egyptian Astrology*

QUADRANT

Chart area. A quadrant is one of the four quarters of the chart, as it is divided by the angles. The oriental quadrants consist of the tenth to twelfth and fourth to sixth houses. The occidental quadrants consist of the first to third and seventh to ninth houses. If applied to the zodiac, the oriental quadrants are from Aries to Gemini and Libra to Sagittarius with the occidental as the remaining signs.

⫸ *Houses*

QUADRUPLICITY

Classification of signs. The signs of the zodiac are grouped in three quadruplicities: cardinal, fixed and mutable. The term refers to each category containing four signs, one of each element. The quadruplicities indicate how the elements are being expressed throughout the signs, i.e. how the individual deals with life after perceiving it in the way suggested by the elements. The cardinal quadruplicity consists of Aries, Cancer, Libra and Capricorn, and is ascribed initiating and motivating qualities. The orientation is extrovert; exchange with the environment and adaptation to outer circumstances are of highest importance. The fixed quadruplicity contains Taurus, Leo, Scorpio and Aquarius and is characterized as securing and stabilizing. The orientation is introvert; personal values and motifs have priority over the demands of the environment. Gemini, Virgo, Sagittarius and Pisces belong to the mutual quadruplicity, which is characterized as a mixture of the two others. The orientation can be either extrovert or introvert, implying adaptability and mediating qualities, but is likely to suddenly change under pressure. The quadruplicities are also called 'qualities' or 'modes'.

⫸ *Cardinal, Fixed, Mode, Mutable, Quality*

QUALITY

Classification of zodiac signs. In astrological language, the term quality refers to certain charac-

ABOVE: The signs of the zodiac, which are grouped into three quadruplicities: cardinal, fixed and mutable.
LEFT: Pisces, the fish, belongs to the mutable quadruplicity.

teristics of the signs. It is used in two ways: it either refers to the quadruplicities, a categorization of the signs as cardinal, fixed or mutable; or it pertains to the nature of the signs as implicated by the combination of elements and the four classic principles. In the first sense, the term 'cardinal', 'fixed' or 'mutable quality' summarizes the energy flow within the sign in question and characterizes the way in which the sign tends to express the element to which it belongs. The second meaning of the term, quality, plays an important role in medical astrology. By linking each triplicity with combinations of the four classic principles, e.g. fire with heat and dryness, earth with dryness and cold, air with heat and moisture, and water with moisture and cold, each sign ends up with a certain quality, which is also reflected in the physical body. To be 'out of quality' refers to an imbalance between the elements, which may result in illness.

⫸ *Cardinal, Element, Fixed, Mode, Mutable, Quadruplicity, Triplicity*

QUERENT

Literally, a questioner. A term used in horary astrology to indicate the person who asks the question for whim the chart is cast. It is symbolized by the ascendant and its ruler, and the Moon in the chart. The querent may be the astrologer or the person asking the astrologer the question.

))))➤ *Horary Astrology.*

QUESITED

Subject of horary question. The quesited is the matter or person enquired about for a horary question. It is symbolized by the planet that rules the sign of the cusp on the house that relates to the question. This is referred to as the 'quesited's significator'.

))))➤ *Horary Astrology.*

QUINCUNX

Minor aspect. The quincunx, also known as 'inconjunct', is an aspect of 150 degrees and is generally allowed an orb of three degrees. Although used by traditional authorities like William Lilly, it was long dismissed by many astrologers as meaningless or too weak in its influence. In recent times, the quincunx has gained greater recognition and some modern astrologers even give it the status and importance of a major aspect. The planets involved, their positions in sign and house, and the houses they rule imply special talents, which the individual can only develop after experiencing and solving a crisis situation. Usually, this crisis involves having to make a seemingly impossible choice between two sides of oneself, which are described by the relevant planets. The realization that both facets of one's personality can simply be used according to circumstance, at different times and according to circumstance may then lead to their further development.

ABOVE: Querent Imperial General Wallenstein consults an astrologer about his future prospects. It is not good news.

))))➤ *Aspect, Finger of Fate, Inconjunct, Minor Aspects, Yod*

QUINDECILE

 Minor aspect. By dividing the zodiac into 15 segments, one arrives at an angle of 24 degrees; this is known as the quindecile aspect. It belongs to the series of aspects introduced by Johannes Kepler in the seventeenth century. Like the other aspects of this group, it refers to special intellectual, occult or creative talents, which are present but need to be developed by the individual. Those who consider it do not agree as to whether it is a harmonious or disharmonious aspect, but the quindecile suggests a focus on an extreme interest, pursued by the individual at all costs.

)))◗ *Aspect, Minor Aspects*

QUINTILE

 Minor aspect. The quintile is an aspect of 72 degrees and is generally allowed an orb of two degrees. If one of the lights is involved, the orb may be as wide as three degrees. The quintile is one of the lesser known and less frequently used aspects, although some astrologers regard it as important. It was introduced by seventeenth-century astrologer Johannes Kepler and is based on the division of the circle into five segments. Because of the numerological implications of the number five and the cabalistic interpretation of the five-pointed star, the quintile is said to denote extraordinary mental powers of invention and creation, which can be used to give spiritual principles a practical, earthly application. Although the individual is given this talent, (s)he still has to develop it through means described by the planets involved, their positions in signs and houses and by the houses they rule.

)))◗ *Aspect, Minor Aspects*

ABOVE: Due to interpretations of the number five and of the five-pointed star, the quintile is said to give great mental and creative powers.

QUOTIDIAN

Prediction rate of movement. The quotidian is the name given to the rate of movement when secondary progressions are used for predictive work. The most commonly used rate is called Q2 and it is based on the ratio of one tropical day for a year (1: 365.24219879). An alternative rate is called Q1 or Bija correction and this is based on the ratio of one sidereal day for a year (1: 366.2563992).

RADICAL

Valid chart. The term refers to the state of the birth chart, also known as the radix. In horary astrology it describes a chart that is fit to be judged. To decide whether the chart is fit the considerations before judgement are considered. If the chart has no factors in it included in the considerations then the chart is judged. Astrologers apply the considerations in different ways so there are differences of opinion over whether certain charts are valid. The radical position of any planet or chart point is the birth position of the planets as distinguished from any directed or progressed positions.

)))◗ *Considerations Judgement, Direction, Horary Astrology, Radix* innumerable works on astrology and other occult subjects and gained huge popularity. Smith's favouring of the Placidean house system led to the spread in popularity of this system. After his death in 1832, John Palmer took over editorship of the *PM* until his death in 1837. A man called Medhurst was the next Raphael until 1847, followed by Wakely until 1852 and Sparkes until 1875. Finally, the name was adopted by Robert Thomas Cross. Cross became as renowned as Smith, and was an equally prolific writer.

RADIX

Birth chart; another name given to the chart or horoscope. This name carries the additional implication that the chart cast is radical, or valid. In horary astrology a chart needs to go through a number of tests before it can be deemed valid to read.

))➤ *Horary Astrology*

RAPHAEL

Nineteenth-century astrologers. The name Raphael means 'God has healed' and it is associated with the planet Mercury, the traditional ruler of astrology. The first time Raphael was adopted as a pseudonym was by Robert Cross Smith (1795–1832). At the age of 25 he became the editor of *The Prophetic Messenger* which survives today in the form of Raphael's *Ephemeris*. There were few astrologers at this time and Smith led the revival of nineteenth-century astrology. He wrote

RAPT MOTION

The apparent daily motion of a body from east to west. The daily motion of the Earth on its axis. This is used to calculate 'rapt parallels' which are equal distances from the meridian formed by rapt motion. They are not related to the positions of the planets in the signs. Rapt parallels are interpreted in the same way as ordinary parallels, which are calculated according to planetary latitude. The term is obscure and rarely used today.

RAY

Traditional astrological theory. A ray is a force or energy with the emphasis on the quality that force exhibits rather than the form it creates. The astrologer Al-kindi (AD 800–873) attempted a rational explanation of astrological effects in terms of rays in his book *On the Stellar Rays*. The book also invokes terrestrial rays as an explanation for the efficacy of amulets, incantations, curses and sacrifice. He explained how the stellar

rays interacted with various elements as they passed through space and came into contact with an individual. This work was influential in creating a belief in astro-logical magic. Medieval astrologers took hold of the idea of a physical cause for astrological influence. For years planets were held to emit rays that carried the nature of that planet – what might now be called its characteristics.

From 1936 the theosophist Alice A. Bailey wrote a series of books entitled *Esoteric Astrology*. She took various traditional views and presented them in a more elaborated form. Central to her theories was the idea of the Seven Rays – one for each of the planets.

RECEPTION

Planetary placement. Reception may take two forms. Mutual reception occurs when two planets are in each other's dignity. For example, Mars in Gemini and Mercury in Aries are in mutual reception because Mars rules Aries and Mercury rules Gemini. Mutual reception by ruling sign is the strongest. Mixed reception occurs when two planets are in dignities assigned to the other, but the nature of the dignities are different. For example, Mars is in Cancer, ruled by the Moon, and the Moon is in Capricorn where Mars is exalted. It is stronger if the two planets concerned are also making an aspect to one another. Both types of reception give a bond between the two planets and they can be read as if they had changed places in the chart. Only rulership and exaltation tend to be used although technically any of the five dignities may be applied. In modern astrology only mutual reception tends to be used and it is this type of reception that is generally referred to when using the term.

▶ *Aspect, Dignity, Exaltation, Mixed Reception, Mutual Reception, Rulership*

ABOVE: An amulet from Tekke Turkmenistan. Al-kindi believed that the efficacy of such charms could be explained by stellar rays.
LEFT: A Tarot card of the stars and their effect on earthly life.

RECTIFICATION

Astrological method for ascertaining an individual's time of birth. Rectification is the art of taking an approximate time of birth and refining it through astrological techniques. Many birth times are not recorded accurately – if at all. There are a variety of methods used to rectify the birth chart. Predictive techniques are often used retrospectively. Primary directions were most commonly used in the past but today progressions and transits are most often used. Knowing the astrological patterns that would be expected to coincide with a certain event, the astrologer moves the angles and house cusps in the birth chart until a chart is found which, when predictive techniques are applied, give the expected prediction for the date of the event. Another method of rectification is the pre-natal epoch. Thus, if you know the time the child was

conceived, you know the precise moment of birth. The most condemning objection to its use is the birth of identical twins, which presumably have the same pre-natal epoch, but are nevertheless born at different times.

)))➤ *Pre-Natal Epoch*

REFRANATION

Planetary combination which prevents another combination. Refranation occurs when one planet is travelling towards another, but before it reaches it and the aspect becomes exact, it goes retrograde and so the aspect doesn't occur. Alternatively, the planet it is moving towards moves into the next sign before it reaches it. This is taken as an indicator in horary astrology that the matter under negotiation will not be brought to a successful, or the desired, conclusion. Refranation is another form of prohibition, preventing the results shown on a cursory look at a chart.

)))➤ *Abscission of Light, Frustration, Prohibition, Retrograde*

ABOVE: *The birth of identical twins, like those of the sign Gemini, contradict the principles of rectification.*

REGIOMONTANUS HOUSE SYSTEM

Regiomontanus is one of the house systems most commonly used by horary astrologers. The method is named after Johann Müller (1436–76), more commonly known by his Latin name Regiomontanus. The system is a modification of the Campanus system, in which the celestial equator is divided into equal 30-degree arcs and used as the primary reference instead of the prime vertical. These segments are then projected on to the ecliptic, with the degrees at which they cut the ecliptic marking the house cusps. The cusps are regarded as the centre of the houses. Evidence suggests that this method originated with the Arabs around the eleventh century AD. The popularity of Regiomontanus came about because the house cusps are fixed for an observer at a particular latitude, and can be inscribed on an astrolabe plate, making it possible to calculate the houses quickly, and Müller developed a comprehensive set of tables, called the *Tabulai directionum profectionumquem*, for the system. Between the astrolabe and set of tables, the method grew in popularity across Europe during the sixteenth century, eventually replacing the Alcabitius method.

)))➤ *Alcabitius House System, House System*

REGULUS

Fixed star used by astrologers. Regulus was one of the four stars of the ancient Persian monarchy when, as watcher of the north, it marked the summer solstice. It was seen as one of the four guardians of heaven, one who regulated all things in the heavens. It is now at the end of the twenty-ninth degree of Leo.

)))➤ *Fixed Stars*

RELATIONSHIP CHART

Although sometimes used to describe a chart cast for the start of a relationship, this usually describes a technique whereby the charts of both people in a relationship are combined. An imaginary birth place, date and time is established, based on the halfway point between both people's place, date and time of birth. This chart is then taken to describe the nature and quality of

ABOVE RIGHT: Johann Muller, known as Regiomontanus, expounds the system of Ptolemaius in a sixteenth centruy engraving.

the relationship between the two people concerned. The relationship chart may be compared with the two birth charts used to see what contributions each makes to the relationship. The relationship chart may be treated in the same way as any horoscope and predictive techniques applied to it. This technique may be taken further by calculating a new chart for the halfway point between the relationship chart and the chart of each person individually. This shows the relationship of each to the relationship itself. The technique was first described by Ronald Davison in his book *Synastry* in 1977.

)))➤ *Synastry*

RELOCATION

In relocation astrology, the birth time and date of the person whose chart is being considered is used, but it is recast for either the place they are living at that time, or a place that they are considering living. The new chart describes the likely experiences they will have in that location. This tool is used when someone is deciding whether or not to make a move. The most important factor in a relocated chart is when planets become angular, that is, placed near the cusps of the first, fourth, seventh or tenth houses. More specific techniques such as astro*carto*graphy and local space charts are used to give the same information in a diagrammatic form. Relocation of charts is a traditional technique that has been used for so long in the history of astrology that there is no record of when it was first devised. It is held that predictions based on a relocated chart will be more accurate for an individual as the house placements and ascendant and midheaven may potentially be different to the birth chart.

)))➤ **Astro*carto*graphy, Local Space**

RENAISSANCE ASTROLOGY

By the turn of the eighteenth century, scientific interest in astrology was at a lower ebb than it had been for hundreds of years. Although there had been no concerted attack on the discipline, it was no longer assumed that academia would be automatically interested. By 1720 the last of the notable astrologers of the previous century was dead. The few astrologers that remained fell

far below the expertise of their predecessors. They would certainly not have been capable of writing works such as Lilly's *Christian Astrology*. There had been attempts to bring the study of astrology in line with the new scientific age, and the eighteenth century set off on a course of scientific empiricism and ignored the efforts of astrologers to gain their work scientific credence. Almanacs continued to sell, however, and some were brought out specifically for women. Towards the middle of the

century, there was a turn towards religion, increasing the opposition to astrology. Popular interest still brought clients, but they took astrology far less seriously. By the 1790s the astrological *Conjurers Magazine* appeared – but was short-lived, lasting only seven issues. Astrology would not begin its recovery until Raphael led the revival in the 1820s.

ABOVE: Emigrants can have relocation charts cast, to suit their destinations.
ABOVE RIGHT: Johannes Vermeer's Astronomer, *painted in 1668 at a time when interest in the stargazing sciences was at an all-time low.*

RETROGRADE

The term retrograde is applied to an apparent backward motion in the zodiac of certain planets when decreasing in longitude as viewed from the Earth. After a time, the planet then appears to stop once again and reverse its movement through the sky. The planet then goes 'direct' and is back on its normal cyclic path through the sky. This traditional concept arises in the illusory planetary motion created by the orbital rotation of the Earth, with relation to other planets in our Solar System. Planets are never actually retrograde or stationary, they just seem that way. Except for the Sun and Moon, all planets may be retrograde, but Mercury spends the longest period retrograde, about 20 per cent of the time. A retrograde period is seen as a cycle, beginning when the planet begins to slow to a halt before travelling backwards through the zodiac and ending when the planet returns to the point where it first paused. Retrograde planets in the birth chart were said to be weak or debilitated.

))))➤ *Station*

REVOLUTION

Loosely applied to anything that pursues an orbit. Also used in connection with directions involving the return of the Sun, Moon or any other planet to the place it was in the original chart. These charts are often referred to as return charts in modern astrology. The chart is cast for the time of return and judged as a separate chart as well as in comparison with the original chart for the purpose of making predictions relating to the planet.

))))➤ *Direction, Jupiter Return, Saturn Return*

ABOVE: Ascension, which is an astonomical measurement similar to longitude on Earth, may be calculated by this French navigator.

RIGHT: The planets' orbits around the Sun can be referred to as revolutions.

RIGHT ASCENSION

Astronomical measurement. One element of the astronomical coordinate system on the sky; this can be thought of as longitude on the Earth projected on to the sky. Right ascension is usually denoted by the lower-case Greek letter alpha (a) and is measured eastwards in hours, minutes and seconds of time from the vernal equinox. There are 24 hours of right ascension and the 24-hour line is taken as 0 hours. Right ascension may be expressed in degrees, in which case there are 360 degrees of right ascension to make a complete circuit of the sky.

))))➤ *Longitude*

RISING DEGREE

Ascendant degree. The rising degree is often wrongly called 'ascendant' in popular astrological language. It marks the exact section of the sign rising ('ascending') on the eastern horizon at the relevant time. Some astrologers use corresponding degree symbols in their analysis or ascribe masculine or feminine qualities to certain degrees.

)))))➤ *Ascendant, Degree Symbol, Sabian Symbol*

ROYAL STARS

Type of fixed star. There are four royal stars: Aldebaran, Regulus, Antares and Fomahault. Regulus is usually considered the 'most' royal, although Aldebaran also has proponents. When a chart point or planet is near one of these stars, (within one degree), it promises great success so long as certain conditions are fulfilled. These stars are also known as the 'watchers of the heavens'. Each one of these stars rules over one of the four cardinal points.

)))))➤ *Aldebaran, Antares, Fixed Stars*

RULER

Representative planet. The term has various meanings. Firstly, it indicates a planet incorporating and expressing the characteristics of the sign it 'rules'. If situated in this sign, the planet is dignified. Secondly, astrology works with 'rulers' of houses, which should correctly be called 'lords'. The 'accidental' lord of a house is the ruler of the sign on the cusp, representing matters of this area. The 'natural' lord of a house is the ruler of its corresponding sign. If, for example, Aries is on the cusp of the fifth house, Mars as ruler of Aries is accidental lord of this area. The natural lord of the fifth house is the Sun as ruler of the fifth sign, Leo. Thirdly, a planet, sign or house may represent or 'rule' certain people or phenomena according to the doctrine of congenialities. Lastly, the 'lord of chart' or 'chart ruler' is believed to be the most influential planet.

)))))➤ *Dignity, Lord of Chart, Rulership*

ABOVE: As certain planets are viewed from the Earth, they appear to be moving in a backward or retrograde manner, as illustrated in this diagram.

RULERSHIP

Certain planets are deemed to have strength in certain signs. The traditional scheme does not allow for the modern planets – Uranus, Neptune and Pluto – which are said to have an affinity with, rather than rule, a sign. The Sun rules Leo, Moon Cancer, Mercury Gemini by day and Virgo by night, Venus Taurus by night and Libra by day, Mars Aries by day and Scorpio by night, Jupiter Sagittarius by day and Pisces by night and Saturn Capricorn by night and Aquarius by day in the traditional scheme. In modern terms Uranus is the co-ruler, or has an affinity with Aquarius, Neptune Pisces and Pluto Scorpio. The distinction between day and night rulers is often omitted in modern astrology. A planet in a sign of which it is the Ruler is said to be in its own sign. The ruler of a house is the ruler of the sign on its cusp. The chart ruler is the most strongly placed planet or ruler of the rising sign.

SABIAN SYMBOL

Degree symbol. The sabian symbols probably constitute the most popular system of degree symbols in use today. The system attaches a specific meaning to each degree of the zodiac, which is expressed and summarized by a symbolic image. The symbols were randomly obtained by clairvoyant means in 1925 and recorded by Marc Edmund Jones, who published them in 1931. Their sequence suggests an innate transformational cycle contained in the 360 zodiacal degrees, which was further analysed, reformulated and explained by American astrologer Dane Rudhyar in 1973. Rudhyar also devised several methods of use for the symbols as an oracle. For the application of the sabian symbols to the individual horoscope he gave the following rules: the symbol for the rising degree answers the question 'what?'; the descending degree symbol describes the 'whereto?'; The symbols for immum coeli and midheaven provide information as to the 'how?' and 'why?', respectively.

)))))➤ *Degree Symbol, Descendant, Immum Coeli, Midheaven, Rising Degree*

SAGITTARIUS

Sagittarius is the ninth sign of the zodiac, a member of the mutable triplicity, masculine and of the fire element. A feral sign, the symbol for Sagittarius is the centaur archer and its ruling planet is Jupiter. The Sun enters the sign of Sagittarius around 22 November and exits around 21 December. People whose birthdays fall between these dates are said to be Sun-sign Sagittarius. This is the last month of autumn and the nature and qualities of Sagittarius are closely associated with this time of the year prior to the winter solstice, when the days begin to get longer again, the time for thanksgiving and reflection of past blessings and misfortunes.

In physical terms, Sagittarius rules the thighs and legs, the very tools needed to venture out and travel, see the world, looking for life's adventures. Sagittarius is restless, a traveller keen on exploring and understanding life from a broader perspective, needing to know what is on the other side of the horizon. Like the symbol, the archer, Sagittarius sends out energy like arrows in all directions, following to see where they land, covering enormous ground and latitude of thought, learning and growing in wisdom along the way.

Sagittarius represents a search for self through activity that reaffirms humanity's place in both the physical and spiritual worlds; it does not limit this search to gratify the individual ego but is inclusive of all people. The other aspect of Sagittarius's symbol is the centaur; through the upper human part there is a soaring intellect, seeking inspiration from the heavens, while the lower animal part keeps its legs firmly on the ground, connected to the needs of physical reality. Sagittarius is on a quest for understanding the truth of the higher and lower natures of life, with a desire to coalesce them in a united whole.

Sagittarius is concerned with the philosophy, ideas and concepts upon which human society is built; religion, law and higher education come under the precepts of this sign. Sagittarius has a great need of freedom and independence, both physically and mentally, in order to undertake the journeys of body and mind into the realms of awareness and understanding. Sagittarius cannot be contained or held back, the very energy of the sign is outgoing and expansive.

As one concerned with higher religious and spiritual

ABOVE: Sagittarius, the centaur archer, from from a fifteenth century Italian manuscript by Hyginus.
LEFT: Jupiter, ruler of the sign Sagittarius, rides his eagle.

matters, and how they can be implemented in society, there is something of the religious zealot in Sagittarius. Once an idea or philosophy takes root in the mind, Sagittarius will be fanatical about the method by which it is communicated. This can sometimes be perceived as dogmatic and self-righteous, as Sagittarius tries to gather others to follow the path or faith that has been deemed beneficial for the wellbeing of all.

The ruling planet, Jupiter, gives Sagittarius an optimistic and jovial character; here is the *bon vivant*, pleasure-loving and benevolent soul. There is a touch of good luck connected to this sign, as though the natural good spirits of Sagittarius attract abundance and good fortune. The Sagittarian approach to life is straightforward, rarely subtle, boldly going after many goals, hoping each will turn up a reward. If one doesn't, then Sagittarius will be momentarily disappointed, grateful for the experience and move on to the next with positive expectations.

Sagittarius always wants more of what is pleasurable, evident from the lower, animal nature of the sign: more food, more wine, more sex. It is very difficult for Sagittarius to put a limit on desire, which can often lead to their own undoing. In relationships with others, Sagittarius tries to avoid heavy emotional responsibility, and must have the freedom to come and go as the whim takes them. Commitment is fine; being trapped or limited by a relationship is not. An intellectually stimulating and physically energetic companion is the most desirable mate, one that understands that Sagittarius is a free spirit and will behave accordingly.

Any planet in a horoscope found in this sign will operate through the energies connected with it. The Moon in Sagittarius, for example, might suggest an instinctive feeling for philosophical and religious ideology and a desire to be around many diverse people from all walks of life, but an aversion to deep emotional intimacy. Mars in Sagittarius may operate as an abundance of physical energy, a talent for sports and a fanatical, fighting spirit in matters relating to the human condition and its improvement through spirituality.

Whatever part of the horoscope that Sagittarius is found is the arena of life in which there will be a concern for experience of an expansive nature; for example, Sagittarius on the seventh house cusp suggests that it is through the ideas and philosophies of those with whom one makes close personal relationships that one gains understanding and an ideological framework through which to interpret life.

In its most positive expression, Sagittarius is straightforward, magnanimous and adventurous with an expansive and inspirational mind, an excellent teacher. In its negative expression Sagittarius is tactless and coarse, fanatical, dictatorial and never satisfied.

))))▶ *Feral Signs, Fire Signs, Jupiter, Masculine, Mutable, Sun-Sign*

ABOVE: Perhaps the tutor of this fourteenth century Parisian philosophy lesson was born with the sun in Sagittarius, as such people make excellent teachers.

SAROS CYCLE

Eclipse cycle. Eclipses of the Sun and Moon occur in a pattern that repeats itself every 18 years, a fact that has been known since ancient times. This period is called the saros, a term taken from a Babylonian word and first used by the astronomer Edmund Halley. Eclipses of the Sun and Moon can only occur at new or full Moon respectively, and have to occur close to the nodes of the Moon. The time between successive passages by the Moon through one of its nodes is called the draconic month and equals 27.212220 days. The time between successive new or full Moons is called the synodic month and equals 29.530589 days. If we take 223 synodic months (6,585.321 days) and compare them with 242 draconic months (6,585.357 days) we can see that they are almost the same. This period is the saros and it amounts to 18 years, 10 and a third days.

SATELLITE

Any object that orbits another body. Apart from Mercury and Venus, all planets have satellites, termed moons. The Moon is a satellite of Earth and both may be seen as satellites of the Sun. Minor satellites are small chunks of rock in orbit around planets, as compared with large satellites like the Earth's Moon. In astrology the term is confined to a body which revolves around one of the planets in our Solar System.

ABOVE: Diagram of the movement of Saturn from the Astronomicum Caesareum *by Pedro Apiano, dated 1540.*

SATURN

The outermost of the traditional planets. Saturn orbits the Sun between Jupiter and Uranus with a rotational cycle of 29.458 years. While Saturn is the traditional ruler of zodiacal Capricorn by night and Aquarius by day, modern astrology assigns the latter sign to Uranus. Saturn's nature is traditionally masculine, cold and dry, melancholic and malefic. Mythological Saturn is the Roman equivalent of Chronos, father of the gods, who overthrew his own father Uranos and later, fearing their rebellion, swallowed his own children. Accordingly, astrological Saturn often represents the father, conventional views, generational conflicts and issues of fear, repression and control. Saturn rules all natural and man-made structures, be it the skeleton, any hierarchy, organization, authority, the karmic law of cause and effect, a life plan or time itself. A well-placed Saturn may denote discipline, practical and organizational talents, patience, successful ambition, reliability, responsibility, honesty, frugality and often a very dry sense of humour. Saturn's negative manifestations include rigidity, restriction, narrow-mindedness, depression, excessive limitations and fear of life. Saturn's cycle symbolizes learning through pain, with an inbuilt challenging 'examination' every seven years. Many astrologers regard a person as adult only after the first Saturn return at the age of roughly 29 years.

))))➤ *Malefic, Saturn Return*

SATURN RETURN

Saturn has a rotational cycle of 29.458 years. A Saturn return chart is constructed for the moment when this planet returns to the zodiacal degree it occupied at the native's birth. Since Saturn is connected with the need to structure one's life and with life's learning processes, this chart provides information as to how the individual will tend to process the lessons of the first 29 years and which life direction will henceforth be chosen. The Saturn return roughly coincides with the return of the progressed Moon and often marks the individual's transition into maturity.

))))➤ *Jupiter Return, Saturn, Secondary Progression, Solar Return*

SATURNALIA

Astrological Festival. The Roman festival of Saturnalia is at the root of many Christmas traditions. Saturn, god of the 'seed time' and mythical ruler, presided over a golden age according to Roman myth. His tenure was a time of peace and prosperity, with equality for all men and without private property. Saturnalia was one of the solstice festivals and in early times Christmas was moved to coincide with the celebrations surrounding the solstice to capitalize on the existing celebrations of pagan gods. Many present-day pagans are reviving the celebration of Saturnalia and other solstice festivals.

ABOVE: The phases of the Moon, which is a satellite of the Earth.

RIGHT: A representation of Saturnalia, Portal of the Months, in a thirteenth century Romanesque carving from Ferrara Cathedral.

SCORPIO

Scorpio is the eighth sign of the zodiac and a member of the fixed triplicity, feminine and of the water element. A fruitful sign, the symbol for Scorpio is the scorpion; its traditional ruling planets is Mars, particularly by night, and its modern ruler Pluto. Often both planets are used as co-rulers. The Sun enters the sign of Scorpio around 23 October and exits around 21 November. People whose birthdays fall between these dates are said to be Sun-sign Scorpio. This is the second month of autumn and the nature and qualities of Scorpio are closely associated with that time of year. When the air is cooler and trees drop their dead leaves to the earth (the decay of which becomes fertilizer), they bring a promise of new growth

In physical terms, Scorpio rules the reproductive organs and excretory functions, and is connected with regeneration and new beginnings, but only after the old has been thoroughly explored, the hidden depths uncovered, latent energy released and transformed. Scorpio is referred to as the sign of death and re-birth, and its connection to the reproductive organs illustrates how sex is a process which makes new life possible, as death makes room for new forms of life to develop.

Scorpio represents a search for self through discovering the hitherto unexplored depths of that which is hidden and internal, determining the motivating force behind action and reaction to stimulus from the outside world. It is through exploring the unconscious and making it conscious that Scorpio seeks to transform and effect change in the world. Scorpio is fascinated by mystery and is an excellent detective looking for truth, meaning and the purpose behind all existence. There is an innate understanding and acceptance in Scorpio of what others may find are the more unpleasant aspects of nature. Scorpio has little fear of delving into the places of dark secrets – only in this way can they be exposed to the light and transcended. This is a very personal pursuit, however, and Scorpios are surrounded by an air of mystery themselves, jealously guarding their privacy, rejecting any encroachment of the inner world from the outside, knowing that in giving over secrets they are vulnerable to attack and injury. Scorpio will not expose any personal weakness and is loathe to display any sign of vulnerability. This does not stop Scorpio from attempting to uncover the secret depths of others; with the determination of a blood-hound, Scorpio will follow any whiff of information, whether it be emotional, physical or mental to

ABOVE: Scorpio, the sign of death and re-birth.
RIGHT: The night sky of Mars, Scorpio's ruler, with its two small moons and, at the appropriate seasons, Earth gleaming like the evening star.

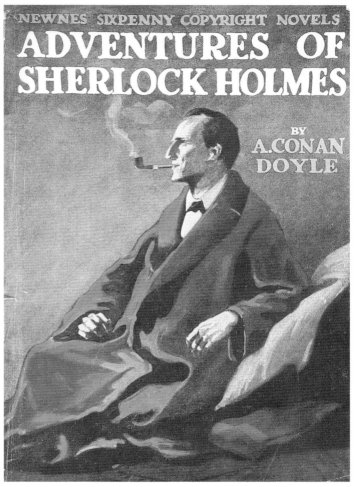

RIGHT: Scorpio has a fierce determination and will follow the slightest scent of information, like Arthur Conan Doyle's fictional detective Sherlock Holmes.

NEWNES SIXPENNY COPYRIGHT NOVELS
ADVENTURES OF SHERLOCK HOLMES
BY
A.CONAN
DOYLE

achieve a deeper understanding of the human psyche. For Scorpio knowledge brings power, and knowledge of another's secrets brings the power of control. This is a self-defence mechanism for Scorpio, insurance against any threat by being in a position to do damage first before suffering the humiliation of attack and defeat. The symbol for the sign, the scorpion, has been observed stinging itself to death rather than be subject to annihilation from an outside attacker.

There is a seductive quality to Scorpio that draws others in; their powerful self-control alludes to a strength of character and an intensely passionate nature which is extremely attractive to the opposite sex. The desire to merge completely with another is a powerful imperative and intimate relationship is often the arena in which Scorpio looks to satisfy that desire. Scorpio can go to extremes in the power of emotions – love and hate are felt forcefully. Scorpio takes a long time to accept another into their personal territory, testing the prospective lover or friend to determine their worthiness, but once a commitment has been made the love and devotion of Scorpio is complete and all-consuming. Equally, if Scorpio is betrayed then the full force of hate and fury is unleashed on the betrayer, and nothing less than total destruction will satisfy the vengeful scorpion. There is something of the destroyer in Scorpio, that which does not stand up to test of truth must be destroyed in order to make way for re-birth and a new expression of reality.

Any planet in a horoscope found in this sign will operate through the energies connected with it. Venus in Scorpio, for example, might display a desire to experience love and relationships with a life-or-death intensity, or a taste for emotionally powerful and evocative art forms. Neptune in Scorpio might promote a belief in life after death, reincarnation and a fascination with psychic and occult mysteries.

Whatever part of the horoscope that Scorpio is found is the arena of life in which there will be a concern for deep understanding, connection and transformation. Scorpio on the fifth house cusp, for example, might operate as a talent for creatively turning discarded items into a work of art, or having a powerfully protective and controlling relationship with one's children.

In its most positive expression, Scorpio is tenacious, strong, passionate and sensitive, loyal and creative, inspiring faith with an ability to help others transform themselves through a deep understanding of the human psyche. In its negative expression, Scorpio is destructive, manipulative and jealous, sadistic, secretive and vindictive, totally ruthless.

))⯈ *Feminine, Fixed, Mars, Pluto, Sun-Sign, Water Signs*

SECOND

Unit of measurement. The sixtieth part of one minute, derived from Babylonian mathematics. One second is the time that elapses during 9,192,631,770 cycles of the radiation produced by the transition between two levels of the caesium 133 atom. One second is equal to 1/86,400 of a mean solar day.

))))▶ *Minute*

SECONDARY PROGRESSION

Prediction method. Secondary progressions are based on the formula of one day = one year. In this system the astrologer casts a chart for the year in question by casting it for that many days after birth using the ephemeris of the year of birth. It gained popularity as in the past astrologers would not have the availability of ephemerides for different years, and this was a simple method to secure an approximation. Secondary progressions are based on the actual motions of the planets along the Ecliptic, on the assumption that the conditions encountered on the second day of life will be those which will govern the second year of life; hence an error of four minutes in the actual birth moment makes a difference of only one day in the timing of the prognosticated condition or event. Although not used as extensively as transits nowadays, there are still many adherents to this system.

))))▶ *Direction, Primary Direction, Progression, Tertiary Progression, Transit*

SECOND HOUSE

Sector of a chart. In modern astrology the second house is associated with money and possessions, income and expenditure, personal values and gain and loss. It describes what we possess or hope to possess and resources or attributes that give a sense of substance, value, worth and security. It shows what constitutes personal security. In horary astrology it represents the finances and assets of the person asking the question. In political astrology it refers to the nation's assets and financial status. It represents the treasury, revenue and all places and

activities concerned with money-making, such as banks. In lawsuits or conflicts it represents the friends, assistants and witnesses, and anyone who acts as a resource for the prosecution. In event charts it represents the friends and allies of whoever initiates the action. In medical astrology it represents the throat and neck, as far down as the shoulders. It is associated with the colour green. It is succedent, feminine and nocturnal in nature. It shows the direction east-north-east. It is associated with Jupiter and Taurus and it is considered particularly unfortunate in traditional astrology if the Sun or Mars are in the second house. It is also known as anaphora ('rising up'), gate of Hades or the house of wealth

))))▶ *Houses*

BELOW: Johannes Kepler, who introduced the quintiles, the group of aspects to which the semi-decile belongs
BELOW LEFT: Claude Vignon's Treasure, *represented by the second house.*

SEE-SAW

Chart shape. The 'see-saw' is one of the so-called 'Jones patterns' – a distinctive planetary formation which informs the natal astrologer about certain characteristics of the individual in question at first glance. The 'see-saw' consists of two groups of planets, which are separated by at least two empty houses on each side. There should be no more than one empty house in each group and the pattern should contain at least one opposition. This chart shape suggests a strongly dualistic individual nature. The subject is constantly aware of antagonistic views or conflicting possibilities which should be considered.

))))▶ *Bucket, Chart Shape, Locomotive, Tripod*

SEMI-DECILE

Minor aspect. The semi-decile is one of the lesser known and used minor aspects. It is sometimes also called vigintile and belongs to a group of aspects, known as the quintiles, which were introduced by Johannes Kepler in the seventeenth century. It covers an angle of 18 degrees, with an orb of maximum one degree. The semi-decile is regarded as positive and harmonious, indicating new beginnings, the constructive exchange of old conditions for new ones. It relates to the assessment of an old situation before creating new circumstances and is said to create favourable conditions for new enterprises.

)))⏵ *Aspect, Johannes Kepler, Minor Aspects*

SEMI-QUINTILE

Minor aspect. The semi-quintile, also known as 'decile', is an aspect of 36 degrees and is generally allowed an orb of only one degree. It belongs to a range of aspects which were introduced by seventeenth-century astrologer Johannes Kepler and are based on the division of the zodiac into five segments. The semi-quintile carries similar connotations as the quintile, but is regarded as weaker. The practical resourcefulness or interest in occult matters it may indicate are not as pronounced and depend even more on being consciously developed by the individual than is the case with the quintile.

)))⏵ *Aspect, Decile, Johannes Kepler, Minor Aspects, Quintile*

SEMI-SEXTILE

Minor aspect. The semi-sextile is an aspect of 30 degrees; the relevant planets are one sign apart. It is usually allowed an orb of no more than two degrees. The

ABOVE: A see-saw planetary formation suggests a dualistic nature; maybe they were present in the charts of these fourteenth century knights.

opinions about its significance and interpretation differ greatly. Whereas some astrologers regard it as a preparatory phase for individual strengths to emerge, and interpret it as beneficially providing good opportunities, others call it 'dissociate' and connect it with disturbing, albeit minor, incidents. This could be due to the fact that some semi-sextiles operate from signs that harmonize in their expression, while others involve signs of a conflicting nature.

)))⏵ *Aspect, Minor Aspects, Orb*

SEMI-SQUARE

Minor aspect. The semi-square is an aspect of 45 degrees. It is usually allotted an orb of no more than three degrees, sometimes five degrees if the lights are involved. Most astrologers are content to compare it to the square and simply call it weaker. Both aspects do indeed manifest in similar ways, indicating an inner feeling of irritation, which possibly could be released through constructive action, were it not that the action is obstructed, either by circumstances or by the individual himself. There is a difference in strength between semi-squares that stand by themselves, and may indeed be called weaker squares, and those which activate an existing square, for example, when a planet transits a square's midpoint, in which case the semi-square may work out quite explosively. It is probably for this reason that some astrologers regard it as a perfect tool to time forthcoming events.

)))⏵ *Aspect, Minor Aspects, Sesquiquadrate, Square*

SEPARATION

Movement of a planet in relation to a chart. This indicates the movement of one planet away from another planet, house cusp or sensitive point, after the formation of an aspect or angular relationship. The two are moving away from each other and so the effect is becoming weaker. A separating aspect is weaker than an applying one. It is often used in timing events, especially in horary astrology, but rarely taken into account in modern astrology.

SEPTILE

Minor aspect. The septile is one of the 'abstract' minor aspects. It is based on a division of the zodiac into seven segments, which gives it an angle of 51 degrees 25 minutes 43 sec of arc. This makes it difficult to discern in the chart, which may be one of the reasons why the septile is seldom used. Interpretations vary from 'inspiring but weak' to 'emotional and practical difficulties'. The septile appears to have a Neptune/Uranus connotation and its positive or negative manifestations probably depend on the compatibility of the relevant planets and of the signs they occupy.

))》 *Aspect, Minor Aspects, Novile*

SERPENTIS

Degree of the zodiac. Also known as the accursed degree, serpentis lies at 19 degrees of Scorpio and signifies tragedy and misfortune. It is similar in nature to a combination of the planets Mars and Saturn. This chart point is rarely used today except in horary astrology.

))》 *Critical Degree, Horary Astrology*

SESQUIQUADRATE

Minor aspect. The sesquiquadrate involves two planets positioned in an angle of 135 degrees from each other. It is usually given an orb of three degrees, sometimes five degrees if the lights are involved. The sesquiquadrate is one of the 'minor

BELOW: These medieval surgeons, operating on the eye and nose, are ruled by the seventh house, as is their ability to cure the ailment.

squares', which is an indication of its disharmonious nature. Whereas the square itself, and also the semi-square (the other 'minor square') in many cases, hold the possibility of turning their tension into productivity through a conscious act of will, the sesquiquadrate does not seem to hold this option. Natally, it often indicates dangerous over-impulsiveness, domineering tendencies and a propensity towards anger and irritation. Some mundane astrologers relate it to radicalism and even terrorist activities, when Mars and Neptune are involved. It has even been suggested that a sesquiquadrate transit to the ruler of the eighth house may imply danger of death when supported by other aspects.

))》 *Aspect, Minor Aspects, Semi-Square, Square*

SESQUIQUINTILE

Minor aspect. The sesquiquintile, also known as tredecile, is part of the aspect group also known as quintiles or Keplerian aspects. It involves two or more planets positioned at an angle of 108 degrees from each

Albule oculorum sic excitauntur;

other and is given an orb of two degrees. Most textbooks ignore this aspect, possibly because it may interfere with the trine, depending on the orb given to either aspect. Lilly interpreted it as mildly beneficial, similar to trine and sextile, while others regard it as an 'almost major' aspect, indicating the laying of mental or practical foundations for further personal growth.

))))➤ **Aspect, William Lilly, Minor Aspects**

SEVENTH HOUSE

Sector of chart. The seventh house has the descendant on its cusp and is an angular house. In modern astrology it is the house of marriage, as well as of relationships in general and of open enemies. It is associated with any sort of partnership, including business partnerships and litigation and the opponent – defendant – in any lawsuit or conflict. It represents the person against whom action is taken, the spouse or lover. It also represents fugitives and runaways and thieves, as well as the destination in a journey. If there is a need to discriminate between the father and grandfather, it represents the grandfather. In horary astrology this house represents the astrologer. In political astrology it shows the marriage and divorce rate and issues pertaining to them. It describes public enemies to the nation and whether war or peace may be expected. In medical astrology it shows the doctor treating the ailment and their ability to cure the disease. It rules from the navel to the top of the legs, including the buttocks, bladder, womb and reproductive organs. It is a masculine, angular and western house. It is also called the angle of the west, setting, dysis (west/sunset) and the house of marriage.

))))➤ **Houses**

BELOW: The Fountain of Eternal Youth under the influence of Venus. As the goddess of love, Venus can trigger sexual appeal in individuals.
LEFT: An astrologer, represented by the seventh house, prepares a horoscope.

SEX

Fifth-house matter. There are many horoscope factors pertaining to sexuality. For example, a strongly placed Mars or Sun may indicate great sexual appetites in a male horoscope, while females with a strong Venus often exude a sex appeal befitting the goddess of love. Among the signs, Scorpio is especially noted for its interest in sex. Accordingly, modern astrology looks at eighth-house factors in this context, because of the psychological connection between sex and death. But traditionally, the main indicators for 'venereal sports' are all horoscope factors of the fifth house, the area associated with creation, recreation and procreation .))))➤ **Love**

SEXTILE

Major aspect. The sextile aspect involves two or more planets at an angle of 60 degrees from one another. The permissible orb for this aspect is far from agreed among modern astrologers, but is mostly given as four degrees, or six degrees when the lights are involved. Although it equals half a trine and is therefore often belittled as a 'minor' or 'weaker' trine, the sextile is one of the major aspects, which are based on Pythagorean mathematics and were already used in ancient Greek astrology. The aspect usually combines signs of the same polarity, though not of the same element and is symbolically related to the third and the eleventh house. It denotes the ability to turn intellectual understanding into productivity, to develop one's talents and to make use of fortunate opportunities for growth and for the fulfilment of one's hopes and wishes, which often arise under sextile transits.

)))➡ *Aspect, Major Aspects, Semi-Sextile, Trine*

BELOW LEFT: William Shakespeare, English playwright and poet, who used astrology as a rich source of imagery.

SHAKESPEARE, WILLIAM

The works of William Shakespeare are full of imagery from many sources. Mythology, magic and science all find a place in his texts. One of the richest sources of imagery in his works is astrology. In Shakespeare's 37 plays there are more than 100 allusions to astrology and many of his characters' actions are said to be favoured or hindered by the stars. The signs of the zodiac are mentioned in six plays and the planets are blamed for disasters. The references would have made sense to his audience and are no indicator of whether or not he personally believed in astrology. In Shakespeare's time the discipline was held in high regard. Both highborn and commoners employed astrologers and were familiar with astrological terms and concepts. *King Lear* in particular contains numerous references, most famously: 'This is the excellent foppery of the world, that, when we are sick in fortune (often the surfeit of our own behaviour) we make gaiety of our disasters the sun, the moon and the stars…'.

SHORT ASCENSION

Speed that sign rises. Some signs rise more quickly than others. The signs of short ascension – Capricorn, Aquarius, Pisces, Aries, Taurus and Gemini – are often found intercepted in horoscopes; in other words the cusp of the third house may be in Cancer and the fourth in Virgo. That would mean that the sign Leo was intercepted. In the southern hemisphere, long and short ascension are reversed and the signs of long ascension become the signs of short ascension. In horary astrology if the ascendant is less than three degrees, especially in a sign of short ascension, the chart is not fit to be judged. In the past aspects occurring in signs of short ascension were shrunken to the next smaller major aspect. For example, a square between a planet in Capricorn and a planet in Aries might act more like a sextile.

)))➡ *Aspect, Long Ascension*

SIDEREAL ASTROLOGY

The sidereal zodiac is a star-based zodiac that uses a fixed star as a reference point. It is more commonly used in the East, although a minority of western astrologers prefer to use the sidereal zodiac. In the West the tropical zodiac is used, which has been moving away from the sidereal zodiac at a rate of about one degree every 72 years since the third or fourth century AD. There is now a gap of about 24 degrees between the two zodiacs. A planet in the sign of Aries under the tropical zodiac falls in Pisces in the sidereal. Many of the 700 million people in the Indian subcontinent use a form of sidereal astrology. There are differences in opinion as to the exact starting point of the sidereal zodiac but they are small. There is a western sidereal astrology movement that uses slightly different interpretations. The sidereal zodiac is held by many to be more astronomically correct. Various occult groups, such as the Golden Dawn, have also used the sidereal zodiac by preference.

SIDEREAL TIME

Time measurement system. Sidereal time is time measured relative to the stars (the period between successive conjunctions with any star). One sidereal day – 23 hours and 56 minutes – is the period during which the Earth completes one rotation on its axis (this is the same as the time it takes to come into alignment with a particular star). Because the stars are so distant from us, the motion of the Earth in its orbit makes a negligible difference in the direction to the stars; hence, the Earth rotates 360 degrees in one sidereal day. Sidereal time may be considered the same as right ascension when seeking to align star maps to the sky. The right ascension that you find at your zenith is the current sidereal time. Astrological tables are published using sidereal time and a conversion is necessary to give clock time in order to cast the horoscope.

))))▶ *Right Ascension*

ABOVE: Taurus, the bull, is an example of a sign of short ascension, which means that it rises more quickly than some of the other signs.

SIGNIFICATOR

A planet pertaining to a particular issue. A planet may be taken as a significator of a person, an event or of affairs ruled by a house. Its strength by virtue of its sign and house position, and its relationship by aspect, are all consulted when judging a horary chart. In horary astrology the Moon always acts as a secondary significator. In a birth chart the strongest planet is usually taken as the significator of the person for whom the chart is cast. The ruler of the sign on each house cusp is taken as the significator of matters related to that house.

)))➤ *Horary Astrology, Houses, Ruler*

SIGNS

Term referring to the division of space on the zodiac belt into 12 sections to create a frame of reference by which the positions of celestial bodies can be identified. The Sun, Moon and planets all appear to move in a circular path around the Earth; this path is called the ecliptic. Each of the 12 divisions of 30 degrees is called a sign and given a name: Aries, Taurus, Gemini, Cancer, Leo, Virgo, Libra, Scorpio, Sagittarius, Capricorn, Aquarius and Pisces. These names refer to the constellations, or groups of stars, that rise and set within the path of the ecliptic, although, due to a phenomenon known as the Precession of the Equinoxes, the signs and constellations no longer coincide. The divisions each mark the apparent movement of the Sun through the sky in one yearly cycle. The Sun takes approximately one month to pass through each sign, while the Moon passes through all 12 signs in approximately 271/3

days. The rate at which the rest of the planets pass through the signs varies greatly.

)))➤ *Constellation, Equinox, Zodiac*

SINISTER

Direction of aspect. Sinister means 'on the left-hand side'. A sinister aspect is one in which the faster planet is waning, or decreasing in light, with respect to the slower one. The faster planet is casting its rays to the left because the slower planet is on the left side when viewed from the Earth.

)))➤ *Dexter*

ABOVE: The Moon, the secondary significator in horary astrology, is shown here with its movement in relation to the Sun (red is day, night is blue).
LEFT: A medieval representation of the twelve signs of the zodiac.

SIXTH HOUSE

Method of chart division. In modern astrology the sixth house is the house of service. It represents the day-to-day routine of work, employment in general, pets and employees. It is also the house of health. Illness and disease, their causes and curability and health-industry workers are shown by this house. Also uncles and aunts on the father's side of the family. In horary astrology it represents these issues related to the person asking the question. In political astrology it represents the nation's food reserves and those who keep public records such as libraries and book-keepers. It represents the working classes generally, public employees and services such as the civil service, the armed forces and the police. It is also held to represent trade unions and social services. In medical astrology it represents the nature of illness and whether it is physical or psychological. It rules the lower part of the belly and small intestine, the guts, liver and kidneys. It is associated with the colour black and is a cadent and feminine house. It represents the direction west-north-west. Mars has joy here and Virgo and Mercury are associated with it. The sixth house is also known as mala fortuna ('bad fortune') or the house of sickness and bad fortune.

)))⏵ *Houses*

SLOW IN COURSE

A planet is said to be slow in motion when its travel in a 24-hour period is less than its mean motion. The average daily motions of the planets are: Moon 13 degrees 10 minutes 36 seconds, Sun 0 59 08, Mercury and Venus 0 59 08 (same as Sun), Mars 0 31 27, Jupiter 0 4 59, Saturn 0 2 1.

)))⏵ *Swift in Motion*

SOLAR APEX

Astronomical term and prediction method. In astronomy the solar apex is the point on the celestial sphere towards which the Sun and Solar System are moving; currently this point is approximately 10 degrees south-west of the star Vega. It is the point on the sky in the constellation Hercules towards which the Sun appears to be moving relative to its closest stellar neighbours. It is also the name given to a method developed by the astrologer Sepharial (Walter Gornold, 1864–1929), which summarized information found in many of his other works and offered techniques to apply in financial speculation.

ABOVE: The policeman from this nineteenth century songsheet is represented by the sixth house, along with the civil service and the armed forces.

SOLAR ARC

The angular distance between the Sun in the birth chart and the Sun moved by secondary progression. This value is used for a method of direction called solar arc directions. A solar arc direction is when the Sun is first progressed as in a secondary progression – that is, one day after birth is equivalent to one year of life. The position of the Sun in the birth chart is subtracted from this position. This figure, called the solar arc, is then added to all the bodies and chart points to give new positions that are then used for prediction.

))))▶ *Direction, Secondary Progression*

SOLAR RETURN

In modern astrology, the solar return chart is calculated when the Sun returns to the exact degree and minute of the Sun in the natal chart. This occurs around one's birthday. The effects of a solar return chart last for about one. Some astrologers claim the chart can take hold a few months prior to the birthday. The location used for the solar return chart is in dispute among astrologers. Some prefer to use the same location for the birth chart. Others calculate the chart using the primary living location for that year. Still others claim that the location where a person has travelled to on the birthday should be used for the chart for the entire year. This method is not accepted generally. The primary living location is a better contestant with the birth location. If you consider the ascendant and the houses as a major factor in the chart, shifts in location can make a huge difference in interpretation.

))))▶ *Planetary Returns*

SOLAR SYSTEM

Groups of celestial bodies. The Solar System is the planetary system that contains the Sun, the nine planets, about 90 satellites of the planets, comets and asteroids. The Sun is

BELOW: A nineteenth century diagram of the Solar System, which contains the Sun, the planets and their satellites and various comets and asteroids.

the focal point and the planets orbit the Sun. The planets move in regular orbits and each has a pull of gravity which varies according to its mass and size. The planets can be divided into two groups: the terrestrial planets include Mercury, Venus, Earth and Mars; these are rocky and Earth-like, rotate more slowly than the gas giants and are closer to the Sun. The gas giants are Jupiter, Saturn, Uranus and Neptune. These are large and composed of gaseous elements. Pluto is the most remote planet in the Solar System. The orbits of the planets are ellipses with the Sun at one focus, although the orbits of Mercury and Pluto are almost circular. The orbits of the planets are all more or less in the same plane (the ecliptic); they all orbit in the same direction.

))))▶ *Galaxy, Orbit, Universe*

SOLSTICE

Seasonal measurement. In the northern hemisphere the summer solstice is the longest day of the year when the Sun is furthest north. The winter solstice is the shortest day of the year. In the southern hemisphere, winter and summer solstices are exchanged. The summer solstice marks the first day of summer. At the time of the solstices (around 21 June and 21 December) the maximum and minimum periods of daylight are experienced. The Sun is above the horizon for different lengths of time at different seasons. At the June solstice in the north the direct rays produce about three times as much heat as at the December solstice.

SOLSTICE SIGNS

Solstice signs refers to Cancer and Capricorn. When the Sun is at zero degrees of Cancer, it is the time of the summer solstice, i.e. it appears to reach its furthest point north of the ecliptic and marks the longest

day of the year in the northern hemisphere. Consequently when the Sun is at zero degrees of Capricorn, it is the winter solstice, reaching its furthest point south of the ecliptic, marking the shortest day of the year in the northern hemisphere.

SOUTH NODE

Chart point; also called descending node, cadua draconis, dragon's tail and ketu. The Moon's nodes are points that indicate where the orbit of the Moon around the Earth crosses the ecliptic – the apparent path of the Sun through the zodiac. These nodes form an axis,

ABOVE: The Sun rises above the stones of Stonehenge, Wiltshire, at dawn on the day of the 2001 summer solstice.

ABOVE RIGHT: Cancer, the crab, one of the two solstice signs.

rather than being separate points opposite each other, although are generally interpreted separately. Often only the north node is entered on the chart. The nodes move backwards about three degrees a day. The position of the node can show whether there was an eclipse shortly before or after birth, whether a planet near the node would shortly be accented by the Moon. The ancients held that the Moon's north node partook of the nature of Saturn. A planet in close conjunction to the south node at birth represents karmic repression or tendencies that restrict growth. In modern astrology the nodes are often taken to show the soul's journey and provide information about past lives. Interpretation of the nodes varies widely.

SOUTHERN SIGNS

Southern signs, also referred to as austral or meridional signs, are so called because they decline from the equinoctial or celestial equator (the Earth's equator projected into space) in a southward direction. They are Libra, Scorpio, Sagittarius, Capricorn, Aquarius and Pisces. The southern signs are measured from zero degrees of Libra, the point where the Sun's path intersects the celestial equator at the autumn equinox, and contain the final half of the zodiac.

⟫⟫➤ *Equinox*

SPECULUM

Astrological tool. The term speculum, from the Latin *specere*, meaning 'to look at', has been used to describe a number of tools. In astrology it is primarily a table of data used as an aid in calculating directions. A speculum of aspects is a table of every degree in the horoscope that may be in aspect with the planets. A speculum may include information such as declination, right ascension or latitude. Any drawing or table that gives information showing the relative positions of the planets may be called a speculum. An instrument used to ascertain the true horizon is also called a speculum.

SPICA

Fixed star used by astrologers. Now at almost 24 degrees of Libra, Spica is a binary, brilliant flushed white star that originally marked the ear of wheat shown in the Virgin's left hand, in Virgo. Its name is derived from *stakhus*, or ear of corn. It is said to confer renown, riches and success.

SQUARE

Major aspect. An aspect between two or more planets positioned at an angle of 90 degrees is called a square. The allotted orb for this aspect is usually six to eight degrees. The square combines planetary energies operating from different elements and from signs of opposite polarity; hence it is a tense and disharmonious aspect. Traditional astrology regards it as malefic and in horary charts the square denotes severe difficulties in the way of a positive outcome – although success is not necessarily impossible. Modern astrology regards the square as an aspect of constant inner tension, urging the individual towards action in order to relieve it. Success is frequently delayed or thwarted, either by circumstances or by inconsistent behaviour on the part of the individual himself, and often demands great effort sustained over long periods. The element background of the relevant signs may give an indication as to the severity of the square in question. On the positive side, the square offers numerous opportunities for learning and personal development usually lacking in more harmonious aspects.

)))➤ *Aspect, Major Aspects, Malefic, Semi-Square, T-Square*

LEFT: Virgo, the constellation in which the star Spica was originally located.
BELOW: The coming of railways and trains, such as this North British Railway Express Locomotive, necessitated a national standard time system.

STANDARD TIME

Originally time was a local matter, based on true noon, when the Sun was at its highest point in the sky for that particular location. With the coming of railways it became necessary to establish a consistent time system. Standard time-zone meridians were spaced at 15-degree intervals of longitude east and west of Greenwich in the UK, and all clocks in each zone were adjusted to the mean solar time of the midpoint of the zone. Although standard time was legally adopted on 18 November 1883, it was not in common use in many areas for a number of years.

)))➤ *Time*

STATION

A planet makes a station when it appears motionless before reversing direction in its orbit, as viewed from Earth. Thus, a planet can make a station when going from retrograde to direct, or from direct to retrograde. Stationary planets are considered to be quite influential. When turning retrograde, they symbolize a reversal or delay. When turning direct, they indicate a renewal or revitalization. Mercury is the planet most frequently retrograde, and therefore makes the most stations. The Sun and Moon are never stationary and never retrograde.

)))➤ *Retrograde*

NORTH BRITISH EXPRESS ENGINE.

STELLIUM

Multiple conjunction. A stellium, also known as satellitium, is a gathering of three or more planets, grouped together in the same sign or house, preferably within less than 30 degrees of arc. The planets involved are connected by conjunction, even if the orb between the first and the last planet of the stellium is wider than usually accepted. A conjunction describes the combined forces of the planets involved; therefore, the stellium indicates a massive concentration of energies in the sign and house in question. In mundane astrology a stellium, often called planetary line-up, indicates a quick succession of events in accordance with the nature of the planets involved and the zodiacal area they occupy. Natally, the characteristics of the sign will be clearly recognizable in the individual's character and may even override the characteristics of the Sun-sign. The area of life signified by the house in question will be of great importance to the native. It often provides a multitude of challenging or even confusing experiences, which offer ceaseless opportunities for personal development.

))➤ *Conjunction, Mundane Astrology, Orb*

SUCCEDENT

Type of house. The succedent houses are those that follow ('succeed') the angular houses. That is, the second, fifth, eighth, and eleventh houses. A succedent planet is one that occupies a succedent house. These are houses of stability, where the ideas developed in the angular houses can be administered. All succedent houses are connected with possessions. Succedent houses are said to be in the middle ground and succedent activities are aimed at managing and controlling things. There is a correspondence between succedent houses and the fixed signs. The succedent houses are related to the accumulation of resources, developing stability and reserves, maintaining or developing things. In western astrology the eleventh house is considered the strongest whereas in Vedic astrology the fifth house holds more strength. Traditionally, the eleventh house was regarded as a powerful house, considered equal in some sources to the fourth and seventh houses. When timing an event from a chart, a succedent planet indicates that it is likely to take weeks, rather than months or days.

ABOVE RIGHT: The Sun-signs, whose characteristics may be overridden by the those of the stellium, or planetary line-up, in mundane astrology.

SUMMER TIME

Summer Time was first defined in an Act of 1916, which ordained that for a certain period during the year legal time should be one hour in advance of Greenwich Mean Time. The Summer Time Acts of 1922 to 1925 extended the period during which Summer Time was in force and, from 1916 to World War II, clocks were put in advance of GMT by one hour from the spring to the autumn. During the war, double summer time (two hours in advance of GMT) was introduced and was used when normally ordinary Summer Time would have been kept. During the winter clocks were kept one hour in advance of GMT. In 1968 clocks were advanced one hour ahead of GMT on 18 February and remained so until British Standard Time, during which clocks were kept in advance of GMT all year, came into force between 1968 and 1971.

))))➤ *Daylight Saving Time, Time*

SUN

Astrological planet. Although the Sun is not a planets in the astronomical sense, astrology refers to it as such because astrological nomenclature was established when our Solar System was still seen as geocentric. Western solar astrology is based on the apparent annual path of the Sun around the Earth, which is divided into 12 equal parts. The Sun is the traditional and modern ruler of Leo, is exalted in Aries and in its fall in Libra. Its nature is described as masculine, hot and dry. The Sun's glyph, a circle with a point in the middle, illustrates its astrological meaning: the central, all-encompassing life force and the individual as the centre of its own universe. In the chart, a favourably placed and well-aspected Sun indicates creativity, self-reliance, courage, strength, success, a healthy physical disposition, generosity, a warmly affectionate nature, authority, grand-scale undertakings and leadership qualities. An afflicted Sun suggests a lack of self-esteem or, at the other end of the scale, over-confidence, as well as egotism, selfishness, dictatorial behaviour, bad fortune, fear, physical weakness and problems with authorities. In the physical body, the Sun rules the heart and the blood as carrier of life-sustaining substances.

))))➤ *Leo, Lights, Luminary, Ruler, Solar Return*

SUNRISE CHART

Chart analysis method. When the time of birth is unknown, a chart is cast for an arbitrary time and the house cusps ignored. Although it is common to use noon for the time of such a chart, it may also be cast for any other time. Sunrise is often used, as people are statistically more likely to be born early in the morning than at midday. If the birth is assisted, e.g. by caesarean, this is unlikely to apply.

ABOVE: The Sun, masculaine, hot and dry in nature, is represented in a fourteenth century Treatise on Astronomy.

SUN-SIGN ASTROLOGY

Sun-sign astrology is what most people think of when hearing the term astrology. It is based on assuming that the sign on which the Sun falls on the date of birth is the first house of the chart. The other planets are placed around this chart and it is interpreted accordingly. Sun-sign astrology is comparatively new. It was not until the beginning of the twentieth century that the Sun gained prominence over the other planets in the horoscope. The astrologer R. H. Naylor invented the Sun-sign column in 1930. He had to find a way of writing so that each reader could feel involved, and chose to divide his essays into 12 paragraphs, one for each person born when the Sun was passing through a particular zodiac sign. Immediately following the publication of Naylor's column, other newspapers followed suit and Sun-sign columns are a regular feature of most newspapers and women's magazines all over the world and remain extremely popular.

))))➤ *R. H. Naylor*

SUPERIOR CONJUNCTION

Planetary position. The conjunction of an inferior planet (one which orbits between the Earth and Sun), Mercury or Venus, with the Sun is a superior conjunction when the Earth is between the Sun and the planet. It is an inferior conjunction when that planet is between the Earth and the Sun.

))))➤ *Inferior Conjunction*

SUN-SIGN

Sun-sign refers to the zodiac sign that the Sun was passing through on the date of birth. The Sun passes with regularity through each of the 12 signs in the period of one year. For example, if someone's birthday was 28 November, his or her Sun-sign would be Sagittarius. The Sun, at the centre of the Solar System and around which all other celestial bodies rotate, is the source of life and growth; therefore the Sun-sign represents the qualities and behavioural nature that an individual feels happiest and most comfortable projecting.

))))➤ *Sun-Sign Astrology*

SUPERIOR PLANET

A superior planet is one that has its orbit around the Sun, outside the Earth's. The superior planets are Mars, Jupiter, Saturn, Uranus, Neptune and Pluto. The planets that have orbits between the Earth and Sun – Mercury and Venus – are termed inferior planets.

))))➤ *Inferior Planet*

ABOVE: Manuscript showing the seven stages of the Sun and the signs of the zodiac, or Sun-signs, from Loqman's 1583 The Fine Flower of Histories.

SWIFT IN MOTION

A planet is said to be swift in motion when its travel in a 24-hour period exceeds its mean motion. The average daily motions of the planets are: Moon 13 degrees 10 minutes 36 seconds, Sun 0 59 08, Mercury and Venus 0 59 08 (same as Sun), Mars 0 31 27, Jupiter 0 4 59, Saturn 0 2 1.

SYNASTRY

The word synastry comes from the Greek prefix *syn* ('bringing together') and *astron* ('star'). It is the comparison of two or more horoscopes to determine compatibility. Any relationship can be analysed synastrically (business partners, parent–child, teacher–student, etc.). This technique will identify areas of strength and weakness, harmony and disharmony in relationships. The charts of each of the people in the relationship are cast first. Then the astrologer studies the charts, noting connections such as what houses the planets belonging to one person fall into in the second person's chart, and what aspects are formed between the planets in one chart and planets and chart points in the other. Some astrologers use techniques such as relationship charts (charts cast for the halfway point between the place, time and date of birth of both people) or composite charts (charts derived from the arithmetical mean of the planetary positions and chart points of the charts of both people). Sun-sign compatibility as appears in the popular press is synastry at its most basic level.

ABOVE: The relationship between this pregnant woman and her child can be analyzed synastrically – by comparing their two horoscopes.
RIGHT: Psychologist Carl Jung, who coined the term 'synchronicity'.

SYNCHRONICITY

Synchronicity is a term coined by the psychologist Carl Jung to describe a connectedness of events that cannot be related causally. Jung quotes astrology as an excellent example of manifest synchronicity, and this theory is at the basis of modern, psychological astrology. Jung described astrology as representing 'the summation of all the psychological knowledge of antiquity'. The origin of the principle of synchronicity is linked with Jung's acquaintance with the I-Ching, although the Chinese regard the working of this oracle in terms of the operation of spirits – in other words an animistic causality.

 Carl Jung

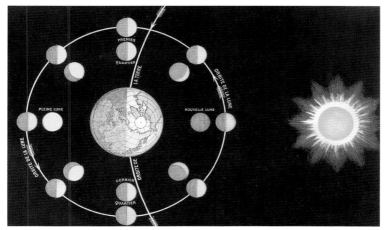

SYZYGY

Syzygy occurs when the Moon (or a planet) is in opposition or conjunction with the Earth and Sun; the three bodies are positioned in a straight line. At syzygy, the Moon (or planet) is seen as new or full (from Earth). In astronomy the term refers to an alignment of three bodies of the Solar System along a straight or nearly straight line. A planet is in syzygy with the Earth and Sun when it is in opposition or conjunction, i.e. when its elongation is 180 degrees or 0 degrees.

SYNODIC PERIOD

Cycle of phases of the Moon. The synodic period is a cycle from new Moon to new Moon, lasting 29 days, 12 hours and 44 minutes. The Moon spends two-and-a-half days travelling through each astrological sign. In astronomy the term synodic period refers to the length of time during which a body in the Solar System makes one orbit of the Sun relative to the Earth, i.e. returns to the same elongation. Because the Earth moves in its own orbit, the synodic period differs from the sidereal period, which is measured relative to the stars. The synodic period of the Moon is called the lunar month, or lunation.

SYNTHESIS

Integrated chart interpretation. To arrive at a detailed judgement, the astrologer has to consider all horoscope factors and weigh them against each other. Beginning and advanced students alike are often overwhelmed by the volume of information and turn to so-called 'cookbooks' or interpretational computer software. But whereas these tools may be of great help in memorizing the different rules and ways of interpretation, they do not and cannot provide a synthesized analysis. This task remains with the astrologer who has to combine strict adherence to the framework of rules with intuition and sensitivity.

)))⏵ *Interpretation, Key Words*

ABOVE: The phases of the Moon. The complete cycle from one new Moon to the next is referred to as a syndonic period.

T-SQUARE

Aspect pattern. The t-square is an aspect figure involving two planets in opposition, which are both squared by a third planet. The aspects contained in this figure mark it as highly active and conflicting, similar to the 'grand cross'. The relevant planets usually occupy signs of the same quadruplicity, automatically emphasizing the cardinal, fixed or mutable quality in the chart. The t-square indicates vast energies at work within the individual, constantly searching for outlets through action. The tendency to focus on the negative may be overcome by acts of conscious willpower, and may also lead to great accomplishments.

)))⏵ *Aspect, Grand Cross, Opposition, Quadruplicity, Quality, Square*

TABLES OF HOUSES

Sets of tables that show the degrees of the signs which occupy the cusps of the houses in different latitudes for every degree of right ascension, or for every four minutes of sidereal time. Each different house system requires a different set of tables, although the ascendant and midheaven remain consistent whatever system is used. Astrologers use them when calculating charts and, as the most readily available for a number of years were Placidus tables, this tended to be the most used system. As most astrologers now use computers there is more variance in house systems used.

)))⏵ *House System, Placidus House System*

TAURUS

Taurus is the second sign of the zodiac, a member of the fixed triplicity, feminine and of the earth element. A bestial sign, the symbol for Taurus is the bull; its ruling planet is Venus. The Sun enters the sign of Taurus around 20 April and exits around 20 May. People whose birthdays fall between these dates are said to be Sun-sign Taurus. This is the second month of spring and the nature and qualities of Taurus are closely associated with this period when the beauty and creative aspects of nature are clearly visible all around, fresh green leaves are covering trees, flowers are in bloom, the earth is rich!

In physical terms, Taurus rules the neck and throat; it is also connected to the lymphatic system of the human body, and the metabolizing of energy. The neck connects the head, and therefore thought, to the rest of the body, which must respond to the thought and use the skills inherent in the body to fulfil its desires. Taurus is a sensual sign and is prone to indulging the senses of the body. For this reason Taurus is often, in physical terms, fairly solid and robust, luckily because the sign is ruled by Venus; this does not come across as crude and coarse but rather as a luxurious beauty. However, there is a natural tendency to excess so sometimes Taurus can become heavy and sluggish.

Taurus represents a search for self through an instinctive understanding of the physicality of life. There is a need to experience reality through the sense of touch; indeed anything that cannot be seen and touched has very little impact on Taurus; abstract ideas and concepts must be made manifest in reality. That is not to say that Taurus has no sympathy with spiritual and philosophical matters, rather that there is an intuitive understanding of how the spirit manifests itself through nature, as though there is a deep understanding that for any dream to be realized there must first be a solid object with which to work. Taurus is concerned with the material world – possessions have value as they offer security that is obvious and not merely ephemeral.

Taurus does not rush at anything without forethought, or decide on a course of action without first being sure that it will work out as expected; once the course is decided then the bull will steadily, with determination, follow it to conclusion. Equally, Taurus is slow in forming opinions; again once the opinion is formed it is almost impossible to shift it, for Taurus has devoted much energy and thought to making sure that they are secure with such

BELOW: Taurus, the bull, and man with a tree branch, from a French fifteenth century Calendar and Book of Hours.

an opinion. This is a quality inherent in all the fixed signs of the zodiac, and the one that gives Taurus its reputation for stubbornness. Taurus builds a strength of character that is permanent, that only changes under extreme pressure, but never loses its core virtues.

Being ruled by Venus, Taurus has a great love of beauty, luxury and over-abundance. Taurus likes to surround itself with objects d'art, and indulge in the pleasures of fine wine and dining. In love there is a need for romance, and as an earth sign, a need for the constant demonstration of physical affection; although Taurus may be slow in trusting another enough to give their heart, once they do, it is given with loyalty, devotion and a desire to protect and care for the loved one with the best things in life. Due to the need for

ABOVE: Venus, ruler of Taurus, by Michelangelo Buonarroti
ABOVE RIGHT: Taurus likes to collect objets d'art, such as these Navajo native vase and seed pots.

ownership, this can be most evident in their relationships where possessiveness and jealousy make frequent appearances.

Taurus is ambitious and will patiently pursue any task that is seen to have a worthwhile outcome. Taurus is very productive, and can take any seed project or idea and turn it into a practical and working concern. Through determined and steadfast effort, that is not flighty or easily distracted, Taurus will make the most of the inherent potential in any occupation to achieve the financial rewards that is so important to this sign.

Any planet in a horoscope found in this sign will operate through the energies connected with it. Mercury in Taurus, for example, suggests that communication will not be frivolous or ill considered and there will be little waste of words. Jupiter in Taurus will manifest as an even greater need to expand the self through sensual pleasure and luxury, a true hedonistic approach to life.

Whatever part of the horoscope that Taurus is found is the arena of life in which there will be a concern for pleasurable physical experience and a need for material rewards that can be possessed. Should Taurus be found on the descendant or seventh house cusp there will be a strong desire for relationships or marriage in which the two can work together to build a materially safe and secure existence, with much attention to the physical aspects of the partnership.

In its most positive expression, Taurus is determined, sensitive and understanding, loyal with a love of beauty in all its forms. In its negative expression, Taurus is stubborn, possessive and over-indulgent in sensual appetites.

)))➤ ***Bestial Signs, Earth, Feminine, Fixed, Sun-sign, Venus***

TENTH HOUSE

Sector of chart. With its cusp of the midheaven, the tenth house is an angular house, second only to the first house in importance. In modern astrology it refers to what we would like to be remembered as having contributed to the world. It is the house of ambition, associated with career and profession. It is also associated with fame, notoriety, reputation, public work, and the mother. It describes the trade of a person, employers, prestige, reputation, power, and success. It is associated with those in dignified positions such as royalty, the government and any form of authority. In political astrology it refers to those in authority over a nation, including prime ministers and presidents. It represents the police or armed forces when they assert authority, credit and power, national trade and influence. In legal matters it represents the judge or magistrate and the ruling in a law court. In medical astrology it describes the curing of illness, and is also associated with the knees, calves and shins. It is associated with the colours red and white and is a feminine house. It is associated with Capricorn and Mars. It is also known as the medium coeli, Mesouranema, angle of the south and house of profession.

)))) **Houses**

TERM

Term is the fourth of the five essential dignities. The word means 'boundary', or 'termini of signs'. There are two sets of terms, the Egyptian and Ptolemaic, now known as Chaldean. The basis for assigning terms is to reward those planets with greater numbers of essential dignities in a sign, and to assign the benefics, Jupiter and Venus, more degrees than the malefics, Mars and Saturn. The planet that rules the sign being considered as that sign's ruler, or by being its own exaltation or triplicity, tends to be granted the first position most frequently The last few degrees of a sign are always ruled by Mars or Saturn. This appears to be the origin of the idea that the final degrees of a sign have bad qualities. Planets in their own terms denote participation of matters in the business of that planet, but not from a position of power. In horary astrology they are used to describe the person in question. For example, the term 'ruler of the ascendant' is used to describe the person asking the question.

)))) *Dignity, Exaltation, Horary Astrology, Malefic, Triplicity*

TERTIARY PROGRESSION, MINOR PROGRESSION, LUNAR PROGRESSION

Prediction method. Tertiary progressions are based on the lunar return cycle. Following the day of birth, each return of the Moon to its zodiacal position is equal to a year of life. One day in the ephemeris represents one lunar month of life. Usually a day is held to represent a year of life as in secondary progressions. In minor or tertiary progressions, one day can be held to represent a month or week of life. There are numerous variations on this theme. In one form of minor progressions a month in the ephemeris represents a year of life. This gives faster motion than with tertiary progressions but slower than the actual movement of the planets. With secondary progressions the outer planets move too slowly to be considered. However, with minor or tertiary

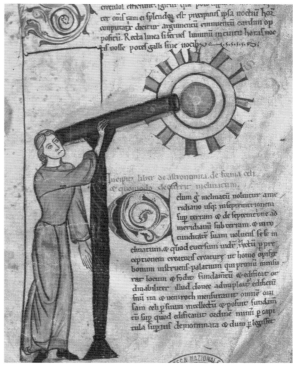

progressions additional trend from these planets may be considered. Whatever method is used a chart is cast and may be read as a stand-alone chart as well as in comparison to the birth chart.

))▶ *Direction. Progression, Secondary Progression*

THIRD HOUSE

Sector of chart. In modern astrology the third house represents communication, our ability to express ourselves, short journeys, siblings, cousins and neighbours. It is associated with early schooling and our attitude and relationship with knowledge itself as well as the environment in which we live and work. Any tools of communication such as the telephone also come under the third house. In horary astrology it represents the ability of the person asking the question to communicate well. In political astrology it represents rumours and propaganda, the media and all means of disseminating news and information. It also represents the transport system and the education system and

neighbouring nations. In lawsuits or conflicts it represents all written statements, contracts, deeds, writs and the ability to affect the situation through correspondence. In medical astrology it represents the shoulders, arms, hands and fingers. It is associated with orangey-yellow or rusty colours. It is a cadent, masculine, nocturnal house. It represents the direction north-north-east. The Moon is said to have joy, or be happily placed in the third house. It is associated with Gemini and Mars. The third house is also known as *dea* (meaning 'goddess') or the house of brothers.

))▶ *Houses*

TIME

There are two methods of time-keeping based on the rotation of the Earth. Solar time is kept with reference to the Sun and sidereal time with reference to the stars. The time required by the Sun to pass over the meridian twice is known as an apparent solar day, but as this varies with the time of year, the mean solar day is used as the average day. This is about four minutes longer than a sidereal day. The time shown by a sundial is apparent or true solar time. Local time means the time used in a particular place, now normally equivalent to standard time. Standard time-zone meridians are spaced at 15 degree intervals of longitude east and west of Greenwich and all clocks in each zone adjusted to the mean solar time of the midpoint of the zone. Daylight saving time or summer time involves moving the clocks one hour forward allowing more light in the working day. Time is usually now expressed in the 24-hour clock format.

))▶ *Daylight Saving Time, Greenwich Mean Time, Standard Time, Summer Time, Time Zones*

TIME DIFFERENCES

The primary reason for time differences at different locations is the adoption of time zones. In order to create consistency within a given area, time zones are 15 degrees apart and use the mean solar time of the midpoint of the zone. The international date line at 180 degrees longitude is the point at which, by convention, the date changes. It is a day later to the west of the line than east. Most countries also operate a summer-time system, where the clocks are moved forward in the spring and back again to standard time in the autumn, usually by one hour, although this may vary. The dates on which this is done also vary from country to country and from year to year. Prior to the establishment of the railway network, local mean time was kept in most areas. Although standard time was introduced in the late nineteenth-century, for some years many places would use two different time systems, the local time and railway time.

))))➤ *Standard Time, Time Zones*

TIME ZONES

Time measurement system. Originally time was a local matter, based on true noon, when the Sun was at its highest point in the sky for that particular location. With the coming of railways it was necessary to establish a consistent time system. Standard time zone meridians were spaced at 15-degree intervals of longitude east and west of Greenwich and all clocks in each zone were adjusted to the mean solar time of the midpoint of the zone. The present system employs 24 standard meridians of longitude (lines running from the North

Pole to the South, at right angles to the equator) 15 degrees apart, starting with the prime meridian through Greenwich. These meridians are theoretically the centres of 24 standard time zones; in practice, the zones have in many cases been subdivided or altered in shape for the convenience of inhabitants. Time is the same throughout each zone and differs from the international basis of legal and scientific time, Greenwich Mean Time, by an integral number of hours; minutes and seconds are the same.

))))➤ *Greenwich Mean Time*

TOPOCENTRIC HOUSE SYSTEM

Method of chart division. The Topocentric house system was derived from the timing of events, in the 1960s, by South American astrologers Anthony Page and Vendel Polich. The methods of calculating are rather complex, but this system tends to give house cusps similar to Placidus. Their research was established entirely through practical experiments focused on the nature and timing of events, the naibod arc and use of primary directions to determine house cusps that related to those events. They found that the cusps lay on a great plane passing through the birth location rather than a great circle that they labelled a 'cone of rotation'. They determined the house cusps by the natural rotation of the geocentric horizon around the topocentric axis. It could thus be seen as a combination of space and time. Fundamentally, it is an amendment to the Placidus house system. The Topocentric system is apparently used more for fatalistic fields of astrology as opposed to the psycho-logical, when Placidus is the more popular choice. It does not seem to be commonly used, perhaps due to its complexity.

))))➤ *House System, Placidus House System*

ABOVE: The Royal Observatory at Greenwich, from which time zones are measured, with the park in the foreground and ships on the Thames to the left.

TRANSIT

 Prediction method. Transits are based upon the actual motions of the various planets. The transits in effect at any time are the actual positions the planets occupy, considered in relation to the places they occupied on a given date of birth. Apart from very detailed work only the planets lying outside the orbit of Mars are considered in transits. As there is no actual calculation involved – an astrologer simply looks up the positions of the planets for a given date and places them around the outside of the birth chart – this is the easiest and most popular prediction technique. Transits are considered to be more event-oriented than other forms of direction, such as secondary progressions. Particular attention is paid to the returns of the planets to their original positions and to the halfway points in their cycles. They are often used in conjunction with other techniques to provide more comprehensive information as, in this way, all of the planets in the chart may be moved and considered from their new vantage points.

)))➤ *Direction, Progression, Secondary Progression.*

TRANS-NEPTUNIAN PLANETS

Hypothetical Planets. The trans-Neptunians are the planets of the 'Neptunian Chain' in esoteric astrology. This scheme assumed that Neptune did not belong to our Solar System and that there were two other relevant planets outside its orbit; one of them may have been Pluto, which had not been discovered at the time.

)))➤ *Esoteric Astrology, Hypothetical Planets*

TRANS-SATURNIAN PLANETS

Planets outside Saturn's orbit. The trans-Saturnian planets used by modern astrology are Uranus, Neptune and Pluto, discovered in 1781, 1846 and 1930 respectively. Also known as the 'new' or 'outer' planets, they are believed to be indicators of human evolution and of the individual's connection with the collective mind.

)))➤ *Neptune, Pluto, Transpersonal Planets, Uranus*

TRANSLATION OF LIGHT

Planetary combination. Translation occurs when a swifter planet leaves a heavier one and then catches up with another heavier planet. The swift one then translates, or passes on, the light from one to the other. The two heavier planets can be separating from an aspect, or approaching an aspect. Ideally, the translating planet should share a dignity with the first heavier planet, showing sympathy. It indicates help that may be given by another party in a horary question. It can also indicate contact being made between the people indicated by the planets.

)))➤ *Prohibition*

ABOVE: A Victorian representation of human evolution, thought to have been indicated by the trans-saturnian planets.
ABOVE LEFT: Ebenezer Sibly's birth chart, around which transits are placed.

TRANSPERSONAL PLANETS

Planets outside Mars's orbit. In natal astrology, Saturn, Jupiter, Uranus, Neptune and Pluto are also referred to as the transpersonal planets. Saturn and Jupiter are seen as mediators between the individual and society, while Uranus, Neptune and Pluto are interpreted as being linked with collective tendencies, i.e. human evolution.

))))➤ *Planet, Trans-Saturnian Planets*

TRAVEL

Astrology divides the subject of 'travel' into two parts: short and long journeys. Short journeys, like the daily trip to work, a weekend visit or any travel inside the country, are described by planets in the third house and by its ruler, also by Mercury or Gemini. A (temporary) affliction may indicate traffic jams, train strikes and the like, as is often the case during Mercury's retrograde periods. International travel and 'travelling in the spirit', as in watching travelling programmes or reading about foreign countries, belongs to planets in the ninth house and the ruler thereof.

))))➤ *Gemini, Mercury, Ninth House, Retrograde, Third House*

BELOW: *Journeys undertaken in Rickman's helicopter could belong to the third or the ninth house, depending on their extent.*

TRINE

Major aspect. The trine is one of the classic Ptolemaic aspects, consisting of two or more planets positioned at an angle of 120 degrees from each other. The orb given to this aspect is usually eight degrees, or 10 degrees in cases where lights are involved. The trine combines planetary energies working from the same element background as well as from the same masculine or feminine polarity. Therefore, the relevant planets are said to cooperate in the most harmonious way, which is why traditional astrology calls it a 'benefic' aspect, bestowing special talents and fortunate circumstances on the native and a positive result on the matter at hand. Modern astrology associates the trine with inspiration and creativity, based on the ability to intellectually penetrate universal principles and to link them to mundane circumstances. But since the trine is so completely void of friction, its gifts may be taken for granted and, unless other factors of the horoscope indicate more activity, the native may miss the opportunity for personal development the trine has to offer.

))))➤ *Aspect, Benefic, Feminine, Grand Trine, Major Aspects, Masculine*

WILL'S   CIGARETTES.

"RICKMAN" HELICOPTER.

TRIPLICITY

In modern astrology, triplicity refers to the breakdown of the signs into the four elemental groups: fire, earth, air and water. The fire signs – Aries, Leo and Sagittarius are the inspirational group. The earth signs – Taurus, Virgo and Capricorn - are the practical group. The air signs – Gemini, Libra and Aquarius - are the mental group. The water signs – Cancer, Scorpio and Pisces - are the emotional group. However, there is another form of triplicity that refers to day and night triplicity rulers. For example, Aries is ruled by the Sun by day and Jupiter by night. Water signs have Mars as both day and night ruler. Planets in their own triplicity are generally considered lucky. Good things happen not because they are worked at but because you have stumbled on a good result. The triplicities were derived from the sign and exaltation rulerships and in medieval astrology used in preference. Originally each triplicity had a mixed ruler in addition to those of day and night.

))) *Element, Exaltation, Rulership, Sign,*

TRIPOD

Chart Shape. The 'tripod' is one of the so-called 'Jones patterns', a distinctive planetary formation which tells the natal astrologer about basic characteristics of the individual at first glance. In this pattern the planets are placed in three separate groups and each group is connected to the other by at least one trine aspect. A 'group' may also consist of only one planet, which is why this pattern is sometimes confused with the 'bucket'. The tripod suggests a focus on spiritual growth through understanding, the ability to blend opposites and to transcend the dualities inherent in life on Earth.

))) *Bucket, Chart Shape, Locomotive, See-Saw*

BELOW: Tropic of Capricorn, with a navigator studying the horizon.
LEFT: The four elemental groups – fire, earth, air and water. Triplicity signifies the breakdown of the signs of the zodiac into the elements.

TROPICS OF CANCER AND CAPRICORN

The Tropic of Cancer and the Tropic of Capricorn each lie at 23.5 degrees latitude. The Tropic of Cancer is located at 23.5 degrees north of the equator and the Tropic of Capricorn lies at 23.5 degrees south of the equator. They mark where the Sun is overhead at noon on the solstice. The Sun is directly overhead at noon on the Tropic of Cancer about 21 June and on the Tropic of Capricorn about 21 December .

))) *Equator, Latitude, Solstice*

TROPICAL ASTROLOGY

In western astrology the start of the zodiac begins with the spring equinox, when the Sun enters the sign of Aries. Owing to the astronomical phenomenon called precession, this starting point moves backwards about one degree every 72 years. Originally both sidereal and tropical zodiacs coincided. Since the third or fourth century the two zodiacs have been separating from one another. There is now a gap of about 24 degrees between the tropical and sidereal zodiacs. In the west we continue to use the tropical zodiac, the zodiac as it originally was. This means that although a planet may be spoken of as being in the sign Aries, for example, astronomically it is actually in Pisces. Astrologers know this discrepancy but it is one of the arguments used to refute astrology by astronomers. The sidereal zodiac, which is a star-based zodiac that uses a fixed star as a reference point, is more commonly used in the east although a minority of western astrologers also use the sidereal zodiac.

ABOVE: In tropical astrology, a planet said to be in the sign of Aries, the ram, could astronomically be in Pisces.

TROPICAL YEAR

Time measurement. The solar or tropical year is a period of time in which the Earth performs a revolution in its orbit around the Sun, or passes from any point of the ecliptic to the same point again. It is 365 days, 5 hours, 48 minutes and 46 seconds in length. It is about 20 minutes shorter than the sidereal year. The tropical year is what is generally meant by the term year.

TRUE NODE

Lunar chart point. A method of calculation for the point at which the Moon's orbit crosses the ecliptic (the apparent path of the Sun). The nodes do not move at a predictable speed and vary from day to day. The mean node is the position based on average speed. With the assistance of computer software it is now easy to calculate the position of the true node, the actual position.

))))➤ *Node*

TWELFTH HOUSE

Sector of chart. In modern astrology the twelfth house represents dissolution, sacrifice, withdrawal, and past lives, secret enemies, conspiracies and behind-the-scenes activities, the unconscious, fantasy and daydreams and also institutions, including prisons and hospitals. It represents hidden, restrained and secret matters. Traditionally, it is an unfortunate house, associated with sad events, sorrow, anguish, captivity, imprisonment and persecution. It represents places that are denied access to public view, particularly those concerned with seclusion or isolation. It is associated with scandal and skeletons in the closet. It is also connected with large animals. In political astrology it is associated with the prison system, criminals, spies and enemies of the nation, underground movements and secret societies. It represents those who are in need of support and therefore the welfare state. In medical astrology it is associated with the feet. In legal matters it is the house of incarceration. It is associated with the colour green and the direction east-south-east. It is a feminine, cadent house and reputed to be the most unfortunate in the chart. It is associated with Pisces and Venus and Saturn joys (is happy in) this house. It is also known as Bad Daemon, bad fortune and the house of enemies.

))))➤ *Houses*

Representation of **FREDERICK BARON TRENK,** *Confined and Loaded with 68 Pounds weight of Iron and Chains in a Dungeon at* **MAGDEBURG,** *by order of The* **KING** *of* **PRUSSIA.**

UNDER SUNBEAMS

Planetary position related to the Sun. A planet is said to be under sunbeams if it is between 8 1/2 and 17 degrees away from the Sun. It is slightly weakened in its effect, less so if it is not in the same sign as the Sun. Mars, however, is strengthened in this position as it is of the same hot and dry nature as the Sun. The term tends to be used in horary astrology.

))))➤ *Cazimi, Combust, Horary Astrology*

UNIVERSAL TIME

System of time measurement. The times of various events, particularly astronomical and weather phenomena, are often given in Universal Time (UT), also referred to as Greenwich Mean Time (GMT). The two terms are used to refer to time kept on the Greenwich meridian (longitude zero). Universal Time is used by news agencies, and other organizations and is the standard international time system. It is the civil time for the UK and Ireland in the winter.

UNIVERSE

The total sum of all that exists; the physical system that encompasses all known space, matter and energy, existing now, having existed in the past or postulated to exist in the future. There cannot be more than one Universe. Most physicists and astronomers refer to the known universe as the Universe. The Universe is infinite. The observable portion which is within the grasp of our senses with the aid of technology is infinitesimal.

))))➤ *Galaxy, Solar System*

BELOW: The according to ancient Indian cosmology: the Earth is sustained on the backs of elephants who are in turn standing on the back of a cosmic turtle.
BELOW LEFT: Baron Trenk's imprisonment was a matter of the twelfth house.

URANIA

 Astrological mythology. Urania, one of the nine muses in Greek mythology, is the muse of astrology and is represented by a staff pointed at a celestial globe. Her name is derived from the Greek *ouranos*, meaning 'sky'. Urania was also occasionally used as a byname for Aphrodite. Her attributes were the globe and compass; she is often depicted with her foot on a turtle, symbol of silence and retreat. Urania can tell the future by the position of the stars; she is able to disclose the secrets of the sky, the eclipses and phases of the Moon.

URANIAN ASTROLOGY

Modern astrology technique. Uranian astrology was an invention of the German astrology school which had its heyday in the 1920s. It is notable for its number of Uranian or Trans-Neptunian points – hypothetical planets located far beyond the orbit of Pluto. The technique is closely related to cosmobiology. Uranians also developed a system of midpoints, similar to the Greek formulae for Arabic Parts. The midpoints are degrees sensitive to transits and the presence of other points in that location. A configuration of midpoints, a planetary picture, shows a complex of traits, issues and likely events. Alfred Witte, the founder of the Hamburg School of Astrology and a German surveyor, along with others devised sets of key words and concepts assigned to each planetary picture. Because the effects of the planets on human behaviour is considered more plausible than the divisions of life into 12 regions of the sky, (houses), the use of houses fell out of favour with Uranian astrologers. This was compatible with their attempt to pare astrology down to the essentials. Harmonious aspects such as trines and sextiles are also typically eliminated in favour of more difficult aspects (conjunction, square, opposition, semi-square) which are considered more intense.
))) *Aspect, Cosmobiology, Reinhold Ebertin*

URANUS

First Trans-Saturnian planet; modern ruler of Aquarius. Originally named after the astronomer William Herschel, who discovered it in 1781, Uranus orbits the Sun between Saturn and Neptune with a rotational cycle of 84.015 years. In modern astrology, it

ABOVE: Urania, the muse of astronomy.
RIGHT: A view of Uranus, or Herschel as it was also known, after the astronomer William Herschel who discovered it in 1781.

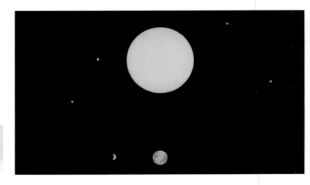

became the ruler of zodiacal Aquarius, a sign associated with non-conformity and revolutionary tendencies, which upholds the creed of 'freedom, equality and brotherhood' of the French Revolution, which took place shortly after Uranus's discovery. Accordingly, modern mundane astrology views Uranus as an indicator of new discoveries, sudden and unexpected events, disruptive disturbances such as explosions, uprisings and revolutions and of unpredictable occurrences. It is linked with electricity and modern technology like computers, aviation or space travel. Natally, Uranus represents the individual's need for self-realization and freedom from traditional restrictions. A prominent, well-aspected Uranus suggests originality and inventiveness to the point of genius, independence, unconventionality and an interest in the latest global fashions and develop-ments. An afflicted Uranus may indicate disruptive or anti-social behaviour, impracticality, uncontrolled emotional outbursts, stubbornness and delusions bordering on madness. Transiting Uranus's opposition to its natal position, at about 42 years of age, often marks the beginning of the mid-life crisis.

)))➡ *Aquarius, Opposition, Ruler, Transit, Transpersonal Planets, Trans-Saturnian Planets*

URSA MAJOR

One of the best-known constella-tions in the northern sky, known as the Great Bear. The third-largest constel-lation, it is probably the most widely recognized of the northern hemisphere's constella-tions because of its distinctive asterism that forms the rump and tail of the Great Bear. It is also known as the Plough or Big Dipper.

BELOW: This representation of Ursa Major is from a seventeenth century Persian manuscript on the constellations.

URSA MINOR

Constellation. The two Bears, Ursa Major Ursa Minor, and the northern-hemisphere sky, revolve around a star that doesn't appear to move – Polaris, the North Star; and the orientation of the bear figures changes dramatically through the course of the night. From earliest times the two bears have been paired together.

VALENS, VETTIUS

Ancient astrologer. Valens led an ascetic life, believing the pleasures of men would interfere with his knowledge and learning of astrology, and it is reported that he lost all his money searching for an astrological teacher. Valens ran an astrology school, where students swore oaths, and believed in a process of initiation. He worried that his astrology would fall into the wrong hands and had a disdain for people who only learned small bits of the discipline. While Valens made many remarks against other astrologers who hid their lack of knowledge with difficult speaking and writing skills, he would also make his own writing difficult in order that the ignorant could not just pick up one of his books and understand his methods. When astrological predictions failed he believed it to be the fault of the astrologer. Astrology to Valens was a means of participating in the divine and attain union with God. He made many mentions of keys hidden throughout, and weaving the general matters with the specifics. It is believed by many that he was the originator of the Porphyry house system. His *Anthologiae* is the longest extant astrological work from antiquity and contains more than 100 horoscopes.

VEDIC ASTROLOGY

Eastern astrology system. Vedic (meaning 'knowledge' or 'truth' from the *Vedas*), or jyotish, astrology is the form of astrology most commonly used in the East, particularly in the Indian subcontinent. It was perceived through visions by the sage Parasara, who is considered the original author of the Vedic texts. It uses the sidereal (star-based) zodiac, rather than the tropical zodiac, as used in the West. Vedic astrology was developed in India over 5,000 years ago. It is part of the Vedic wisdom that includes sciences such as Ayurveda, Vastu (Vedic architecture) and Yoga. The information has been passed down from generation to generation and astrology forms a large part of Indian culture. Charts are drawn in a square, rather than circular form and the most important planet is the Moon, rather than the Sun as in western astrology. Dasas,

BELOW: Scholars observe the Moon, the most important planet in Vedic astrology, and note sown their observations.
BELOW LEFT: The planet Venus and Love under her influence.

routinely called planetary periods or cycles, are intervals during which the person's life corresponds to the energies of individual planets and used as a predictive tool.

▶ *Sidereal Astrology*

VENUS

Personal planet, night ruler of Taurus and day ruler of Libra. Venus orbits the Sun between Mercury and Earth, with a rotational cycle of 224.7 days. Because the planet sometimes moves faster than the Sun, but also has periods of retrograde

motion, it can appear behind the Sun (when it is known as the evening star) or rise before it (when it called the morning star). Venus's nature is traditionally described as feminine, moderately cold and moist. Also known as 'the lesser fortune', its influence is generally benefic. As a personal planet, Venus describes the manifestation of spiritual values in daily life. Named after the Roman goddess of love, the planet rules affections, diplomacy, harmony and beauty. In the male horoscope it describes the type of woman the native feels attracted to. Psychologically, Venus represents the need for emotional or material security and therefore indicates how the individual tends to relate to others and handles financial affairs. A dignified Venus suggests physical beauty, pleasant manners, a good sense for colours, shapes and proportions, diplomatic skills, artistic talents, warm affections, popularity and financial success. An afflicted Venus may indicate laziness, debauchery, unfaithfulness, jealousy, selfishness, emotional coldness and an excessive need for entertainment and the 'good life'. Physically, Venus rules the kidneys, bladder and sexual organs.

))))➤ *Affliction, Dignity, Libra, Retrograde, Ruler, Taurus*

VERNAL EQUINOX

The vernal equinox (Latin for 'equal night of spring') occurs when the Sun moves to 0 degrees Aries in March. At this point day and night are of equal length, hence the name. Seen from northern latitudes, the Sun will now be above the equatorial plane, until it moves into Libra in September, at which point the autumnal equinox occurs.

))))➤ *Cardinal Points, Ecliptic, Equator, Equinox, First Point of Aries, Solstice*

VERNAL POINT

The first degree of the chart. Another word for zero degrees Aries, or the Aries point. The point where the celestial equator intersects the ecliptic in the east. This is the beginning of the tropical zodiac. It is considered significant when working with midpoints, especially if a birth time is not available.

))))➤ *Aries Point*

VERTEX

Point on a chart. Vertex comes from the Latin *vertere*, 'to turn'. The word refers to a summit, the highest point reached in the apparent motion of a celestial body or other points. In astronomical terms the vertex is the point where the prime vertical intersects the ecliptic in the west. The anti-vertex is the same point in the east. It is usually viewed as an axis, comprising the vertex and anti-vertex, although some astrologers see them as discrete points. It is usually found in the fifth, sixth, seventh or eighth house. By combining the meaning of turning point with those of the houses, the vertex is related to meeting people. It is a sensitive point on the chart and often relates to a compulsive, yet fortunate experience. It is mainly used for examining issues connected with relationships and can represent a particular person in your life.

))))➤ *Ecliptic, Houses, Prime Vertical*

VESPERTINE

Planet that sets in the west after the Sun has set; the reverse of matutine. The name was traditionally given to the planet Venus by the Greeks, as it was noted for its brightness in the evening. (Venus was also occasionally called Herald of the Dawn as it can also rise before the Sun.) It was originally believed that the evening and morning views of Venus represented two separate planets.

))))➤ *Matutine*

VIA COMBUSTA

Area of the zodiac; 'the combust path'. The term refers to the area between 15 degrees Libra and 15 degrees Scorpio. It maintains the influence of the fixed stars that were once in that section of the sky. In horary astrology, when the Moon is in the via combusta, the chart is discarded as not fit to be judged. It is considered to be an unfortunate zone and associated with danger.

ABOVE: Perhaps Venus was responsible for the artistic talent of Francis Hayman, shown here in his studio with Robert Walpole, First Earl of Oxford.

VIRGO

Virgo is the sixth sign of the zodiac, a member of the mutable triplicity, feminine and of the earth element. A human sign, the symbol for Virgo is the virgin maid; its ruling planet is Mercury. The Sun enters the sign of Virgo around 23 August and exits around 22 September. People whose birthdays fall between these dates are said to be Sun-sign Virgo. Any planet in a horoscope found in this sign will operate through the energies connected with it. This is the second month of summer and the nature and qualities of Virgo are closely connected with this time of harvest, and reaping the bounty of the earth, a time for work and the use of tools to earn a livelihood.

In physical terms, Virgo rules the stomach and digestive system, and the mental facilities of the sign operate in a similar fashion. There is a huge mental hunger in Virgo, but all information taken in must be processed through an analytical and critical system, discarding that which is useless and storing that which is considered of practical value, separating the wheat from the chaff. Virgo has an abundance of nervous energy which, if not converted through productive channels, can result in anything from mild butterflies in the stomach to full-blown hypochondria. As an earth sign, Virgo is connected to physical reality, and the vehicle or human body must also operate at maximum efficiency. There is an understanding that, as a system, the body is the sum of its many parts; its health, therefore, is of major concern to Virgo, who will maintain regular routines of exercise and a balanced diet to keep it working to the best of their ability.

Virgo represents a search for self through the acquiring of knowledge and practical talents, affirming their validity by putting them to use in the service of self and others. Virgo is referred to as the sign of service; there is an instinctive knowledge that all individuals must operate within a system, using unique talents for the good of the whole. The development of a talent or idea, taking it to its highest potential, is of importance to Virgo – perfection is the goal in any pursuit. Virgo rejects that which is faulty or imperfect, and manifests intellectual skill into a skill of labour. In this way Virgos implement their own critical facilities to purify the material of their business to its essence, in order for it to operate at maximum efficiency and to ward off criticism from the outside. There is something of the craftsman in Virgo – the patient attention to detail, and the developing of routines that hone skills and perfect ability come under this sign. Virgo can be very humble and does not really require recognition for being helpful, but values acclaim for being highly efficient in the performance of duty. The ego is served by affirming its own usefulness in the community. Virgo needs to be needed, and will stand up for others less fortunate in a way that they would not stand up for themselves. One way in which Virgo will measure their contribution is by reaping material benefits in direct correlation to the amount of energy invested. Virgo has a

ABOVE: The sign of Virgo, the virgin maid, from the sixteenth century publication Liber Phisiognomiae.

reputation for being an excellent employee, motivated by the need to live up to the expectations of those in authority over them and excelling in the ability to organize and multi-task. Should the benefits not fit the high quality of service and expenditure of talent, however, Virgo will move on to another employer or environment more deserving of their skills.

In human relationships Virgo is thoughtful, solicitous and kind. Even the manner in which Virgo criticizes is meant to be helpful and constructive, for Virgo wants their loved ones to be the best and as pure as they can. Virgo is devoted, but not sentimental, highly sensual, but not given to dramatic passionate display; their charm is subtle and alluring.

Sometimes Virgo is guilty of manipulating those around them by setting up a feeling of obligation on another's part for all that is done by Virgo in the name of service.

Any planet in a horoscope found in this sign will operate through the energies connected with it. Venus in Virgo, for example, might suggest a talent for perfecting artistic ability, excelling in the techniques of creating beautiful objects or becoming highly skilled in the practicalities of romantic relationships. Mars in Virgo might operate as a conscientious hard worker, or display great physical stamina, focusing an enormous amount of energy on perfecting the health and fitness of the body.

Whatever part of the horoscope that Virgo is found is the arena of life in which there will be a concern for performing a service; for example, Virgo on the third house cusp may indicate an ability for clear thinking and the communication of ideas to others in an efficient manner that promotes understanding.

In its most positive expression, Virgo is precise, dependable, helpful and kind, with an exceptional intuitive intellect and thirst for knowledge. In its negative expression, Virgo is critical, manipulative, nervous, underhanded and prone to hypochondria.

))))▶ *Earth, Feminine, Human Signs, Mercury, Mutable, Sun-Sign*

ABOVE: *Being rather prone to hypochondria, perhaps Virgo would enjoy the play by Moliere of the same name.*
ABOVE LEFT: *Mercury, messenger of the gods and ruler of Virgo.*

VOID OF COURSE

Planetary placement. A planet is said to be void of course if it makes no complete major aspect before it leaves the sign in which it is placed. Although any planet may be void of course, the term is most frequently applied to the Moon. It is a technique used in horary astrology and one of the considerations before judgement, as it means that there is nothing that can be done about the matter under question. The Moon is void of course every few days for a length of time ranging from a few minutes to a day or more.

VOICE SIGNS

Term used in traditional and ancient astrology; it refers to all the signs not considered mute or of slow voice. The voice signs are Aries, Taurus, Gemini, Leo, Virgo, Libra, Sagittarius, Capricorn and Aquarius. In the judging of a horary chart, when a voice sign appears on the ascendant or the more so if the planet Mercury should be in a voice sign, it suggests that there will be further news pertaining to the matter questioned.

))))➡ *Horary Astrology, Mercury, Mute Signs*

BELOW: The waning Moon, as it appears to decrease in size from Earth, is shown over a mountainous landscape.

WANING MOON

A waning Moon is one that is decreasing in size from the perspective of someone on Earth. The waning gibbous Moon can be seen after the full Moon, but before the last quarter Moon. The amount of the Moon that we can see will grow smaller and smaller every day. The waning crescent Moon can be seen after the last quarter Moon and before the new Moon. The crescent will grow smaller and smaller every day, until the Moon looks like the new Moon. In astrology a waning Moon is a time to break negative habit patterns.

))))➡ *Waxing Moon*

WAR TIME

Time-keeping system. During World War II England set the clock ahead by two hours, creating double summer time. During the same period, beginning 9 February 1942, the United States had created war time, setting the clock ahead by one hour. Summer time had been observed in previous years but not consistently so in the US.

))⋙ *Daylight Saving Time, Summer Time*

WATER SIGNS

Signs of the water triplicity. The signs expressing the element water are Cancer, Scorpio and Pisces. Traditionally, the water element refers to the spiritual aspect of life, while modern astrology links it to the emotional realm, though both systems find their analogies in actual water. Cancer, the cardinal water sign ruled by the Moon, reflects its environment, keeps the memories of childhood and seeks containment within the home and the

TOP: A house in Surrey devsatated by a German air raid during World War II, when England kept a different time system from usual.
ABOVE: Scorpio, one of the three water signs.

family. Scorpio, the fixed water sign ruled by Mars (traditional) and Pluto (modern) probes into every available emotional space, often through sexual experience, and resembles deep water, where death and resurrection are waiting beneath the dark surface. Pisces, the mutable water sign ruled by Jupiter (traditional) and Neptune (modern), dissolves and crosses the boundaries between the physical and the spiritual realm, often through poetry or music. Modern astrology associates the water signs with the feeling type of Jungian psychology, focusing on emotional experience which sometimes stands in the way of logic and depends on outside impulses, which may cause neediness in relationships.

))⋙ *Air Signs, Earth Signs, Element, Fire Sign, Triplicity*

WAXING MOON

A waxing crescent can be seen after the new Moon, but before the first quarter Moon. The crescent will grow larger and larger every day, until the Moon looks like the first quarter Moon. The waxing gibbous Moon can be seen after the first quarter Moon, but before the full Moon. The amount of the Moon that we can see will grow larger and larger every day. Waxing means increasing, or growing larger. In astrology the waxing Moon shows a time for action and growth. It is a regeneration period.

))⋙ *Waning Moon*

WEEK, DAYS OF

Traditional astrology assigns a planetary ruler to each day of the week, which is the basis of the system of planetary hours. The sequence of these planetary rulerships is widely believed to be based on the Chaldean order, but this assumption has not been proven conclusively.

))⋙ *Chaldean Order, Planetary Hour*

WEST POINT

Point on a chart. The West Point (also called the equatorial descendant), is where the western horizon intersects the prime vertical and the celestial equator. It is an unfortunate place for the Moon to be, especially in horary astrology, but is a term rarely used in modern astrology.

YEAR

Unit of time. The solar, or tropical year, is a period of time in which the Earth performs a revolution in its orbit around the Sun. The sidereal year is the time in which the Sun's centre, passing eastwards from the ecliptic meridian of a star, returns to the same point.

YOD

Aspect pattern. The Yod is a triangular pattern consisting of two planets in a sextile aspect (60 degrees), while both of them connect to a third planet in a quincunx (150 degrees). The resulting shape resembles a finger, which is why the Yod is also known as 'Finger of God' or 'Finger of Fate'. The apex planet at the tip of this finger is often referred to as the action point that provides clues as to the probable solution of problems or conflicts arising from this aspect combination. The quincunxes of the Yod disharmoniously connect planets in signs of opposite polarity, while the sextile combines planets in signs of

BELOW: The Earth, the revolution of which lasts a solar year.
BOTTOM: Zadkiel, the pseudonym of two astrologers, means 'angel of genius of the planet Jupiter', shown here in a colour photograph from 1973.

the same polarity harmoniously. This contradiction characterizes the workings of the whole pattern and signifies a mixture of inner tension combined with constructive insight and the ability to act. While the quincunx aspects confront the individual with the urgent necessity of making apparently impossible choices, the sextile provides the ability to create favourable circumstances or to use such conditions to one's advantage. The Yod frequently indicates an individual's urge to accomplish something extraordinary and important against all odds; it is often interpreted as pointing out a karmic debt and as focusing the individual's energies on a special life purpose, which can only be accomplished after a crisis and through sustained effort.

))➤ *Feminine, Inconjunct, Masculine, Quincunx, Sextile*

ZADKIEL

Nineteenth-century astrologer. Zadkiel means 'angel of genius of the planet Jupiter' and was the pseudonym of two astrologers – Richard James Morrison (1795–1874) and A. J. Pearce (1840–1923). Morrison worked in the Royal Navy until 1818; he became a professional astrologer in 1830. He launched *Zadkiel's Almanac* at this time. He studied astrometeorology and was a member of the London Meteorological Society. Morrison's speculative activities bordered on the fraudulent and in 1862 he brought a libel action against

Sir Edward Belcher after an article published in the *Daily Telegraph* accused him of taking money for using a crystal ball. He won the case but was refused costs. He is best known for his *Grammar of Astrology* and an abbreviated version of *Lilly's Christian Astrology*. He died in 1874 and the name of *Zadkiel* was handed down to a Mr Sparkes. Unfortunately, Sparkes also died soon afterwards, and Alfred Pearce became the new *Zadkiel*. Son of a notorious homeopath convicted of manslaughter, Pearce edited *Zadkiel's Almanac* until his death in 1923.

))⟩➡ *William Lilly*

ZENITH

Highest point in the sky relative to a position on the Earth. The zenith lies directly opposite the nadir, the lowest point in the sky. Astronomically it is situated at the intersection of the meridian and the prime vertical circles. The term is sometimes used interchangeably with the cusp of the tenth house, or midheaven, which – strictly speaking – is the point on the zodiac where the meridian circle passes through.

ZENITH HOUSE SYSTEM

Method of chart division. The zenith house system was proposed by the astrologer Zariel (David Cope) and is also known as the horizontal system. The zenith system divides the horizon into 12 equal sectors and has great circles passing through the zenith and nadir. Thus, instead of being based around the north–south axis, or midheaven and immum coeli, it is based around the zenith–nadir axis. The cusp of the first house will not be the ascendant as the houses are divided equally from the zenith, similar to the division from the midheaven in the Porphyry system. This point is also known as the anti-vertex. The anti-vertex and vertex (the opposite point to the anti-vertex) are used by astrologers, who do not use this house system, to describe how a person relates to others and conducts their relationships. Because the system bears a relationship to the Campanus system, tables used for Campanus may be used to find Zenith system cusps with minor alterations. The Zenith house system is also sometimes used to describe the Equal house system.

))⟩➡ *House System*

ZODIAC

Basis of all horoscopes. The term zodiac is derived from the Greek *zodiacus*, which means 'little animals' or 'little creatures'. The zodiac is a small band of the sky, about eight degrees on either side of the ecliptic, which contains the motions of most of the planets. Modern astronomers have widened this band to nine degrees because of the extreme latitudes attained by Venus and Mars. The position of any planet is measured by a perpendicular to the ecliptic, giving its geocentric longitude and therefore its position in the horoscope. This band is divided into 30-degree sections called signs, which are defined and described in the study of astrology. There are 12 signs in the zodiac: Aries, Taurus, Gemini, Cancer, Leo, Virgo, Libra, Scorpio, Sagittarius, Capricorn, Aquarius and Pisces. Each sign of the zodiac has a particular graphical representation called a glyph that relates to an animal or a part of the human body. Each of the 12 signs is a unique combination of one of the four elements and one of the three qualities.

ABOVE: The zodiac, on which all horoscopes are based, from the introduction to the Song of Songs in an eleventh centruy bible.

ASTROLOGICAL GLYPHS

Astrologers use a number of symbols, known as glyphs, to represent the planets, signs and aspects. These are used as a type of shorthand amongst astrologers and on the horoscope itself. As well as the symbols there is an internationally accepted convention of abbreviations astrologers use when writing. These abbreviations are also listed below.

The glyphs have evolved over centuries of use. Those used to represent the signs are derived from the images that are associated with the signs. For example, the symbol for Aries is a stylised representation of the horns of the ram. The glyphs that represent the planets are related to the planets meanings and are combinations of the circle, crescent, cross and line. The glyphs for the aspects are simple representations of the shape formed by the aspect if lines are drawn between the two planets concerned.

SIGNS

Aries ♈ AR
The glyph for Aries represents the horns of the ram.

Taurus ♉ TA
The glyph for Taurus represents the head and horns of the bull.

Gemini ♊ GE
The glyph for Gemini represents twins and duality.

Cancer ♋ CA
The glyph for Cancer represents breasts and relates to the association of the sign with the mother figure and sustenance.

Leo ♌ LE
The glyph for Leo represents the mane of the lion.

Virgo ♍ VI
The glyph for Virgo represents an ear of corn and the harvest that takes place during the time that the Sun is in Virgo.

Libra ♎ LI
The glyph for Libra represents a set of scales.

Scorpio ♏ SC
The glyph for Scorpio represents the sting of the scorpion.

Sagittarius ♐ SAG
The glyph for Sagittarius represents the arrow fired by the centaur.

Capricorn ♑ or less commonly ♑ CAP
The glyph for Capricorn represents the horns of the goat.

Aquarius ♒ AQ
The glyph for Aquarius represents the water flowing into the jug of the water carrier and therefore the flow of ideas.

Pisces ♓ PIS
The glyph for Pisces represents two fish swimming in opposing directions.

PLANETS

Sun ☉ SO
Moon ☽ MO
Mercury ☿ ME
Venus ♀ VE
Mars ♂ MA
Jupiter ♃ JU
Saturn ♄ SA
Uranus ♅ UR
Neptune ♆ NE
Pluto ♇ or ♇ PL

MAJOR ASPECTS

Conjunction (0 degrees) ☌ CNJ
Square (90) □ SQ
Trine (120) △ TR
Opposition (180) ☍ OPP
Sextile (60) ⚹ SEX

COMMON MINOR ASPECTS

Quincunx (150) ⚻ QCX
Semi-square (45) ∠ SSX
Semi-sextile (30) ⚺ SSQ
Sesquiquadrate (135) ⚼ SQQ

LESS COMMON ASPECTS

Quintile (72) **Q** Q
Septile (51°26') ⑦ s
Novile (40) ⑨ n
Biquintile (144) **Bq** Bq
Parallel ‖ P
Contra-Parallel ⧺ Cp

OTHER ASTROLOGICAL GLYPHS

☊ North Node of Moon   NN
☋ South Node of Moon   SN
⚷ Chiron   CH
⊕ Earth   EA
⊗ Part of Fortune   PF

COMMONLY USED ABBREVIATIONS

A^sc Ascendant or Rising Sign
D^sc Descendant or Seventh House Cusp
Mc Midheaven or Tenth House Cusp
I^c Imum Coeli or Fourth House Cusp
℞ Retrograde
St Stationary
D^t Direct
T^r Transiting Planet
Pr Progressed Planet or House Cusp
N^tl Natal Chart
V^x Vertex

MINOR PLANETS

Ceres ⚳
Pallas ⚴
Juno ⚵
Vesta ⚶
Transpluto ◌

URANIANS

Cupido ⚴
Apollon ♃
Hades ♇
Vulcanus ⚼
Zeus ⚹
Cronos ♈
Poseidon ⚹

CALCULATING THE HOROSCOPE

There is now a wealth of computer software available to calculate horoscopes and free programmes are available through the Internet. Additionally, a quick search will reveal a number of websites that enable you to calculate a chart online. Most astrologers, however, learn to calculate horoscopes by hand using sets of tables. The mathematics needed are straightforward. Even if you rely on software for calculation it is worth knowing calculation methods as you will then be aware of any possible errors made by the software.

To calculate a horoscope by hand you need the relevant sets of tables. Firstly, you need an ephemeris for the year the chart is to be calculated for. This gives the positions of the planets for each day of the year at midnight or noon. These positions are adjusted according to the time of day that you were born. Ephemerides are available for individual years or for a number of years at a time. Many astrologers find it more cost effective to buy an ephemeris for the whole century, although they may also buy an ephemeris for the present year so that they can have it easily to hand to check on that day's planetary phenomena.

To calculate house cusps you need a set of tables of houses. These enable you to calculate the rising sign and midheaven of the chart. If you use Equal or Porphyry house systems the intermediate house cusps are derived from the ascendant. For other house systems the intermediate house cusps are listed in the tables. The most easily available tables are for the Placidus house system. Annual ephemerides often carry tables of houses for common locations, including London. House cusps vary with latitude so tables give cusps for a variety of latitudes. If you are calculating a chart for a place between the latitudes given you need to work out the position of the cusps by using the tables for the two closest locations.

Ephemerides and tables of houses may be bought through major booksellers such as Amazon.com, the Astrology Centre of America (*http://www.astroamerica.com/*) or from specialist New Age bookshops. Major booksellers such as WH Smith sometimes stock them, or can order them for you on request.

Raphael's annual ephemeris is the most popular and is easily available. The most popular tables of houses, Raphael's Tables of Houses for the Placidus house system, are no longer being published although second hand copies are often available. Many ephemerides include a selection of tables of houses and a selection of tables published by the American Federation of Astrologers, amongst others, are available from the Astrology Centre of America and specialist bookshops. The log tables referred to in the following text are reproduced in Raphael's annual ephemeris as well as in tables of houses and many astrology textbooks.

CALCULATING A HOROSCOPE

Before beginning calculation you need to ensure that you have the correct information. The first thing you need is the time that the chart is being calculated for. In the UK birth times are not recorded on birth certificates (unless you are one of a set of twins). The exception to this is for people born in Scotland. People born outside the UK may find that their time of birth is recorded on their birth certificate. Apart from asking family members if they remember your time of birth, it may be recorded in a baby book or in medical records.

SUMMER TIME IN THE UK

1950 16 Apr – 22 Oct	1963 31 Mar – 27 Oct	1979 18 Mar – 28 Oct
1951 15 Apr – 21 Oct	1964 22 Mar – 25 Oct	1980 16 Mar – 26 Oct
1952 20 Apr – 26 Oct	1965 21 Mar – 24 Oct	1981 29 Mar – 25 Oct
1953 19 Apr – 4 Oct	1966 20 Mar – 24 Oct	1982 28 Mar – 24 Oct
1954 11 Apr – 3 Oct	1967 19 Mar – 29 Oct	1983 27 Mar – 23 Oct
1955 17 Apr – 2 Oct	1968 18 Feb – 31 Oct 1971	1984 25 Mar - 28 Oct
1956 22 Apr – 7 Oct	1972 19 Mar – 29 Oct	1985 31 Mar – 27 Oct
1957 17 Apr – 6 Oct	1973 18 Mar – 28 Oct	1986 30 Mar – 26 Oct
1958 20 Apr – 5 Oct	1974 17 Mar – 27 Oct	1987 29 Mar – 25 Oct
1959 19 Apr – 4 Oct	1975 16 Mar – 26 Oct	1988 27 Mar – 23 Oct
1960 10 Apr – 2 Oct	1976 21 Mar – 24 Oct	1989 26 Mar – 29 Oct
1961 26 Mar – 29 Oct	1977 20 Mar – 23 Oct	1990 25 Mar - 28 Oct
1962 25 Mar – 28 Oct	1978 19 Mar – 29 Oct	

If you were born in hospital it may be possible to find out from there, but if there is no way of finding out an accurate time of birth, it is best to work with the closest time you have. If you do not know your birth time, the chart is drawn up with Aries being placed on the middle of the left side and the planets drawn in with no houses marked. There will still be enough information to partially interpret the chart.

Assuming that you have a time to work with the next step is to convert that time to Greenwich Mean Time. You should always work in the 24-hour clock system to avoid error. Greenwich Mean Time operates in the UK between late October and early March. If you were born in the UK between late March and late October when British Summer Time was in operation, you need to begin by taking one hour off. The exact dates the clocks change vary each year, but it is usually the third Sunday in March and the fourth Sunday in October. From 25 February 1940 to 7 October 1945 Summer Time remained throughout and an additional hour was deducted for Double Summer Time during the summer months. If you were born between 18 February 1968 and 31 October 1971 British Summer Time was in operation throughout this period, so you need to deduct one hour for GMT whatever date you were born on. Ireland uses the same time as Great Britain. Before 1981 the times changed at 2 am on the dates given below. From 1981 onwards the times changed at 1 am.

If you were born overseas, then you need to find out the time difference between your place of birth and Greenwich Mean Time. If you were born around midnight this could mean that the date changes. For example, if you were born at 11 pm in New York on 11 April, which is five hours earlier, you would add five hours for GMT. This would give you the time of 4 am on 12 April, five hours later. You also need to check if your country was keeping summer time when you were born. In the case of New York, in summer months the time difference would be four hours, rather than five.

The next step is to find the latitude and longitude of the place where you were born. This will be needed to calculate the ascendant and house cusps. A good atlas will give the longitude and latitude of most places. But most astrologers use *The International Atlas or The American Atlas* by Thomas Shanks published by ACS, which also gives time zones and time changes.

CALCULATING THE ASCENDANT AND HOUSE CUSPS

When you have worked out the sidereal time all you need to do is look up the time in a set of tables and read across to see what the ascendant is. Looking at a table of houses for London we take Katie's time of 4:05:33. The closest listed to this time is 4:03:48 and 4:08:00. The tables list the following figures.

Sidereal time	10	11	12	Asc	2	3
	Gemini	Cancer	Leo	Virgo	Libra	Libra
4:03:48	3	10	13	9 33	1	28
4:08:00	4	11	14	10 17	2	29

The column headed 10 gives the position of the midheaven and the other columns give the house cusps as numbered. The time we want lies approximately halfway between the sidereal times given. The first time given is 1:12 earlier than the time we want and the second is 2:27 later. Unless there is a sign change using the first figure in this type of case would normally be sufficiently accurate. However, as the Ascendant is given more accurately we can interpolate to find a more accurate Ascendant. The difference between the later figure and the one we want is about twice as much as that between the earlier figure and the one we want. Therefore if we calculate the difference between the first and second Ascendant position given, halve that and add it to the earlier figure we will have a more accurate Ascendant.

10 17 – 9 33 = 44
44 / 2 = 22
9 33 + 22 = 9 55 Our Ascendant is therefore 9 55 Virgo.

If the chart was to be set using Placidus house cusps at this stage we would simply take note of the figures given for the relevant cusps as listed. The signs are now drawn on the chart wheel with the Ascendant sign on the left. The positions we have calculated above are marked where they fall in the signs. If lines are drawn from these points straight across the wheel we then have the remaining house cusps.

If the chart was to be set using Equal houses we simply mark the Ascendant on the wheel. Each sign following is then

marked at the same degree as the Ascendant. Drawing lines across the chart we then have the house cusps. The midheaven is marked with an arrow pointing upwards where it falls.

If the chart was to be set using Porphyry houses the midheaven is marked on the top of the chart. Each sign is marked at the same degree, in a similar fashion to the Equal house system. The Ascendant is then marked by an arrow on the left of the chart.

For other house systems, tables for that particular system are required.

SOUTHERN HEMISPHERE CHARTS

The tables of houses are calculated for the northern hemisphere and so an adjustment must be made when calculating charts for the southern hemisphere. When looking up the ascendant and house cusps, the OPPOSITE sign to the one given is the correct one to use. For example, if the tables show that the Ascendant is in Capricorn, for a southern hemisphere chart it will be in Cancer.

LONGITUDE AND LATITUDE OF MAJOR TOWNS AND CITIES IN THE UK AND IRELAND

ENGLAND

Barnsley 51N33 1W30
Basingstoke 51N16 1W07
Bath 51N22 2W23
Bedford 52N08 0W29
Berkshire 51N30 1W20
Birmingham 52N30 1W50
Blackpool 53N50 3W03
Bletchley 52N00 0W46
Bognor Regis 50N47 0W41
Bolton 53N35 2W26
Bournemouth 50N43 1W54
Bradford 53N48 1W45
Brighton 50N50 0W08
Buckinghamshire 51N45 0W48
Bury St Edmunds 52N15 0E43
Cambridgeshire 52N20 0E05
Canterbury 51N17 1E05
Carlisle 54N54 2W55
Cheltenham 51N54 2W04
Chester 53N12 2W54
Cirencester 51N44 1W59
Cornwall 50N30 4W40
Coventry 52N25 1W30
Crewe 53N05 2W27
Cumbria 54N30 3W00
Darlington 54N3331 1W34
Derby 53N55 1W29
Derbyshire 53N00 1W33
Devon 50N45 3W50
Doncaster 53N32 1W07
Dover 51N08 1E19
Essex 51N49 0E40
Exeter 50N43 3W31
Frome 51N14 2W20
Gateshead 54N58 1W37
Glastonbury 51N06 2W30
Gloucester 51N53 2W14
Great Yarmouth 52N37 1E44
Grimsby 53N35 0W05
Guildford 51N14 0W35
Halifax 53N44 1W52
Hampshire 51N05 1W15
Hove 50N49 0W10
Huddersfield 53N39 1W47
Ipswich 52N04 1E10

Kent 51N15 0E40
Lancashire 53N03 2W30
Lancaster 54N03 2W48
Leeds 53N50 1W35
Leicester 52N38 1W05
Leicestershire 52N46 0W53
Liverpool 53N25 2W55
London 51N30 0W53
Maccelsfield 53N16 2W07
Manchester 53N30 2W15
Margate 51N24 1E24
Middlesex 51N29 0W22
Newcastle 52N26 3W06
Newcastle under Lyme
  53N00 2W14
Newcastle upon Tyne
  54N59 1W35
Northamptonshire
  52N20 0W50
Norwich 52N38 1E18
Nottingham 52N58 1W10
Nottinghamshire
  53N00 1W00
Oldham 53N33 2W007
Oxford 51N46 1W15
Oxfordshire 51N39 1W10
Peak Forest 53N13 1W50
Penzance 50N07 5W33
Plymouth 50N23 4W10
Portsmouth 50N48 1W05
Preston 53N46 0W12
Rotherham 53N26 1W20
Rugby 52N23 1W15
Salisbury 53N47 1W48
Scunthorpe 53N36 0W38
Sheffield 53N23 1W30
Shrewsbury 52N43 2W45
Shropshire 52N40 2W00
Skegness 53N10 0E21
Slough 51N31 0W36
Somerset 51N08 3W00
South port 53N39 3W01
Stafford 52N48 2W07
Staffordshire 52N50 2W00
Stockport 53N25 2W10
Stoke 51N27 0E37

Stratford upon Avon
  52N12 1W41
Suffolk 52N15 0E43
Surrey 51N10 0W20
Sussex 50N55 0E15
Taunton 51N01 3W06
Torquay 50N28 3W30
Warwick 52N17 1W34
Warwickshire 52N13 1W34
Weymouth 50N36 2W28
Wiltshire 51N15 1W50
Winchester 51N04 1W19
Woking 51N20 0W34
Wolverhampton 52N36 2W08
York 53N58 1W05
Yorkshire South 53N30 1W15
Yorkshire W 53N45 1W40

SCOTLAND

Aberdeen 57N10
Ayr 57N28 4W38
Balmoral 57N02 3W13
Dalkieth 55N54 0W04
Dumfries 55N04 3W27
Dundee 56N28 3W00
East Kilbride 55N46 4W10
Edinburgh 55N57 3W13
Falkirk 56N00 3W48
Fort William 56N49 5W07
Glasgow 55N53 4W15
Gretna Green 554N59 3W04
Inverness 57N27 4W15
Kilbride 57N05 7W27
Leith 55N59 3W10
Motherwell 55N48 4W00
Oban 56N25 5W29
Paisley 55N50 4W26
Peebles 55N39 3W12
Perth 56N24 3W28
Selkirk 55N33 2W50

WALES

Abergaveny 51N50 3W00
Aberystwyth 52N25 4W05
Bangor 53N13 4W08
Barry 51N24 3W15

Caernarvon 53N08 4W16
Caerphilly 51N35 3W14
Cardiff 51N29 3W13
Cardigan 52N06 4W40
Harlech 53N52 4W0007
Hay on Wye 52N04 3W07
Holyhead 53N19 4W38
Llandudno 53N19 3W49
Merthyr Tydfil 51N46 3W23
Monmouth 51N50 2W43
Pembroke 51N41
Pontypool 51N43 3W02
Rhyl 53N19 3W29
Swansea 51N38 3W57
Tenby 51N41 4W43
Wrexham 52N03 3W00

NORTHERN IRELAND

Antrim 54N43 6W13
Armagh 54N21 5W36
Belfast 54N35 5W55
Derry 55N00 7W19
Omagh 54N36 7W18

EIRE

Adare 52N34 8W48
Carlow 52N50 6W55
Cavan 54N00 7W21
Ennis 52N50 8W29
Shannon 52N41 8W55
Cork 51N54 8W28
Donegal 54N39 9W07
Dublin 52N30 6W15
Galway 53N16 9W03
Dundalk 54N01 6W25
Kildare 53N10 6W55
Kilkenny 52N39 7W15
Leitrim 54N00 8W04
Limerick 52N40 8W38
Longford 53N44 7W47
Louth 53N37 6W53
Roscommon 53N38 8W11
Sligo 54N17 8W28
Tipperary 52N39 8W10
Wicklow 52N59 6W0

CALCULATING TIME

Having found Greenwich Mean Time the next step is to convert this to sidereal, or star, time. Looking in the ephemeris for your date of birth you will find that the sidereal time at noon or midnight of that date is given. You now need to calculate the difference between then and the time you were born to give the precise sidereal time for the time of your birth. The interval between the given time and noon is subtracted if it is earlier and added if later.

As a solar day is shorter than a sidereal day (about 10 seconds per hour) we need to make an adjustment. So, if we were looking at a set of tables for noon for each hour after noon you add 10 seconds for each hour. If before noon, you subtract 10 seconds. (Strictly the difference is 9.86 seconds but this level of accuracy is not normally required.) For each part of an hour you add, or subtract, the correct portion of ten seconds, with one second being equivalent to every six minutes. For example, fifteen minutes = 2.5 seconds. (The same method is used for midnight tables, except that there you are looking at the interval to and from midnight.)

This gives the sidereal time for your time of birth if you are born on the Greenwich meridian: at 0 degrees of longitude. A correction needs to be made for longitude if you are born elsewhere. Each degree of longitude is equivalent to four minutes of time, or 15 degrees of longitude is equivalent to one hour. Therefore the longitude of your place of birth needs to be divided by 15 and added, if you are born east of Greenwich, or subtracted, if you are born west of Greenwich.

EXAMPLE ONE

Katie is born at 10:15h on 3 July 1976 in London. As this is during summer time we need to begin by deducting one hour to convert this time to GMT. Katie's birth time is, therefore, 9:15 GMT. Looking at a set of accurate tables for the sidereal time at noon on her date of birth we find that it is 6:46:33. As she is born two hours and forty minutes before noon, we need to subtract that figure. Remembering that there are 60 seconds in a minute and 60 minutes to the degree that gives us:

6	46	33 -
2	40	00
4	06	00

We now need to subtract 10 seconds per hour, which in this case, is 20 seconds for the two hours and 6.66 seconds (rounded up to seven seconds) for the 40 minutes.

4	06	00 -
		27
4	05	33

EXAMPLE TWO

Nathan is born at 17:35h on 2 October 1978 in New York. The sidereal time at noon on this date is 12:43:24. New York keeps Eastern Standard Time, which is normally five hours behind GMT. However, a check reveals that Summer Time was in operation then so the difference is actually four hours. Therefore four hours need to be added giving 21:35 GMT. This is nine hours and 35 minutes after noon and so this figure needs to be added to the sidereal time.

12	43	24 +
09	35	00
22	18	24

We then add 50 seconds for the five hours and six seconds for the 35 minutes giving a total of 56 seconds to be added. This gives us a sidereal time of 22:19:20. In this case we also need to make an adjustment for longitude. New York is 73 degrees 57 minutes west of Greenwich. Divided by 15 this gives four hours, 55 minutes and 48 seconds.

22	19	20 -
04	55	48
17	23	32

This is the sidereal time for Nathan.

CALCULATING THE POSITIONS OF THE PLANETS

The positions of the planets are given in the ephemeris for noon (or midnight) for the date being considered. To calculate the correct positions for the horoscope we therefore need to amend the positions as given for the time of birth. In the case of Katie the positions given would be:

Sun	Moon	Mercury	Venus	Mars
Cancer	Virgo	Gemini	Cancer	Leo
11 40 10	25 34 49	27 51.5	15 52.8	27 54.3

Jupiter	Saturn	Uranus	Neptune	Pluto
Taurus	Leo	Scorpio	Sagittarius	Libra
22 34.8	3 14.3	3 3.6	11 49.4	8 59.1

We would note at this stage that Uranus and Neptune are marked with an R in the ephemeris, showing that they are retrograde on this date.

Firstly we need to note the difference between noon and the birth time we are using. Katie was born at 10:15h: one hour and 45 minutes before noon. The easiest way to calculate the difference in the planetary positions between our birth time and noon is by using log tables. The log tables used are proportional logarithms using 24 hours as their base and are specifically designed for this type of calculation. They are often included in ephemerides and tables of houses.

To find the figure we need, we simply look along the top of the table for hours – in this case 10, and look down the table to the horizontal column for the minutes, in this case 15. That would give us the number 3695.

Next we take note of how fast the planet we are looking at is moving. In annual ephemerides the motion of the planets is given so no calculation is needed. If it is not given you simply calculate the difference between the planet's position on the date you want and the previous or following day, depending on whether you are looking at a chart for before, or after, noon. For example, on Katie's date of birth the Sun is at 11 40 10 Cancer. As she was born in the morning we note that on the previous day it was at 10 42 57 Cancer. By subtracting the second number from the first we find that in one day it has moved 57 minutes and 13 seconds.

Using the log tables we look up the log for 57 minutes, discarding the seconds. That gives us 1.4025. The two logs are added together; they should always be added irrespective of whether the birth time is before or after noon.
3695 + 1.4025 = 1.7720

We then look within the log tables to find the closest number to this and read what is given as degrees and minutes. In this case the closest number is 1.7781 and shows a difference of 24 minutes. As we are looking at a morning birth wethen deduct 24 minutes from the position given for noon 11 40 10 – 00 24 00 = 11 16 10 of Cancer. This is the position of the Sun in Katie's horoscope. If the result of this calculation is over 30 degrees that simply means that the planet has moved into the next sign and you deduct 30 from your answer while noting the sign change. Similarly, if the answer is less than zero that means that the planet has moved into the preceding sign, which may happen if the planet is retrograde. If this is the case, simply add 30 degrees to your answer.

The same process is undertaken for all of the planets. As Uranus, Neptune and Pluto move so slowly, it is often sufficient to take the noon position with no further adjustment. Once the positions of the planets are calculated they are drawn on the chart in their correct places.

CALCULATING ASPECTS

Whether you have calculated a chart by hand or on the computer you may need to calculate aspects. No actual calculation is needed for many of the aspects as with practice they can be seen by eye. However, minor aspects are not so easily recognised and some simple calculation is needed. Firstly, you decide what type of aspect you are looking for. Normally we begin by making a search for the major aspects, starting with the conjunction. A decision needs to be made from the outset what orbs you are allowing for the aspects. Although an exact number is given for each aspect, the orb is the 'give and take', or the range in which the aspect may take effect. In modern astrology the aspects themselves are given an orb, whereas in traditional astrology it is the planets that give the orb of influence. The orbs will become clear in the examples that follow.

The orbs accepted by most modern astrologers are:- conjunction, square, trine, opposition and square: eight degrees, sextile: four degrees, quincunx: two degrees and all minor aspects: one degree. Some astrologers will allow a greater orb when the Sun or Moon are involved in the aspect.

The orbs used by most traditional astrologers are referred to as moieties. This gives the range either side of the planet that may be considered. An orb, as it is used in modern astrology, is half of the moiety of a planet. The moieties of the planets are as follows: Sun 17, Moon 12, Mercury 7, Venus 8, Mars 7 30, Jupiter 12,

Saturn 10. There is no consensus on the moieties of Uranus, Neptune and Pluto, but they are often treated in the same way as Saturn, or given a moiety of eight degrees.

The moieties of each of the planets being considered are added together and this total is halved to give the orb of an aspect between those two planets. For example, for the Sun and Venus 17 + 8 = 25 25 /2 = 12 30. This is the orb for any aspect.

CONJUNCTION

The conjunction is an aspect of 0 degrees. Two planets next to each other in the chart will be in conjunction. As an orb of 8 degrees is used by modern astrologers they may be up to 8 degrees apart. They need not be in the same sign; if they are in different signs this is a dissociate conjunction. For example, if the Sun is at 26 degrees of Cancer, and Venus at one degree of Leo, these two planets are conjunct.

OPPOSITION

This is an aspect of 180 degrees, so the planets are directly opposite on the chart. (They may not be in opposite signs.) If the Sun is at 26 degrees of Cancer and the Moon at 20 degrees of Capricorn they are in opposition.

SQUARE

This is an aspect of 90 degrees, or three signs apart. Occasionally two planets will be in square separated by four signs. The easiest way to spot a square is to count three signs along in either direction from the planet you are looking at and see if there is another planet there. If the Sun is at 26 degrees of Cancer and Jupiter at 29 Libra they are in square.

TRINE

This is an aspect of 120 degrees, or about four signs apart, and is worked out in the same way as the square.

SEXTILE

This is an aspect of 60 degrees, or two signs apart, and worked out as above.

QUINCUNX

This is an aspect of 150 degrees or five signs apart.

MINOR ASPECTS

Although, with experience, it is possible to see minor aspects by eye many of them need to be calculated, especially in the early stages of learning astrology. The position of each planet is converted to absolute longitude. Remembering that each sign is 30 degrees long the degree within the sign is added to the longitude degree at the start of that sign.

Aries begins at 0 degrees, Taurus 30, Gemini 60, Cancer 90, Leo 120, Virgo 150, Libra 180, Scorpio 210, Sagittarius 240, Capricorn 270, Aquarius 300 and Pisces 330. A planet at 22 Libra is therefore at 202(180 + 22) degrees of the circle.

After noting the absolute longitude of each planet, and chart point if you are calculating aspects to them, take note of the angular distance of each aspect you're searching for so that you can see if any combination is in their range. The most commonly used minor aspects are: semi sextile 30, semi square 45, sesquiquadrate 135, quincunx 150.

Rarely used minor aspects are:- decile or semi quintile 36, novile 40, septile 51 25, quintile 72, sesquiquintile 108, bi quintile 144.

Beginning with the Sun each planet is considered in relation to the Sun's position. If the Sun is at 26 Cancer, it is at 116 degrees of the circle. If Venus is at 10 Virgo, it is at 160 degrees of the circle. Taking the lower number from the higher (160 –116) we get 44. As the semi-square is an aspect of 45 degrees and has a one degree orb these two planets are in semi-square. Many astrologers use only major aspects unless the commonly used minor aspects are exact, in which case they may be considered.

When the aspects have been calculated they are listed and a note is made as to whether they are applying: – the two planets are approaching each other, – or separating: the aspect has already been exact. For example, if the Sun is at 4 degrees of Scorpio and Mercury at 8 degrees of Scorpio they are in conjunction. The Sun is the faster planet and is moving towards Mercury, therefore in a few days time they will be at the same degree. This is an applying aspect. If the Sun were at 10 degrees of Scorpio it would be separating from Mercury. Applying aspects are generally thought of as being stronger.

JUDGING THE STRENGTH OF THE PLANETS

In traditional astrology the dignities and debilities of the planets are considered in interpretation. Modern astrologers generally only take note of rulership. The dignities and debilities of the planets are set out in the table below. To read the table you look at the sign the planet is in and read across the columns. For example, if considering 15 degrees of Aries we would note the following:

- It is ruled by Mars (by day).
- The Sun is exalted (especially at 19 degrees).
- It is the Sun's triplicity in the day and Jupiter's at night.
- As it is over 14 degrees and under 21, it is in Mercury's term.
- It is in the Sun's face.
- Venus is in detriment there and Saturn in fall.

If Venus was at this degree it would be in a difficult and weak position, being in detriment.

SIGN	EX	TRIP D/N	TERMS					FACES			DET	FALL
♈ ♂ D	☉ 19	☉ ♃	♃ 6	♀ 14	☿ 21	♂ 26	♄ 30	♂ 10	☉ 20	♀ 30	♀	♄
♉ ♀ N	☽ 3	♀ ☽	♀ 8	☿ 15	♃ 22	♄ 26	♂ 30	☿ 10	☽ 20	♄ 30	♂	
♊ ☿ D	☊ 3	♄ ☿	☿ 7	♃ 14	♀ 21	♄ 25	♂ 30	♃ 10	♂ 20	☉ 30	♃	
♋ ☽ D/N	♃ 15	♂ ♂	♂ 6	♃ 13	☿ 20	♀ 27	♄ 30	♀ 10	☿ 20	☽ 30	♄	♂
♌ ☉ D/N		☉ ♃	♄ 6	☿ 13	♀ 19	♃ 25	♂ 30	♄ 10	♃ 20	♂ 30	♄	
♍ ☿ N	☿ 15	☿ ☽	☿ 7	♀ 13	♃ 18	♄ 24	♂ 30	☉ 10	♀ 20	☿ 30	♃	♀
♎ ♀ D	♄ 21	♄ ☿	♄ 6	♀ 11	♃ 19	☿ 24	♂ 30	☽ 10	♄ 20	♃ 30	♂	☉
♏ ♂ N		♂ ♂	♂ 6	♃ 14	♀ 21	☿ 27	♄ 30	♂ 10	☉ 20	♀ 30	♀	☽
♐ ♃ D	☊ 3	☉ ♃	♃ 8	♀ 14	☿ 19	♄ 25	♂ 30	☿ 10	☽ 20	♄ 30	☿	
♑ ♄ N	♂ 28	♀ ☽	♀ 6	☿ 12	♃ 19	♂ 25	♄ 30	♃ 10	♂ 20	☉ 30	☽	♃
♒ ♄ D		♄ ☿	♄ 6	☿ 12	♀ 20	♃ 25	♂ 30	♀ 10	☿ 20	☽ 30	☉	
♓ ♃ N	♀ 27	♂ ♂	♀ 8	♃ 14	☿ 20	♂ 26	♄ 30	♄ 10	♃ 20	♂ 30	☿	☿

The planets are given points according to their position in this scheme. A commonly used system is that outlined in the table below.

ESSENTIAL DIGNITY	SCORE	ESSENTIAL DEBILITY	SCORE
Planet in Own Sign	5	Planet in Detriment	-5
Planet in Mutual Reception	5	Planet in Fall	-4
Planet in Exaltation	4	Peregrine	-5
Reception by Exaltation	4	In Own Triplicity	3
In Own Terms	2	In Own Face	1

ACCIDENTAL DIGNITY	SCORE	ACCIDENTAL DEBILITY	SCORE
On MC or Ascendant	5	In 12th House	-5
In 7th, 4th, or 11th house	4	In 8th or 6th house	-4
In 2nd or 5th house	3	Retrograde	-5
In 9th house	2	Slow in Motion	-2
In 3rd house	1	♄ ♃ ♂ Occidental	-2
Direct	4	☿ ♀ Oriental	-2
Swift in Motion	2	☽ Decreasing in Light	-2
♄ ♃ ♂ Oriental	2	Combust	-5
☿ ♀ Occidental	2	Under Sunbeams	-4
☽ Increasing in Light	2	Partile ☌ with ♄ or ♂	-5
Not Combust, nor Under Beams	5	Partile ☌ with ☋	-4
Cazimi	5	Partile ☍ with ♄ or ♂	-4
Partile ☌ with ♃ or ♀	5	Besieged by ♄ or ♂	-5
Partile ☌ with ☊	5	Partile □ with ♄ or ♂	-3
Partile △ with ♃ or ♀	4	Conjunct Algol, or within 5°	-5
Partile ✳ with ♃ or ♀	3		
Partile ☌ with Cor Leonis	6		
Partile ☌	5		

TECHNIQUES FOR JUDGING RELATIONSHIPS

CALCULATING A COMPOSITE CHART

A composite chart is a chart that combines the charts of two people in a relationship and represents the relationship itself, and the shared energies of the people involved. It is formed by determining the midpoints between pairs of planets, angles and the focal points of the two horoscopes concerned. The midpoint is the halfway point between two planets.

Firstly, the birth charts of the two people concerned need to be calculated. The positions of the planets and angles are then listed in terms of absolute longitude, or where they lie on the circle. Remembering that each sign contains 30 degrees, the degree within the sign is added to the longitude degree at the start of that sign. Aries begins at 0 degrees, Taurus 30, Gemini 60, Cancer 90, Leo 120, Virgo 150, Libra 180, Scorpio 210, Sagittarius 240, Capricorn 270, Aquarius 300 and Pisces 330.

The position of the planet in its sign is added to the 0 degree equivalent of that sign. For example, if Jane's Moon is at 21 34 Cancer we add 90 to this position giving an answer of 111 34. If her boyfriend, Paul's Moon is at 16 12 Aquarius we add 300 to this position giving an answer of 316 12.

To find the position of their composite Moon these figures are added together and divided by two.

$$111 \ 34 \ +$$
$$316 \ 12$$
$$\overline{}$$
$$427 \ 46$$

Divide this total by two and you get 213 53 (remembering that sixty minutes equal one degree when carrying over numbers)

The nearest beginning of a sign to this figure is Scorpio at 210. As Scorpio is 13 degrees 53 minutes later, the position of the composite Moon is therefore 13 53 Scorpio. The same procedure is applied to each of the planets, the Midheavens, Ascendants, Moon's nodes and, if a quadrant house system is

used, house cusps. There is no need to refer to a table of houses when calculating the new cusps.

(A slightly different technique involves calculating the midpoints of the latitudes and longitudes of each chart and using the composite midheaven in the relevant set of tables to find the Ascendant and house cusps.)

Each of the new positions are drawn on the circle as a new chart and the resultant aspects calculated. This chart can then be interpreted in a similar way to a birth chart. Transits can be applied to the composite chart to judge the outcome of the relationship. The composite chart cannot be progressed, although if the progressed charts of the two people concerned are calculated, a composite chart can be made from these progressed charts. It is also possible to derive a composite chart for more than two people. If, for example, four people are involved in a relationship, all four positions are added together and then divided by four to find the positions in the composite chart representing that relationship.

THE RELATIONSHIP CHART

An alternative method of deriving a chart for a relationship between two people is to cast a new chart for a birth date, time and place that lies halfway between those of the two people concerned. Whereas the composite chart is a mathematical abstraction, based on the theory of midpoints, the relationship chart is a real chart existing in time and space.

INTER ASPECTS AND THE SYNASTRY GRID

The most common way to compare two people's charts in detail is to examine the aspects made from a planet in one chart to a planet in the other. For example, if Jane's Sun is at 22 34 Cancer, and Paul's Venus is at 24 12 Capricorn, these two planets will be in opposition. The orbs for the aspects used in synastry are smaller than those used in judging birth charts. Generally, five degrees are used for the conjunction, four for the opposition, square and trine, three for the sextile and one for all other aspects. There is no accepted consensus on the exact orbs to be used although it is agreed that the closer to exactitude the aspect, the more

	Sun	moon	merc	ven	mars	jup	sat	ur	nep	pl	asc	mc	NN
Sun													
Moon													
Merc													
Ven													
Mars													
Jup													
Sat													
Ur													
Ne													
Pl													
Asc													
mc													
Nn													

important it is for the relationship. To make it easier to gain an overview of the inter aspects a grid is drawn up with one person's planets along the top and the other persons down the side as shown above.

The aspects between each pair are then marked in the grid. Stressful aspects may be drawn in red, harmonious aspects in blue and neutral aspects in green. This enables you to see at a glance how problematic the relationship is likely to be.

PREDICTION METHODS

TRANSITS

Transits are the simplest prediction method available to the astrologer. A transit occurs when a planet, moving in its orbit, forms an aspect to any planet or point in the birth chart. Once the birth chart has been calculated it is possible to look in an ephemeris, or check with a computer programme where the planets are on a chosen date. The transiting planets are drawn around the outside of the chart should be noted. Any aspects that are formed between the transiting planet and points on the birth chart. These are then interpreted according to the nature of the planets involved and the particular aspect formed.

Although transits can be calculated using any of the planets, normally only the planets from Mars outwards are used. This is due to the fact that the inner planets move too quickly for practical use. Inner planet transits are only used in very detailed predictive work. There is no general consensus for which of the orbs of the aspects should be used, although they should be smaller than those used in interpreting the birth chart. Many astrologers will only use an orb of one degree, whatever the aspect. Although technically any aspect may be used, only the major aspects

are generally considered when interpreting transits. An awareness of the speed of orbit of the planets means that estimates can be made of upcoming transits. Although their speeds differ, owing to retrograde motion the Sun, Mercury and Venus take about one year to travel through the whole chart, spending about one month in each sign. Mars takes about two years to go around the chart and spends about two months in each sign. Jupiter takes 11.86 years to go round the chart and spends about a year in each sign. Saturn takes about 28 years to go around the chart and spends about two and a half years in each sign. Uranus takes 84 years to go around the chart and spends about seven years in each sign. Neptune takes about 165 years to go around the chart and spends about 14 years in each sign. Pluto takes about 249 years to go around the chart and spends between 12 and 31 years in each sign, owing to its eccentric orbit.

The regular patterns of movement of the planets means that they will transit their position in the birth chart at approximately the same age for each person. The type of aspects made are expressed in the table below.

Age	Saturn	Uranus	Neptune	Pluto
7	Square	Semi sextile		
14	Opposition	Sextile	Semi sextile	
21	Square	Square		Semi sextile
28	Conjunction	Trine	Sextile	
35	Square	Quincunx		
42	Opposition	Opposition	Square	Sextile
49	Square	Quincunx		
56	Conjunction	Trine	Trine	
63	Square	Square		Square
70	Opposition	Sextile	Quincunx	
77	Square	Semi Sextile		
84	Conjunction	Conjunction	Opposition	Trine

Knowing that these types of transits occur at these particular ages means that instead of checking regularly to see if there are any relevant transits upcoming in the birth chart, the astrologer will check the exact date that these transits are likely to take place for the individual concerned. Aspects made to other planets in the birth chart will be considered as well.

of life in the progressed chart. This date is generally known as the noon date. Someone born in the early part of the day will have a noon date later in the year than the birth date while someone born later in the day will have a noon date earlier than their birth date. The following table gives the equivalent periods of life compared with time in the ephemeris.

Ephemeris	Life
1 day	1 year
12 hours	6 months
6 hours	3 months
2 hours	1 month
1 hour	15 days
30 minutes	About 7 and a half days
10 minutes	About 2 and a half days
5 minutes	About 1 day

To calculate the noon date you begin by noting the interval to, or from, noon of the birth time. As the ephemeris is calculated using GMT all calculations need to be in GMT.

EXAMPLE

Laura was born on 6 February 1970.

Her birth time was 10 am.

The interval from 10 am to noon is two hours.

As her birth time is before noon her noon date will be later than her birth date.

Two hours = one month (see table above).

Therefore her noon date is 6 January.

Occasionally the noon date may fall into the preceding or following year.

An alternative method is to work out what number day in the year the birth date is. 6 February is day number 37 of the year.

A birth time of 10 am gives an interval of two hours from noon.

This interval converts to one month or approximately 30 days. Subtracting 30 from 37 gives a noon date of 7 January.

Although these methods may yield slightly different results they are adequate for most predictive work. There are more complex arithmetical methods to calculate progressions more accurately, but if greater accuracy is required most astrologers use computer software, which provides exact results.

SECONDARY PROGRESSION CALCULATION

Secondary progressions are also simple to calculate. Taking the ephemeris for the year of birth you simply count one day forward for each year of birth. Remember that at the age of one you have completed one year of life, so the day AFTER birth represents that year. Again the progressed positions are drawn around the birth chart and aspects made to the planets and points in the birth chart are noted and interpreted.

For greater accuracy than this basic method of calculating progressions some simple arithmetic is required. It is helpful to know the date in the year that corresponds exactly with the noon positions in the ephemeris. (Although the noon ephemeris is described here the methodology remains the same if using a midnight ephemeris – except then we consider the midnight date.) This means that you do not need to recalculate the positions of the planets for each year

PREDICTION METHODS (CONTINUED)

Having found the noon date the next stage is to find the correct day in the year that corresponds to the year in question. Noon in the ephemeris corresponds to the 6 (or 7) of January prior to Laura's birth. Noon on 6 February corresponds to 6 January in progressed terms.

If we wanted to look at her progressions for age 30 we would begin by adding 30 days to her birth date. 30 days on from 6 February is 8 March. The noon positions for the planets on 8 March would equal the progressed positions for 6 January (the noon date calculated above).

Noon position 8 March 1970 = progressed positions 6 January 1970

Noon positions 9 March 1970 = progressed positions 6 January 1971

Noon positions 10 March 1970 = progressed positions 6 January 1972

and so on until we reach

Noon positions 7 April 1970 = progressed positions 6 January 2000

Therefore by noting the positions in the ephemeris for 7 April 1970 we have the progressions for 6 January 2000.

If we want to look at a particular month during the year – usually for the position of the Moon as it moves the fastest – we take the position of the Moon on the date of birth, the position on the following day and subtract one from the other. This gives the motion of the month during that day. Dividing this figure by 12 will give the progressed motion in one month. This figure is then added to the position we have for 6 January to give February's progressed Moon position, added again to give the position for March's and so on.

To calculate the progressed Ascendant and Midheaven you take the date in the ephemeris that corresponds to the year under investigation. In the above case that would be 8 March 1970. The sidereal time for this date is noted. The Ascendant and Midheaven are then calculated in the same manner as the birth chart.

A simpler method is to use solar arc. Subtract the position of the Sun in the birth chart from the position of the progressed Sun. This gives the solar arc. Add this figure to the Midheaven in the birth chart. Using a table of houses for the correct latitude, look up the corresponding ascendant.

It is only worth calculating the progressed Midheaven and Ascendant if the birth time is accurate. A few degrees error in the angles, owing to an incorrect time, will result in a few years error in timing with progressions.

CONVERSE PROGRESSIONS

Converse progressions are calculated exactly like secondary progressions except one day before birth is held to equate with one year of life. The noon date, if used, is also different and needs to be calculated in reverse.

TERTIARY AND MINOR PROGRESSIONS

If the basic premise is accepted that a day in the ephemeris can correlate with a year of life, it is a small step to equate it with a month or week. There are two methods of equating a day with a month. The first, using the calendar month, and calculated as above, substituting a month for a year, is known as monthly secondary progressions. Basing the progressions on a lunar month requires special tables to aid in counting forward the days. These are known as tertiary progressions.

Minor progressions equate a month in the ephemeris with a year of life.

SOLAR ARC DIRECTIONS

To obtain the solar arc subtract the position of the Sun in the birth chart from the position of the progressed Sun. This number is then added to the position of each of the planets (and other chart points) once for each year of life. All the planets move forward at the same rate and the aspects between the planets will always be the same as those in the birth chart.

ONE DEGREE DIRECTIONS

With this basic method of prediction, one degree is added to each planet or chart point. It varies little from the solar arc method but is much easier to calculate.

FIXED STARS

Although there are about 290 stars and 57 constellations that could be used in astrology, only a small number are regularly used. It takes 72 years for a fixed star to move one degree in the zodiac, so the positions below remain valid for a number of years. The fixed stars have an influence when at the

and Pisces 330. A planet at 22 Libra is therefore at 202 (180+22) degrees of the circle.

The formula for a day birth is Ascendant + Moon – Sun = Part of Fortune

Star	Position	Meaning
Caput Algol	26 10 Taurus	Failure, difficulties, disaster
Alcyone	00 00 Gemini	Compassion and disappointment
Aldebaran	9 35 Gemini	Violence and victory
Regulus	29 50 Leo	Success and glory
Vindematrix	9 56 Libra	Misfortune, war and widowhood
Spica	23 50	Libra Success and prosperity
Acturus	29 14 Libra	Success and prosperity
Antares	9 38 Sagittarius	Conflict and violence
Serpentis	19 Scorpio	Disaster
Vega	15 19 Capricorn	Success in politics or finance
Fomalhault	3 52 Pisces	Good or bad depending on aspects
Scheat	29 22 Pisces	Failure and difficulties, especially at sea

Ascendant or angles at birth, or when near the Sun or Moon. Because they so slowly only one degree of orb is allowed and usually only the conjunction is used (although some astrologers also use the opposition and parallel).

ARABIC PARTS

The Arabic Parts are calculated by adding and subtracting the positions of planets and other features in a chart. The most common part in use is that of the Part of Fortune. Many parts are calculated by different formula depending on whether the chart is for a day or night birth. If the Sun is in the upper half of the chart it is of a day birth.
To calculate the Part of Fortune you need to first convert the positions of the Ascendant, Sun and Moon to absolute longitude. Remembering that each sign is 30 degrees long the degree within the sign is added to the longitude degree at the start of that sign. Aries begins at 0 degrees, Taurus 30, Gemini 60, Cancer 90, Leo 120, Virgo 150, Libra 180, Scorpio 210, Sagittarius 240, Capricorn 270, Aquarius 300

The formula for a night birth is Ascendant + Sun – Moon = Part of Fortune

EXAMPLE

In John's chart the Ascendant is at 27 21 Cancer, the Sun at 15 42 Leo and the Moon at 2 16 Taurus.

Converting these to absolute longitude we get

Ascendant = 120 + 27 21 = 147 21

Sun = 150 + 15 42 = 165 42

Moon = 60 + 2 16 = 62 16

As this is a night birth (because the Sun lies in the bottom half of the chart) we use the night formula.

Ascendant + Sun – Moon = Part of Fortune

```
  147 21 +
  165 42
  _____
  313 03 –
   62 16
  _____
  250 47
```

We then convert this absolute longitude position back to zodiacal longitude. Sagittarius begins at 240 degrees. Therefore John's Part of Fortune lies at 10 47 of Sagittarius. It is then placed in the chart at this position and a note is made of any aspects it may make to the planets in the chart. Only a small orb is generally used (1-2 degrees) and generally only the major aspects are used.

The Arabic Parts, listed below, are calculated in the same way. Those that are marked with an asterisk are calculated differently for day and night births. The day formula is given. If a night birth is being used you simply place the plus sign where the minus sign is and vice versa for a night birth.

*Daemon, religion and spirit	Ascendant + Moon – Sun
*Friendship and Love	Ascendant + Daemon – Part of Fortune
*Despair and fraud	Ascendant + Part of Fortune – Daemon
*Captivity and escape	Ascendant + Part of Fortune – Saturn
*Property and goods	Ascendant + 2nd house cusp – Ruler of 2nd house cusp
*Debt	Ascendant + Mercury – Saturn
*Parents	Ascendant + Saturn – Sun
*Grandparents	Ascendant + Saturn – 2nd house cusp
*Children	Ascendant + Saturn – Jupiter
Disease	Ascendant + Mars – Mercury
Captivity	Ascendant + Ruler of house Saturn is in – Saturn
Marriage of men	Ascendant + Venus – Saturn
Marriage of women	Ascendant + Mars – Moon or Ascendant + Saturn – Venus
Trickery and deception of men and women	Ascendant + Venus - Sun
Misconduct of women	Ascendant + Mars – Moon
*Lawsuits	Ascendant + Jupiter – Mars
Death	Ascendant + 8th house cusp – Moon
*Danger and violence	Ascendant + Mercury - Saturn
Journeys	Ascendant + 9th house cusp – ruler of 9th house
*Glory	Ascendant + daemon – Part of fortune
*Friendship and enmity	Ascendant + daemon – Part of fortune
*Success	Ascendant + Venus – Part of Fortune
*Hope	Ascendant + Mercury – Jupiter
Friends	Ascendant + Mercury – Moon
Violence	Ascendant + Mercury – daemon
Bad luck	Ascendant + Part of fortune – daemon
*Trickery and deceit	Ascendant + daemon – Mercury
Realisation	Ascendant + Mercury – Part of fortune
*Retribution	Ascendant + Mars – Mercury
Secrets	Ascendant + Midheaven – Ascendant ruler
Marriage	Ascendant + Descendant – Venus
*Sickness	Ascendant + Mars - Saturn
*Love	Ascendant + Jupiter – Venus
*Luck	Ascendant + Moon – Jupiter
*Passion	Mars + Ascendant - Sun

RECOMMENDED READING

Books suitable for a beginner or the less experienced marked with *

Ancient Classics

Biruni, Al, *Book of Instruction in the Art of Astrology*, Ascella

Bonatus, Guido, *The Astrologer's Guide*, Ascella

Doretheus of Sidon, *Carmen Astrologicum*, AFA

Manilius, *Astronomica*, Loeb Classics

Mathesos Libri VIII, *Firmicus Maternus*, Ascella

Ptolemy, *Tetrabiblos*, Loeb Classics

Angles

Avery, Jeanne, *The Rising Sign, Your Astrological Mask*, Doubleday

Fenton, Sasha, *Rising Signs, Discover the Truth About Your Personality*, Thorsons*

Mason, Sophia, *You and Your Ascendant*, AFA

Aspects

Carter, Charles, *Astrological Aspects*, AFA and Theosophical Society

Marks, Tracy, *Planetary Aspects, From Conflict to Resolution*, CRCS

Pelletier, Robert, *Planets in Aspect*, Whitford *

Sakoian, Francis & Louis S. Acker, *Minor Aspects*, Copple House

Sakoian, Francis & Louis S. Acker, *That Inconjunct, Quincunx, The Not so Minor Aspect*, Copple House

Tompkins, Sue, *Aspects in Astrology*, Element

Tierney, Bil, *Dynamics of Aspect Analysis*, CRCS

General Interpretation

Cunningham, Donna, *An Astrological Guide to Self-Awareness*, CRCS

Goodman, Linda, *Sun Signs*, Bantam Doubleday Dell *

Greene, Liz, *Astrology for Lovers*, Weiser *

Hand, Robert, *Planets in Youth*, Whitford*

Hone, Margaret E., *The Modern Textbook of Astrology*, Fowler *

March, Marion & Joan McEvers, *Only Way to Learn Astrology, Vols 1 to 5*, ACS *

Marks, Tracy, *The Art of Chart Interpretation*, CRCS

Oken, Alan, *Complete Astrology*, Bantam *

Parker, Derek and Julia, *Parkers' Astrology, New Edition*, Dorling Kindersley *

Sakoian, Francis & Louis S. Acker, *The Astrologer's Handbook*, Harper *

Horary

Barclay, Olivia, *Horary Astrology Rediscovered*, Whitford

Goldstein Jacobson, Ivy, *Simplified Horary Astrology*, privately published, available through Astrology Centre of America

Lilly, William, *Christian Astrology*, Ascella

Houses

Houlding, Deborah, *The Houses, Temples of the Sky*, Ascella

Pelletier, Robert, *Planets in Houses*, Whitford*

Sasportas, Howard, *The Twelve Houses*, Harper Collins

Planets

Alexander, Skye, *Planets in Signs*, Whitford

Arroyo, Stephen, *Exploring Jupiter, the Astrological Key to Progress, Prosperity & Potential*, CRCS

Cunningham, Donna, *Healing Pluto Problems*, Weiser

Cunningham, Donna, *Moon Signs, Key to Your Inner Life*, Ballantine

Greene & Sasportas, *Inner Planets*, Weiser

Greene, Liz, *Outer Planets & Their Cycles*, CRCS

Greene, Liz, *Saturn, A New Look at an Old Devil*, Weiser

Greene, Liz, *The Astrological Neptune & the Quest for Redemption* Weiser

Greene, Liz & Howard Sasportas, *The Luminaries*, Weiser

Negus, Joan, *Book of Uranus*, ACS

Sakoian & Acker, *Importance of Mercury in the Horoscope*, CSA

Van Toen, Donna, *Mars Book*, Weiser

Prediction

Brady, Bernadette, *Predictive Astrology: The Eagle and the Lark*, Weiser

Sullivan, Erin, *Saturn in Transit*, Weiser

Marks, Tracy, *The Astrology of Self-Discovery*, CRCS

Mason, Sophia, *Forecasting with New, Full & Quarter Moons*, AFA

Pessin, Dietrech J., *Lunar Shadows, The Lost Key to the Timing of Eclipses*, Galactic Press

Rodden, Lois, *Modern Transits*, AFA *

Relationships

Davison, Ron, *Synastry*, Aurora

Greene, Liz, *Relating*, Weiser*

Hand, Robert, *Planets in Composite*, Whitford

March, Marion & Joan Mcevers, *The Astrology of Human Relationships,* ACS*

Sakoian, Frances & Louis Sacker, *The Astrology of Relationships,* Harper*

Sargent, Lois Haines, *How to Handle your Human Relations* AFA

Townley, John, *Planets in Love,* Whitford

Miscellaneous

Allen, Richard, *Star Names, Their Lore and Meaning,* Dover

Arroyo, Stephen and Robert Zoller, *Fate, Freewill & Astrology, Spica and Ascella, Astrology, Karma & Transformation,* CRCS

Baigent, Michael, Nicholas Campion & Charles Harvey, *Mundane Astrology,* Thorsons

Bailey, Alice, *Esoteric Astrology,* Lucis Trust

Brady, Bernadette, *Brady's Book of Fixed Stars,* Weiser

Cozzi, Steve, *Planets in Locality,* AFA

Curry, Patrick, *A Confusion of Prophets,* Collins and Brown

Davis, Martin, *Astrolocality Astrology, A Guide to What it is and How to Use it,* Wessex Astrologer

Devlin, Mary, *Astrology and Past Lives,* Whitford

Ebertin, Reinhold, *The Combination of Stellar Influences,* AFA

Edmund-Jones, Marc, *The Sabian Symbols in Astrology,* Aurora

Farnell, Kim, *The Astral Tramp, A Biography of Sepharial,* Ascella

Fenton, Sasha, *Astrology ...On the Move! Where on Earth Should you be,* Thorsons

Frawley, John, *The Real Astrology,* Apprentice Books

Hall, Judy, *Patterns of the Past,* Wessex Astrologer

Hamblin, David, *Harmonic Charts,* Aquarian Press

Harding, Mike & Charles Harvey, *Working with Astrology,* Consider

Kempton-Smith, Debbie, *Secrets from a Stargazer's Notebook,* Topquark *

Koestler, Arthur, *The Sleepwalkers,* Viking

Lehman, J. Lee, *Classical Astrology for Modern Living,* Whitford

Lehman, J. Lee, *The Ultimate Asteroid Book,* Whitford

Lehman, J. Lee, *Essential Dignities,* Whitford

Lehman, J. Lee, *Book of Rulerships,* Whitford

Reinhart, Melanie, *Chiron and the Healing Journey,* Penguin Arkana

Robson, Vivian, *Electional Astrology,* Ascella

Schwartz, Jacob, *Asteroid Name Encyclopedia,* Llewellyn

Sullivan, Erin, *Retrograde Planets,* Weiser

Sutton, Komilla, *The Essentials of Vedic Astrology,* Wessex Astrologer

Schulman, Martin, *Karmic Astrology in Four Volumes,* Weiser

Spencer, Neil, *True as the Stars Above, Adventures in Modern Astrology,* Victor Gollancz

Zoller, Robert, *Tools and Techniques of the Medieval Astrologers,* Spica Australia

AUTHOR BIOGRAPHIES

KIM FARNELL

Kim Farnell has been a professional astrologer since 1990 when she gained her Diploma from the Faculty of Astrological Studies. She was a member of the Council of the Astrological Association of Great Britain for nine years and is now on the National Executive Committee of the British Astrological and Psychic Society. She has written sun sign columns and features for a number of magazines as well as articles for specialist astrological publications all over the world. She has also been the editor of a number of astrological publications. Kim's books have been published in English, Serbo-Croat and Japanese. She has frequently lectured at astrological conferences in the UK and overseas, taught astrology and has appeared on TV and radio. She has conducted research into the history of astrology, primarily in the seventeenth and nineteenth centuries. Kim continues to work directly with clients.

CAT JAVOR

Cat Javor began her studies in astrology in Australia in 1983, during which time she worked in radio and television broadcasting. Moving to England in 1988, Cat continued to work in the production of television, live music and theatre whilst maintaining her study of astrology. She became a professional consultant astrologer in 1996 and has written on the subject for the Astrological Journal, various national and international newspapers, magazines and the Internet. She also scripted the Love Match Horoscope Lines and has lectured at the Astrological Lodge of London. Her love of the subject continues to grow with each day.

HELENE SCHNITZER

German-born Helene Schnitzer studied astrology and Jungian psychology at the Achernar School for Astrology in Amstelveen (Holland), and Astro*Carto*Graphy with Arielle Guttman in Santa Fe, New Mexico. She has been a professional astrologer since 1986 and has translated several astrological works, including ' *The Twelfth House*' by Karen Hamaker-Zondag and ' *The Secret Language of Birthdays*', to which she contributed to as a writer. Helene currently works and teaches in London.

PICTURE CREDITS

The Art Archive

10, 11, 12, 42 (l), 59 (r), 68, 70, 113 (l), 153 (t), 160 (t), 181 (l), British Library 14, Museo Correr Venice 17 (t), 35 (l), 82, 105, 142 (l), 148, 171 (r), 172 (t), National Gallery London 17 (b), Biblioteca Estense Modena 18 (l), 52 (t), 102 (r), 115 (r), 150 (l), 165 (b), 190 (l), 192, The British Museum 20, Bauhaus Archiv 21 (t), Biblioteca Nazionale Marciana Venice 24, 31 (l), 41 (r), 47, 48, 73 (r), 86, 90 (b), 97 (l), 142 (r), 146 (r), 163 (t), 174, 181 (r), Museo Nazionale Romano Rome 26, Private Collection Paris 27 (l), British Library 29 (r), 92, 101 (b), San Apollinare Nuovo Ravenna 34, Ethnic Jewellery Exhibition Milan 36, 150 (r), Bodleian Library Oxford (b), 44 (t), Archaeological Museum Naples 49 (r), Tate Gallery London 50 (b), Palazzo Farnese Caprarola 54 (t), Victoria and Albert Museum London 56, Buonconsiglio Castle Trento 58, Real Biblioteca De Lo Escorial 60, 138, 168 (t), University Library Prague 62, 112, Bibliothèque des Arts Décoratifs Paris 67 (b), 193 (t), Biblioteca Bertoliana Vicenza 71 (l), Palazzo Pubblico siena 81 (l), Biblioteca d'Ajuda Lisbon 89, 176, Bibliothéque Nationale Paris 93 (l), 106 (l), 136 (l), 154 (t), Museo de Santa Cruz Toledo 95 (b), Bradford City Art Gallery 98 (b), Bodleian Library Oxford 103, 108, 156 (t), 178, Musée du Louvre Paris 109 (r), 110 (t), 153 (b), Museo della Romana Rome 114, Salamanca University 117 (r), Maison Natale de Pasteur Dole 119 (r), Bibliothèque Municipale Rouen 128, Scrovegni Chapel Padua 132, Galleria Degli Uffizi Florence 139, 179 (l), Ocean Memorabilia Collection 144, National Museum Bucharest 145 (r), Musée de la Renaissance Ecouen 149 (t), Bibliothèque Municipale Castres 157, Museo Naval Madrid 158, Cathedral Museum Ferrara 159 (r), Château de Blois 162 (b), Palazzo Schifanoia Ferrara 167, 186, Turkish and Islamic Art Museum Istanbul 175, Anagni Cathedral Italy 185 (l), Marine Museum Lisbon 185 (r), National Library Cairo 189, NASA 196 (b), Bibliothèque Municipale Arras 197

Mary Evans Picture Library

13, 15 (l), 16, 18 (r), 21 (b), 22, 23 (l,r), 25 (r), 27 (r), 28, 30, 37 (l), 38, 39 (b), 40 (t), 42 (r), 43 (l), 44 (b), 46 (r), 49 (l), 50 (t), 51, 55, 57, 59 (l), 61, 63 (r), 64 (r), 65, 66, 67 (t), 69, 73 (l), 74, 75, 76, 77, 78, 79, 80, 81 (r), 83, 85 (b), 88, 91, 93 (r), 94, 95 (t), 96, 97 (r), 98 (t), 99, 100, 101 (t), 106 (r), 107, 109 (l), 110 (b), 111 (t), 113 (r), 115 (l), 116, 117 (l), 118 (r), 120, 121, 123, 124, 125, 126, 129 (r), 130 (b), 131, 133 (t), 134, 137, 140, 141, 143, 145 (l), 146 (l), 147, 149 (r), 151, 152, 154 (b), 155, 156 (b), 159, 160 (b), 162 (r), 165 (t), 166 (r), 168 (b), 169, 170, 172 (b), 173, 176, 177, 180, 182, 183, 187, 188, 190 (r), 191, 193 (b), 194, 195, The Coupland Collection 161, Explorer Archives 32, 33, 35 (r), 37 (r), 39 (l), 53, 63 (l), Sigmund Freud 102 (l), Arthur Rackham Collection 45

Topham Picturepoint

15(r), 19, 25 (l), 29 (l), 31 (r), 46 (l), 52 (b), 64 (l), 71 (r), 72, 84, 85 (t), 87, 90 (t), 104, 118 (l), 122, 127, 129 (l), 130 (t), 133 (b), 135, 136 (r), 164, 171 (l), 179 (r), 184, 196 (t)

INDEX

Page references in bold indicate major entries on the subject

Adams, Evangeline **11,** 78
affliction 11, 103, 115, 117, 121
air element and signs **12,** 20, 71, 108, 116, 120, 146, 185
see also Aquarius, Gemini, Libra
Al-Biruni 12, 23, 120, 132
Aldebaran **13,** 89, 155
almanacs 14, 28, 122, 153
almuten *def* 13, 112
Antares **16-17,** 89, 155
antiscions **17,** 34
Aquarius **20-1,** 32, 52, 56, 60, 65, 71-2, 80, 117, 120, 130, 136, 146, 166, 168, 197
influence 20-1, 37, 71, 96
mode 20, 116
rulership of 155, 158, 189
triplicities 12, 20, 185
Aquinas, Thomas **23,** 26
Arabic and Islamic astrology 10, 10-11, 12, 13-14, 26, 47, 91, 117, 138, 150, 152
Arabic Parts **23,** 119, 188
Aries **24-5,** 26, 32, 35, 47, 51-2, 56, 60, 66, 74-6, 79, 129, 137, 146, 166, 168, 186, 191, 197
influence 24-5, 37, 71, 78
mode 24, 116
rulership of 24, 61, 65, 115, 155
triplicities 24, 185
Aristotle 23, **26,** 39, 78, 120, 142-3
principles *see* coldness, dryness, heat, moistness
ascendants 12-13, 16, 23, **26-7,** 40, 47, 49, 53, 55-6, 73, 79, 97-8, **111,** 114, 116, 118-19, 125, 133, 138, 142-3, 153, **154-5, 166,** 180
aspects 10, 15-16, 18-19, **27,**

28, 34-5, 54, 58, 60, 65, **66,** 91, 95, 98, **99, 113,** 119, 132-5, 138, 144, 164, 168, 196
aspect patterns 49, 78
see also grand cross, grand trine, kite, mystic rectanlge, T-square
major aspects 27, 34, 53, **114,** 166, 184
minor aspects 27, 36, 61, **119,** 129, 162-3, 164
see also mundane aspects, parallel aspects, *and indivdual aspects*
asteroids **28,** 55, 132, 170
astrocartography **28,** 153
astrolabes 29, 152
Astrologer's Guide, The 18

Babylon 31, **33,** 39, 48, 54, 70, 91-2, 118-19, 158, 162
Bailey, Alice A 75, 97, 150
bi-septile aspects 119
Blavatsky, Helena 75, 97, 103, 124
body parts **37,** 42, 44, 103, 106, 108, 117, 121, 127, 136, 146, 156, 165, 169, 174, 178, 180, 191-2, 197
Bonatus, Guido 18, **38**
Brahe, Tycho **38-9,** 104
Britain 14, 30, 35, 41, 46-7, 58, 60, 62, 73, 89, 93, 107, 110-11, 117, 122, 126, 174, 196-7

calendars 28, 32-3, 37, **40-1,** 70, 102, 105, 118
Cancer 17, 32, 42, **42-3,** 47, 51-2, 56, 60, 65, 76, 81, 94, 102, 106, 111, 115, 123, 129, 146, 168, 171, 197
influence 37, 42-3, 120, 185
mode 42
rulership 121, 155
triplicities 42, 185, 195
Tropic of **185**
Capricorn 17, 32, 35, 37, 44,

44-5, 47, 52, 56, 60, 65-6, 76, 102, 115, 130, 146, 166, 168, 171, 180, 197
influence 44-5
mode 44
rulership 45, 155, 158
triplicity 44, 67, 71
Tropic of 185, **185**
Cassiopeia 50
cazimis *def* **47,** 53, 65
Cepheus 50
Chaldean astrology **48,** 51, 75, 114
chart points 10, 16-17, 27, 47, 68, 118-19, 128, 142-3, 186, 191, 195
charts *see* event charts, composite charts, configurations, flat charts, harmonic charts
charts *see* horoscopes and birth charts, returns
Cheiro (William John Warner) 126
children and childbirth 33, **49,** 77, 136
China 31, 51, 92, 176
Chiron **49,** 140
coldness 66, 120, 146, 190
colours **50-1,** 70, 72, 77, 127, 162, 169, 180-1, 187
combust **51,** 53
comets 11, **51,** 55, 132, 170
composite charts *def* 176, **52,** 101
conjunction aspect 10, 34, **53,** 56, 99, **99,** 114, 128, 142, 173, **175,** 188
contra-antiscia *def* 17, 34
Cope, David ('Zariel') 197
Copernicus, Nicolas **55,** 88, 91, 122
creativity 78-9, 96, 106-7, 189
Crowley, Aleister 11
Culpeper, Nicholas **58,** 62, 92-3
cusps *see under* houses
cycles 58-9, 102-3, 113, 121, 141, 154, 158, 158-9

day and night distinction 15, **59-60,** 66, 91, 97, 128, 133-4, 155, 162, 185
death 13, 15, 47, 70-1, 140, 142, 165
debility 51, **60,** 64-5, 81
decanate *def* **60-1**
decans 114
decile aspects **61,** 119, **164**
declination 34, 47, 54-5, **61**
decumbiture charts **62,** 116
Dee, John **62,** 67
degrees 10, 14-15, **57, 62-3,** 63
descendants *def* **64,** 16, 165
detriment 60, **64-5**
dignity and strength 11-16, 32, 47, 51, 57, 60, 64-5, **65,** 72, 81, 112, 115, 117-18, 120-1, 124, 134, 155, 163, 168, 173, **183,** 190
see also exaltation, face, rulership, term, triplicity
directions 65, 127, 154, 171, 183
Draco 50
dryness **66,** 120, 146

Earth 18-19, 48, 66, **66-7, 67,** 69, 71, 74, 77, 84, 88, 91, 94, 120, 124, 127, 130, 132, 141, 145-6, 167, 170, 177
earth element 76, 178, 185, 192
Ebertin, Rheinhold 56, **68**
eclipses *def* **68-9,** 28, 188
Saros cycle **158**
ecliptic *def* **69,** *def* 168, 26, 80, 105, 116, 130, 132-3, 138, 140, 152, 170, 191, 197
Egypt, ancient 31, **70,** 75, 88, 91-2, 145
elements 26, **71,** 120, 146, 172, 185, 197
see also air element, earth element, fire element, water element
emotions 12, 42-3, 87, 136-

7, 161
ephemerides 28, 59, 72, **73,** 91, 162, 180
equator **74,** 130, 141, 142-3
   celestial equator 26, 47, 61, 79, 130, 152, 191, 195
esoteric astrology 71, **75,** 183
event charts 162
exaltation dignity 57, 60, 65, **75,** 76, 102, 115, 117, 120-1, 124, 150, 185

face dignity *def* 61, 65, **75,** 112, 124, 134
fall 60, **76,** 102, 115, 117, 121
family 42, 81, 98, 169
fate and free will 11, 33, 103, 134, 142, 159, 182, 196
feminine mode 42, **76-7,** 91, 120, 136, 160, 162, 169, 178, 184, 187, 190, 192
finance 42-3, **78,** 137, 162, 179, 191
fire element and signs 66, 71, **78-9,** 92, 120, 146, 156, 185
five-pointed stars 49, 148
flat charts *def* **80**
Fomalhaut 89, 155
Freud, Sigmund 102
frustration 10, **83**

Gemini 13, 32, 51-2, 56, 60, **86-7,** 120, 129, 146, 166, 168, 181, 184, 197
   influence 36-7, 71, 86-7, 96, 185
   mode 86, 116
   and rulership 65, 86, 117, 155
   triplicities 12, 86
Glastonbury 67
glyphs **89,** 174, 197
grand cross aspects 53, **89-90**
grand trine aspects 53, **89,** 105
Gravellaine, Joëlle de 59
Greece, ancient 31, 39, 51, 54, 63, 82, 88, 90-2, **92-3,** 125, 134, 138, 166, 188

Halley, Edmund 158
harmony **90-1, 113,** 114, 123, 148, 184, 188
   harmonic charts 91

heat 66, 102, 120, 146
Hephaestion of Thebes 70
herbalism 58, **92-3**
Hermes Trismegistus 70
Hermes, Trutine of **142**
Herschel, William **93,** 188
Hone, Margaret 104
horary astrology 10, 17, 19, 35-6, 40, 47, 50, 56, 63, 71-2, 75, 77, **94,** 98, 116, 118, 123, 131, 134-5, 147, 162, 165, 180-1, **183,** 194-5
horary charts 34, 47, 53, 76, 79-80, 94, 101, 134, 144
horoscopes and birth charts 10, 15-17, 23, 36, 43, 45, 47, 52-4, 57, 87, 90-2, **94-5,** 96-7, **125,** 126, 134, 148-9, 165-6, 184
   cardinal points 47, 98, 118-19
   casting 26-7, 36, 47, 52, 56-7, 59, 67, 71, 80, 97, 105, 125, 141, 162, 167, 170, 190
   comparing 103, 139, 176, 180-1
   configurations and patterns 18, 49-51, **53,** 135
   interpreting 18-19, 95, **100-1,** 119, 125, 145, 173-4, 177
   'Lord of Chart' 15, **112**
   patterns and chart shapes 39, **39, 49,** 53, 111, **162,** 185, **185**
   and time of birth 80, 97, 128, 133-4, 142-3, 151, 174
   validating 148-9
house systems 56, **96, 182, 197**
   Alcabitius **12-13,** 105
   Campanus **41,** 152, 197
   Equal house **73**
   Koch **105**
   Placidus 13, 105, **138,** 149, 177, 182
   Porphyry **141,** 197
   Regiomontanus **152**
   space-based systems 41, 96
   time-based systems 12-13, 96, 138
houses **16,** 39-40, 47, 49, 56,

58, **63,** 72-3, 80-1, **95,** 104, 112, 129, 131, 147, 153, 168, 173, **177**
   first 53, 63, 73, **79,** 97, 101, 146, 153
   second 80, 109, 146, **162**
   third 40, 60, 101, 146, **181,** 184
   fourth 72, **81,** 94, 98, 132, 146, 153, 173
   fifth 33-4, 49, **77,** 80, 101, 112, 132, 146, 155, 165, 173
   sixth 40, 60, 97, 101, 131-2, 146, **169**
   seventh 53, 63-4, 72, 83, 114-15, 146, 153, **165,** 173
   eighth **70-l,** 80, 146
   ninth 40, 60, **127,** 146
   tenth 58, 63, 73, 118, 131-2, 146, 153, **180,** 197
   eleventh 33, **72,** 80, 83, 101, 132, 146, 173
   twelfth 40, 60, 83, 97, 101, 132, 146, **186-7**
   cadent houses *40,* 60, 123, 169
   cusps *def* **58,** 12-13, 16, 19, 23, 27-8, 34, 41, 49, 57-8, 64-5, 73, 98, 100, 105, 109, 118, 141, 143, 151-3, 155, 164-6, 177, 180, 182, 197
hyleg *def* 13, **97**

immum coeli 16, 81, **98,** 124, 138, 155, 197
inconjunct aspect *see* quincunx aspects
India 12, 31, 39, 73, 92, 103, 190

Jones, Marc Edmund 49, 63, 155
   'Jones patterns' 49, 111, 185
joy 77, 79, **101,** 181
Jung, Carl 12, 71, 80, **102,** 144-5, 176, 195
Jupiter 17, 34-5, 36, 48, 60-1, 65, 67, 75-6, 81, 93, 101, **102-3,** 132, 138-9, 169-70, 175-6
   influence 28, 37, 102-3, 162

mode 91, 116
   rulership 65, 78, 102-3, 118, 136, 155-7, 180, 185, 195

Kepler, Johannes 36, 61, **104,** 119, 122-3, 148, 163-4
kite aspects 49, **105**

latitude **47,** 55, **105,** 132, 138, 152, 185, 197
legal astrology 79, 156, 159, 165, 180-1
Leo 32, 35, 51-2, 56, 60, 65-6, 77, 80, 96, 106, **106-7,** 111, 117, 129, 146, 168, 197
   influence 37, 71, 78-9, 106-7, 116
   rulership 65, 106, 155, 174
   triplicities 106, 185
Leo, Alan 75, **107**
Libra 12, 32, 53, 60-1, 74-6, 108, **108-9,** 111, 120, 130, 146, 168, 172, 197
   influence 37, 47, 71, 83, 96, 108, 108-9, 115-16
   mode 108
   rulership 65, 155, 190
   triplicities 47, 56, 108, 185
life predictions and life expectancy 14-15, 23, 47, 78, 97
   past lives 103
light 10, 50-1, **62,** 99, 138-9, **183,** 184
Lilly, William 14, 18, 58, 110, 120, 132, 134, 147, 153, 165, 197
local space astrology **111,** 153
longitude **10, 47,** 55, **112,** 118, 132-3, 154, 197

Magini, Giovanni Antonio 138
Maltwood, Katherine 67
Manilius, Marcus 95, 114
marriage 64, 71, **114-15,** 165
Mars 16-17, 28, 36, 48, 50-1, 60, 66-7, 75-6, 87, 98, 100-1, 114, **115,** 116, 132, 135, 138-9, 162, 165, 169-70, 175-6, 180-1, 183, 197
   influence 21, 33, 37, 85, 164

rulership 24, 61, 65, 75, 78, 115, 118, 155, 180, 185, 195
masculine mode 91, 102, 108, 115, **116**, 120, 184
medical astrology 29, 37, 62, 66, 70, 77, 79, 81, 83, 85, 93, 97-8, 115, **116**, 120, 140, 146, 162, 169, 180, 187
medium coeli 180
Mercury 18, 47-8, 50, 60, 66, 76, 79, 99, 101, 116, **117,** 132, 135, 138-9, 154, 169-70, 175-6, 184
  influence 36-7, 45, 194
  rulership 12, 61, 65, 67, 75, 86, 117-18, 155, 192
  triplicity 67
meridians 58, **118,** 197
midheaven 13, 16, 58, 72-3, 97-8, **118-19,** 141, 143, 153, 155, 180, 197
midpoints 26, 119, **119,** 163, 188
moistness 102, 120, 146, 190
Montrefelto, Guido de 38
Moon, the 15, 17, 19, 23, 25, 27-8, 30, 33, 37, 42, 48-50, 53, 56, 59-62, 65, 67-9, 75-7, 80-1, 91, 94, 97-8, 101, 107, 109-10, 112, 115-16, 118, 120-1, **121,** 132-3, 135, 137-9, 142, 154, 157, 168-9, 176-7, 180-1, 188, 194
  black Moon 19
  blue Moon **37**
  combust Moon 51
  Dark Moon (Lilith) **59**
  influence 121
  lunar mansions 57, **112-13**
  nodes 27, 33, 35, 103, 116, 128, 134, 139, 158, 171, 186
  phases 28, **57, 83, 88,** 113, **127,** 158, 177, 188, **194,** 194-5
  rulership 65, 118, 121, 155, 195
  void of course 28, 53
Moore, Francis **122**
Morgan, JP 78
Morrison RJ 196-7
mundane aspects 27
mystic rectangle aspects 49,

53, **124**

Naibod, Valentine 125, 182
natal astrology see horoscopes and birth charts
natural astrology def 101
Neptune 36, 51, 60, 76, 98, 102, **126-7,** 170, 175, 183
  influence 127, 161, 164
  rulership 126, 136, 155, 195
nonagesimal aspects def 73, **128**
Nostradamus **129**
novile aspects 119, **129**

occupations and professions 84-5, 87, 102-3, 131, **131,** 169, 180, 193
Oken, Alan 75
Old Moore's Almanac 14, 122
opposition aspect 17, 34, 56, 66, 88-9, 114, **131,** 142, 177, 188
orbs 27, 34, 61, 120, **132,** 148, 163-4, 166, 172, 184

Paracelsus 92
parallel aspects 54, **132-3**
Pars Fortuna 97, **133**
Paul of Alexandria 70
Pearce, AJ 196-7
perihelion 18, **135,** 140
Persia 13, 39, 89
personal relationships 12, 21, 25, 42-3, 45, 52, 64, 72, 79, 87, 92, **94,** 130-1, 139, 193
personality and character 16, 27, 94, 98, 105, 106-7, 123, 125, 127, 135-7, 146, 177
Pisces 32, 52, 56, 60, 76, 120, 123, 130, **136-7,** 146, 166, 168, 185, 187, 195, 197
  influence 36-7, 136-7
  rulership 65, 102, 126-7, 136, 155
  triplicities 136, 185
planets 23, 28, 30, 33-4, 36, 50-1, 53, 55-6, 58, 81, 95, 104, 120, 135, **138-9,** 142-3, 170, 188
  benefic 34-5, 81, 102, 106, 138, 180, 184, 190

besieged def 11, **35**
hypothetical and trans-Neptunian 33, 68, **97,** **183,** 188
inferior def 175, **100**
malefic 11, 59, 98, 100, 112, **114,** 138, 172, 180
matutine def 116
occidental **130**
oriental **132**
peregrine **134**
periods 14, 28, 118, **139,** 190
superior 100, **175**
transiting 18, 23, 27, 57, 183
transpersonal see Saturn, Jupiter, Uranus, Neptune, Pluto
vespertine def 191
see also aspects, conjunction, dignity, Moon, Sun, and individual planets
Pleiades 33
Plotinus 141
Plutino 140
Pluto 51, 60, 76, 97-8, 115, **140,** 170, 175, 183, 188
  influence 36, 140
  rulership 140, 155, 195
Polich, Vendel 182
political astrology 12-13, 21, 24-5, 27, 33, 70, 72, 77, 79, 89, 101, **122-3,** 127, 137, 140, 159, 162, 169, 173, 187, 189
Porphyry 141
precession def **141,** 168, 186
prediction 11, 13, 23, 33, 38, 47, 65, 70, 81, 110, 119, 129, **142,** 144, 170
  methods **54, 88, 113, 125, 139, 142-3,** 162, **169, 180-1,** 182, **183**
  see also life predictions
prime vertical 41, 96, **143,** 152, 195, 197
psychology 57, 61, 67, 70-1, 80, 89, 102, 107, 115, 123, 131, 140, **144-5,** 160, 165, 176, 182, 190, 193, 195
  see also Freud, Jung
Ptolemy, Claudius 27, 37, 39, 46, 54, 66, 73, 88, 90,

113-14, 119, 122, 141-2, **145,** 184
'Ptolemaic aspects' see major aspects under aspects
Pythagoras 51, 92, 123, 141, 166

quadrants 141, **146**
quadruplicities 88, 120, 146, **146**
quincunx aspects 66, 99, 119, **147,** 196
quindecile aspects 119, **148**
quintile aspects 61, 119, **148,** 163-4

'Raphael' **149,** 153
reception 120, 124, **150**
Regiomontanus 152
Regulus 89, **152,** 155
relationship charts def 176, 101, **152**
religion **35,** 55, 59, 76, 82, 91, 101, 103, 127, 140, 142, 148, 156-7, 159, relocation astrology 28, **152-3**
Renaissance astrology 11, 91, **153**
retrogression 28, 33, 60, 151, **154,** 190
returns and return charts 103, 113, 139, 154, 159, 170, 180
Rome, ancient 40-1, 127, 159, 189
Rudhyar, Dane 41, 63, 155
rulership dignity 42, 49, 53, 60, 65, 67, 75, 94, 97, 116, 124, 131, 133-4, 139, 150, **155,** 185
  see also under individual planets

Sagittarius 32, 35, 52, 56, 60, 65-6, 84, 111, 130, 146, **156,** 168, 185, 197
  influence 37, 71, 77-9, 116, 156-7
  rulership 65, 67, 102, 155
  triplicities 156
Saturn 17, 25, 33, 36, 48-9, 53, 60-1, 65-7, 71, 75-6, 79, 81, 91, 93, 98, 100-1, 103, 109, 114, 116, 132, 137-9, **158-9, 159,** 169-

70, 175-6, 180, 187
influence 20, 37, 43, 51,
137, 158-9
rulership 12, 20, 43, 67,
97, 112, 118, 155,
158, 180
Scaliger, Joseph 114
Scorpio 16, 32, 52-3, 56, 60,
71, 76, 80, 111,
120-1, 123, 130, 146,
160-1, 164, 168, 185, 195,
197
influence 37, 146, 160-1,
165
rulership 65, 115, 140,
155
seasons 74-5, 79, 91, 130,
136, 141, 156, 160, 170-1,
178, 186, 191
semi-decile aspects 119, **162-
3**
semi-sextile aspect 119, **163**
semi-square aspects 114, 119,
163, 164, 188
'Sepharial' 88, 169
septile aspects 119, **164**
sesquiquadrate aspect **164**
sesquiquintile aspect **164-5**
sextile aspects 34, 105, 114,
165, **166**, 188, 196
sexuality 77, 112, 115, 140,
157, 161, **165**
see also marriage
Shakespeare, William **166**
significators *def* 76, *def* **168**,
10, 56, 134
signs 11, 17, 20-1, 25, 34,
36, 42-3, 45, 47, 53, 56,
60, 60-1, 65, **76-7**, 80, 95,
100, 104, 112, 116-17,
120, 123-4, 129, **146**, 147,
155, 166, 168, **168**, 185,
188
barren **34**
bestial **35**, 44, 178
bi-corporeal **36**
cardinal 47, 56, 80, 123
commanding **51**
see also Aries, Cancer,
Gemini. Leo, Taurus, Virgo
common **52**
see also Gemini, Leo,
Pisces, Sagittarius
feral **77**, 156
fixed 56, **80**, 123
see also Aquarius, Leo,

Scorpio, Taurus
fruitful **83**
human *see* Gemini, Leo,
Libra, Aquarius
mutable 12, 56, 80, 86,
88, 120, **123**, 136, 146,
156, 192
mute *see* Cancer, Pisces,
Scorpio
Northern **129**
see also Aries, Cancer,
Gemini, Leo, Taurus, Virgo
obeying **130**
solstice **74**, 171
see also Cancer, Capricorn
Southern **171**
see also Aquarius,
Capricorn, Libra, Pisces,
Sagittarius, Scorpio voice
194
see also Aquarius, Aries,
Capricorn, Gemini, Leo,
Libra, Sagittarius, Taurus,
Virgo
water signs 185, **195**
see also Cancer, Pisces,
Scorpio
see also individual signs
Sirius 91
solstices and equinoxes **17**,
74, **74-5**, 79, 86, 95, 141,
156, 168, **170-1**, 186, 191
spirituality 75, 137, 156-7,
190
sports 77, 85, 115
square aspect 34, 56, 88-9,
114, 163-4, 166, **172**, 188
stars, fixed 11, 17, 46, 48, 50,
50, 54, 61, 67, **80**, 89, 93,
113, 138, 143, 152, **155**,
172, 189
see also individual stars
succedence 77, 80, 162, 173
Sun, the 15, 18, 23, 27, 30,
33, 35, 47-51, 53, 55, 58,
60-1, 65-7, 68-9, 69, 72,
74-6, 80-1, 84, 91, 99,
105-6, 110, 112, 116, 118,
127, 132-3, 135, 138-9,
141-3, 154, 158, 162, 165,
168-70, **174-5**, 175-6,
185-7, 191
influence 36-7, 97-8, 174
rulership 78, 106, 118,
155, 174, 185
sunrise charts 174

Sun-sign astrology *def* **175**,
20, 24, 36, 42, 44, 95,
126, 176, 178, 192
synastry *def* 101, 17, 64, 101,
176

Taurus 13, 32, 35, 46, 51-2,
56, 60, 66, 75-6, 80, 129,
146, 162, 166, 168, 178,
178-9, 185, 190, 197
influence 37, 67, 71, 178-9
rulership 65, 155
triplicity 178
term dignity 65, 112, 124,
134, **180**
Thales of Miletus 78, 92
theosophism 103, 107, 150
time 19, 55, 66, 74-5, 79, **89**,
96, 105, 110-11, 119, 125,
139, 158, 162, 172-4,
181-2, 186, **187**, 194-5,
196
sidereal time 13, **167**, 181
see also seasons
tredecile aspect *see*
sesquiquintile aspect
trine aspect 34, 114, 165-6,
184, 188
triplicity dignity 12, 42, 65,
67, 71, 86, 106, 108, 112,
124, 134, 136, 146, 156,
160, 178, **185**, 192
cardinal triplicity 12, 44,
47, 56, 118
tri-septile aspect 119
T-square aspects 18, 53, **177**

Uranus 20, 33, 49, 51, 60,
76, 93, 98, 155, 170, 175,
183, **188-9**
influence 36, 189
as ruler 12, 155, 158, 188-
9

Vedic astrology 32, 36, 53,
71, 90, 129, 139, 173, **190**
Vega 169
Venus 17, 21, 34-5, 48, 60,
65, 75-7, 81, 91, 99, 101,
116, 120, 132, 135, 138-9,
169-70, 175-6, 180, 187,
190-1, 197
influence 21, 36-7, 43, 50,
112, 116, 165, 190-1, 193
rulership 12, 61, 65, 67,
75, 108-9, 117-18,

155, 178-9, 190-1
vertex *def* 68
Villani, Filippo 38
Virgo 32, 51-2, 56, 60, 66,
76, 111, 129, 168, 172,
185, **192-3**, 197
influence 37, 67, 71, 192-3
quadruplicity 146
rulership 65, 117, 155
triplicity 192
Vulcan 75

warfare 70, 81, 115, 140, 164
Warrain, Francis 123
water element 42, 71, 76-7,
120, 136, 146, 160,
185, 195
see also Cancer, Pisces,
Scorpio
Witte, Alfred 68, 90, 188

yod aspect pattern 18, 78, 99,
196

Zadkiel 30, **196-7**
zodiac 33-4, 36-7, 69, 80,
114, 117, **197**
degrees 26, 32, **47**, 50, 53,
57-8, **62-3**, 63, 65, 116,
125, 152, 155, **155**, 163-
5?
divisions 27, 33, 77, 80,
116, 119, 148, 163-4, 168
Earth zodiac **67**
sidereal zodiac 32, 167,
190
tropical zodiac 32, 141,
167, 186, 191